PRAISE FOR STEAL THIS COMPUTER BOOK

First edition

"If ever a book on cyber culture wore a fedora and a trench coat and leaned against a lamp-post on a foggy street, this is the one."

–ELIZABETH LEWIS, AMAZON.COM

"[Wang's] philosophical banter makes his computer guide read like a novel."

–CIO WEB BUSINESS

". . .a delightfully irresponsible primer. . ."

—CHICAGO TRIBUNE

"This book is not going to make a lot of people very happy—and it's going to make a lot of others very nervous."

–HOUSTON CHRONICLE

"If this book had a soundtrack, it'd be Lou Reed's *Walk on the Wild Side*."

–INFO WORLD

"If you're smart, and you work on the Internet, you'll get [*Steal This Computer Book*] before that teen-aged computer geek down the block does."

–THE SARASOTA HERALD-TRIBUNE

". . .this book reminds us that sometimes the best defense is a good offense."

–ELECTRONICS NOW

". . .full of great urban legends about the Internet, proving once again that fact can be stranger than fiction."

–THE SAN DIEGO UNION TRIBUNE

Second edition

STEAL THIS COMPUTER BOOK 3

What They Won't Tell You About the Internet

STEAL THIS COMPUTER BOOK 3

What They Won't Tell You About the Internet

WALLACE WANG

NO STARCH PRESS

San Francisco

STEAL THIS COMPUTER BOOK 3

♺ Printed in the United States of America on recycled paper

1 2 3 4 5 6 7 8 9 10 — 06 05 04 03

No Starch Press and the No Starch Press logo are registered trademarks of No Starch Press, Inc. Other product and company names mentioned herein may be the trademarks of their respective owners. Rather than use a trademark symbol with every occurrence of a trademarked name, we are using the names only in an editorial fashion and to the benefit of the trademark owner, with no intention of infringement of the trademark.

Publisher: William Pollock
Managing Editor: Karol Jurado
Cover and Interior Design: Octopod Studios
Composition: Octopod Studios
Copyeditor: Andy Carroll

Distributed to the book trade in the United States by Publishers Group West, 1700 Fourth Street, Berkeley, CA 94710; phone: 800-788-3123; fax: 510-658-1834.

Distributed to the book trade in Canada by Jacqueline Gross & Associates, Inc., One Atlantic Avenue, Suite 105, Toronto, Ontario M6K 3E7 Canada; phone: 416-531-6737; fax 416-531-4259.

For information on translations or book distributors outside the United States, please contact No Starch Press, Inc. directly:

No Starch Press, Inc.
555 De Haro Street, Suite 250, San Francisco, CA 94107
phone: 415-863-9900; fax: 415-863-9950; info@nostarch.com; http://www.nostarch.com

Library of Congress Cataloging-in-Publication Data

```
Wang, Wallace.
  Steal this computer book 3 : what they won't tell you about the
internet / Wallace Wang.
       p. cm.
  ISBN 1-59327-000-3
  1.  Computer hackers--Handbooks, manuals, etc. 2. Internet--Handbooks, manuals, etc. 3.
Subculture--Computer network resources.  I. Title.
  HV6773.W35 2003
  306.1--dc21
                                2003000475
```

DEDICATION

This book is dedicated to truth, justice, honesty, and the American Way—which are too often mutually exclusive ideas.

BRIEF CONTENTS

CONTENTS IN DETAIL

4
HACKTIVISM: ONLINE ACTIVISM

5
PLEDGING ALLEGIANCE: HATRED AS PATRIOTISM

9
CON GAMES ON THE INTERNET

15
PROTECTING YOUR DATA AND YOUR PRIVACY

16
WAGING WAR ON SPAM

17
WEB BUGS, ADWARE, POP-UPS, AND SPYWARE

PART 5:
PROTECTING YOUR COMPUTER

18
FIREWALLS, INTRUSION-DETECTION SYSTEMS, AND HONEYPOTS

19
COMPUTER FORENSICS: RECOVERING AND DELETING DATA

B
A HACKER'S GALLERY OF ROGUE TOOLS

C
A BIT OF HISTORY: PHONE PHREAKING AND OTHER PHUN

ACKNOWLEDGMENTS

If it weren't for the wonderful people at No Starch Press, this book would still be just another good idea floating around the publishing industry. The most important person involved in the creation of this book is William Pollock, who provided guidance for the book and gently nursed it from a rough idea to a completed manuscript. Two other extremely important people include Andy Carroll and Karol Jurado, both of whom worked tirelessly to ensure that the manuscript was as complete and error-free as possible.

Many hackers deserve credit for their work that directly or indirectly influenced this book. While I have never met many of these people, their books, text files, websites, and software creations have helped influence my thoughts about the "underground" aspect of the computer industry.

I'd also like to thank David Hakala, Jack Rickard, and Todd Erickson of *Boardwatch* magazine (http://www.boardwatch.com) for giving me the chance to write a monthly column for several years that covered the world of computer hacking. Much of the material in this book originally came from these columns, dubbed "Notes From the Underground."

Additional thanks go to Steve Schirripa and Don Learned for giving me my break in performing at the Riviera Comedy Club (http://www.theriviera.com) in Las Vegas. Also a big thanks go out to all the stand-up comedians I've had the pleasure of working with over the years including Dobie Maxwell, Judy Tenuta, Larry Omaha, Kip Addotta, Bob Zany, Gerry Bednob, and Patrick DeGuire.

Final thanks go to stand-up comedians Barry Crimmins, Jimmy Tingle, George Carlin, and Will Durst for their delightfully insightful humor that reveals the truth while making you laugh at the same time. If you want to know what's really happening with our governments, foreign policies, and world leaders, listen to any comedy album from these four comedians. I guarantee you'll learn more about world news, government policies, and international politics from their stand-up comedy acts than you ever could from *Newsweek*, the *New York Times*, the *Wall Street Journal*, the CBS Evening News, or CNN.

Wallace Wang
San Diego, CA

People get mad at me for these views (anti-American government opinions). They say, 'If you don't like this country, why don't you get out of it?' And I say, 'Because I don't want to be victimized by its foreign policy.'

—BARRY CRIMMINS

On the subject of illegal immigrants: The government says we can't let these people in because they're coming for economic reasons, not for political reasons. Oh yeah. Unlike all our ancestors who settled California strictly to exercise that right to vote. 'Where are you going?' 'California!' 'What for?' 'Haven't you heard? They found ballot boxes in the hills!'

—JIMMY TINGLE

Have you noticed that most people who are against abortion are people you wouldn't want to f*** in the first place?

—GEORGE CARLIN

The administration says the American people want tax cuts. Well, duh. The American people also want drive through nickel beer night. The American people want to lose weight by eating ice cream. The American people love the Home Shopping Network because it's commercial free.

—WILL DURST

INTRODUCTION

The successful revolutionary is a statesman, the unsuccessful one a criminal.

—ERICH FROMM

THIS BOOK WON'T TURN YOU INTO A HACKER ANY MORE THAN READING A MILITARY MANUAL CAN TURN YOU INTO A SOLDIER. You won't find step-by-step instructions explaining how to break into a computer, nor will you find technical discussions that show all the flaws inherent in any particular type of operating system. This isn't a technical book about computer hacking. This is a philosophy book about the implications of computer hacking. Hacking isn't just about breaking into computers. Hacking is about exploring, extending boundaries, and searching for knowledge for its own sake.

So if you're looking for detailed information about finding flaws in the latest version of Red Hat Linux or how to configure a Cisco router to protect a corporate network from attack, look somewhere else. But if you want a book that explores both the technical and social implications of the hidden, darker side of the Internet that most people never see, read, or hear about, keep reading. The world of hackers, virus writers, political activism, censorship, racism, and government, religious, and corporate propaganda and intolerance disguised as news, advertising, and press releases awaits you.

Not surprisingly, some people will find the information in this book distasteful, disturbing, and downright dangerous. Yet others will see this same information as an excuse and a reason to cause havoc and make trouble for others. But neither side is correct.

The purpose of this book isn't to teach you how to be a hacker, but rather to teach you to think like a hacker, which means challenging your own preconceived notions about right and wrong and looking beyond the mental limitations that your culture has trained you to think no matter what part of the world you may live in. Computers and the Internet can help open your mind to new worlds that you never dreamed could possibly exist—or it can shut off your mind and funnel your thinking down the narrow confines of a fantasy world that only you choose to see. The choice is up to you.

So if you want to use your computer as a tool to expand your awareness rather than substitute for it, this book is for you. We need you more than ever before. But don't get me wrong. This book isn't advocating the overthrow of your government or the development of a radically different one.

YOUR OWN REVOLUTION

Instead, this book advocates a more personal form of revolution—the revolution within your own thinking. Instead of blindly blaming national governments, international corporations, ethnic groups, sexual preferences, multi-cultural organizations, ideological beliefs, religious institutions, or political parties for all the world's problems, this book suggests that:

→ If you change the way you think, you'll change the way you act.

→ If you change the way you act, you'll be able to change the way others act and think.

→ If you change the way others act and think, you can help change the world— one person at a time.

But it all begins with you.

That's why this book advocates changing your own way of thinking first, because none of us can be correct 100 percent of the time, and the first step toward true change is admitting that neither you nor I—nor your parents, your boss, your spouse, your family, your government, or your church—know everything.

There's no shame in not knowing everything, but there is shame in pretending that we do. We can and must learn from each other, regardless of what we look like, where we live, what we believe in, or which country we might be living in. Open, honest communication is the only way we can change this world for the better, and that's where this book and your personal computer come into play.

Communication's the thing

Although computers are still notoriously difficult, confusing, and downright frustrating to use, they represent a quantum leap in communication similar to the inventions of the alphabet or the printing press. With personal computers and the Internet, people can send and receive email, research information through the World Wide Web, and exchange ideas with people all over the world.

But don't be fooled by the marketing hype designed to suck you into the computer revolution. The world of computers is fraught with hidden dangers that the computer marketing departments don't mention, such as Trojan Horses, electronic espionage, remote computer monitoring, hate groups, con artists, pedophiles, pornography, and terrorism—all just a mouse click away.

This book not only reveals these dangers, but will also help you understand how people create them in the first place. The more you know about anything, the better you can avoid or fight it. Besides exploring the underground nature of the Internet that television and magazine ads conveniently ignore, this book also exposes the darker side of the computer industry itself.

Truth is nothing but a point of view

Although this book won't pretend to be a comprehensive resource for every possible legal and illegal activity you might run across on the Internet, keep in mind that the information provided in this book can help or hurt others. The information itself is neutral. Crash your government's computer network and you may be labeled a terrorist. Do the same thing to an enemy's computer network, and your government may proclaim you a hero. Good and evil depend solely on your point of view.

So welcome to the side of computers that the computer industry doesn't want you to know about, a world where slickly printed tutorials and training classes don't exist.

This is the underground of the real computer revolution, where everyone is encouraged to question, explore, and criticize, but most importantly, to learn how to think for themselves.

And to many governments, corporations, and religions, people who know how to think for themselves can be the most dangerous weapons in the world.

PART 1

INFORMATION OVERLOAD (LIES, DAMN LIES, AND STATISTICS)

1

FINDING WHAT YOU NEED: THE MAGIC OF SEARCH ENGINES

THERE ARE TWO PROBLEMS WITH INFORMATION: NOT HAVING ENOUGH, AND HAVING TOO MUCH. WITHOUT ALL THE NECESSARY INFORMATION ABOUT A TOPIC, IT'S EASY TO MAKE A WRONG DECISION BASED ON AN INCOMPLETE PICTURE OF REALITY. Then again, having too much information can be just as bad, since finding the relevant facts about a topic can be time-consuming and tedious, which encourages people to make snap decisions based on perception rather than accuracy.

The wise man doesn't give the right answers, he poses the right questions.

—CLAUDE LEVI-STRAUSS

Trying to find just enough useful facts without being overwhelmed by too much irrelevant trivia can be a delicate balancing act. Still, if you want to make informed choices based on reason and information rather than on emotion and ignorance, you must take the time to research your topic thoroughly.

As a research tool, the Internet offers a wealth of information about virtually every topic. Unfortunately, the Internet poses a few problems of its own when it comes to research:

→ How do you find the information you need?

→ How do you know if the information you find is accurate, obsolete, misleading, or just plain wrong?

Finding information on the Internet is relatively easy: You just type one or more words into a search engine, and then the search engine lists all the websites (that it knows about) that contain the words or phrases you want to find.

The easy part is sifting through the different websites to find the information you need. The hard part is deciding whether you can trust what you find, knowing that every source of information selectively chooses which facts to report and which ones to omit. Because we all have a natural tendency to interpret facts based on personal biases and experience, don't be surprised to find that one set of facts may cause you to reach a conclusion that's completely different from what someone else might reach.

Sometimes there might be a right answer and sometimes there might be a wrong answer, but more often than not, there won't be any one answer that's either completely right or completely wrong. What you decide may be the right answer depends on your point of view.

SEARCH ENGINES

The key to finding anything on the Internet is to use a search engine, but if you ask different search engines to find the same information, each one will find a number of websites not found by the others. Rather than limiting yourself to the tunnel vision of a single search engine, experiment with some of the different search engines listed below, and you may uncover information that your favorite search engine missed.

Even better, you may find that one search engine is better at finding certain types of data or offers a unique perspective to searching for information. For example, the Teoma search engine tries to cluster search results into subjects. So if you search for "Mustang," the Teoma search engine clusters the results according to "Ford Mustang" and "Mustang horses." The following list includes some of the more powerful search engines:

About	http://about.com
AlltheWeb	http://www.alltheweb.com
AltaVista	http://www.altavista.com
AOL Search	http://search.aol.com/
Ask Jeeves	http://www.askjeeves.com
Google	http://www.google.com
Hotbot	http://www.hotbot.com
LookSmart	http://www.looksmart.com
MSN	http://www.msn.com
Open Directory Project	http://dmoz.org
Teoma	http://www.teoma.com
Yahoo!	http://www.yahoo.com

Meta-search engines

Rather than visit multiple search engines yourself, you can save time by using a meta-search engine, which simultaneously sends your query to two or more general-purpose search engines and eliminates duplicate results. Here are some popular meta-search engines:

DogPile	http://www.dogpile.com
Mamma	http://www.mamma.com
MetaCrawler	http://www.metacrawler.com
Search.com	http://www.search.com

Specialized search engines

Finally, don't ignore specialized search engines designed to search only for websites pertaining to a particular topic. Specialized search engines often find obscure websites that the larger search engines might overlook. There are specialized search engines for everything from caring for fish to the latest crafting fads. Here are a few interesting ones:

AvatarSearch   Finds occult information about witchcraft, vampires, pagan rituals, astrology, tarot cards, and other topics that often panic right-wing conservatives (http://www.avatarsearch.com).

Black Web Portal   Finds websites of particular interest to blacks (http://www.blackwebportal.com).

Crime Spider   Searches for websites providing information about various crime and law enforcement sites and organized by topics such as serial murder, urban legends, and cybercrime (http://www.crimespider.com).

Disinformation   Conspiracy theory–laden search engine that helps you uncover websites offering the "real truth" behind the pyramids of Mars, the sightings of black helicopters over America, film footage of Bigfoot, and the government secrets hidden in Area 51 (http://www.disinfo.com).

Education World   Finds websites that can help students, teachers, and parents learn more about education (http://www.education-world.com).

Federal Web Locator   Lists many of the websites from various government agencies and organizations (except for the really cool ones like the CIA and FBI). Maybe you can use it to find out where all your hard-earned tax dollars are going (http://www.infoctr.edu/fwl).

GovSearch   Collection of government search engines for finding information about the U.S. government: IRS documents, Customs Service, NTIS, U.S. law code, legislative information, OSHA regulations, and information from many other agencies and departments (http://www.nwbuildnet.com/nwbn/govbot.html).

CopSeek Directory and Police Search Engine   Helps you find websites related to law enforcement so you can find a policeman when you need one (http://www.copseek.com).

NerdWorld   Search engine dedicated to computer and technology fanatics (http://www.nerdworld.com).

Que Pasa!   A bilingual search engine geared towards Hispanics and Latinos, available in both English and Spanish (http://www.quepasa.com).

Satanist Net   Search engine geared to helping you find satanic information on the Internet (http://www.satanist.net).

Women.com and **WWWomen**   Two search engines geared toward helping women find information and resources on the Internet (http://www.women.com and http://www.wwwomen.com).

Kid-safe search engines

If you leave your children unsupervised, it's likely that they'll eventually find bomb-making instructions and pornography on the Internet. While keeping children isolated from such information may be impossible, you can at least limit their searching to kid-safe search engines. Unlike general-purpose search engines, kid-safe search engines won't accidentally display links to pornographic or bomb-making websites. Try one of the following:

Ask Jeeves for Kids	http://www.ajkids.com
CleanSearch	http://www.cleansearch.com
Go.com	http://www.go.com
Yahooligans	http://www.yahooligans.com

Multimedia search engines

Most search engines help you find text, but what if you want to find a song, a picture, or a video clip? Rather than waste your time using a general purpose search engine to find an MP3 file of your favorite band, try using a special multimedia search engine instead. These multimedia search engines specialize in searching only for specific audio, graphic, or video files.

Here are some of the more popular multimedia search engines:

Ditto	http://www.ditto.com (see Figure 1-1)
FAST Multimedia Search	http://multimedia.alltheweb.com
SpeechBot.net	http://speechbot.research.compaq.com
MIDI Explorer	http://www.musicrobot.com

Regional search engines

Search engines often include websites from all over the world. If you'd rather limit your search to a specific region or country, try using one of the regional search engines listed in Table 1-1 instead.

Figure 1-1

The Ditto.com website allows you to search the Internet by using pictures.

Table 1-1: International Search Engines

COUNTRY	WEBSITE	URL
ASIA		
General	GlobePage	http://www.globepage.com
China	SINA Online	http://english.sina.com
Hong Kong	Timway.com	http://www.hksrch.com/welcome.html
India	123India	http://www.123india.com
	IndiasWeb	http://www.indiasweb.com
Japan	Search Desk	http://www.searchdesk.com
Philippines	G-Spot	http://www.gsilink.com/gspot
Singapore	Catcha.com	http://www.catcha.com.sg
South Korea	Yahoo! Korea-Seek	http://kr.yahoo.com
AFRICA		
General	Woyaa!	http://www.woyaa.com/
South Africa	Ananzi	http://www.ananzi.co.za
	Max	http://www.max.co.za
EUROPE		
General	Search Europe	http://www.searcheurope.com
France	Francité	http://www.francite.com
	Lokace	http://www.lokace.com

Table 1-1: International Search Engines (continued)

COUNTRY	WEBSITE	URL
Iceland	Iceland on the Web	http://www.vefur.is/iceland
Italy	Italia Mia	http://www.italiamia.com
Malta	Search Malta	http://www.searchmalta.com
Netherlands	Search NL	http://www.search.nl
Russia	Russian Internet Search Engines	http://www.slavophilia.net/russia/search.htm
Switzerland	Swiss Search	http://www.search.ch
U.K.	Everyday UK	http://www.everydayuk.co.uk
	Lifestyle.co.uk	http://www.lifestyle.co.uk
	UK Plus	http://www.ukplus.co.uk
MIDDLE EAST		
General	Ajeeb	http://english.ajeeb.com
Egypt	Egypt Search	http://www.egyptsearch.com
Iran	Iran Index	http://www.iranindex.com
Israel	HaReshima	http://www.hareshima.com
Syria	Syria Gate	http://www.syriagate.com
NORTH AMERICA		
Canada	Canada.com	http://www.canada.com
Mexico	Radar	http://www.radar.com.mx
SOUTH AMERICA		
Bolivia	Bolivia Web	http://www.boliviaweb.com
Brazil	Cadê	http://www.cade.com.br
Chile	Chilnet	http://www.chilnet.cl/index.htm
South Pacific	South Pacific Search	http://www.emaxia.com
Australia	WebWombat	http://www.webwombat.com.au
	WebSearch AU	http://www.websearch.com.au

Searching for more search engines

New search engines seem to appear almost daily (see Figure 1-2). The following sites will help you find the latest and best Internet search engines:

AllSearchEngines	http://www.allsearchengines.com
Search Engine Watch	http://www.searchenginewatch.com

TIPS FOR USING SEARCH ENGINES

Search engines can help you find specific information on the Internet, but they also flood you with large amounts of irrelevant information. With a little bit of extra effort on

Figure 1-2

You can find a search engine in any language.

your part, though, you can make sure that a search engine finds exactly what you want, as quickly as possible. The next time you use a search engine, try some of the following tips.

Search within categories

Many search engines, such as Yahoo!, display categories such as Computers & Internet or Business & Economy. If you click on a category and then use the search engine, you'll have the option of searching the entire Internet or limiting your search to within the currently selected category. Obviously searching within a selected category will take less time and avoid a lot of irrelevant websites.

Still, you might like to search the entire Internet just for the surprise of seeing what the search engine might uncover that is not in your specific category.

Use specific words

If you want to find all websites that focus on birds, you could type the word "bird" into a search engine. Unfortunately, the search engine might return thousands of irrelevant websites that talk about badminton birdies or different ways to cook game birds. Instead of searching for general words, use more specific words such as "ornithology" (which is the branch of zoology dealing with birds). The more precise your search terms, the less likely the search engine will be to return irrelevant websites.

Use multiple words

You can also narrow your search by typing in multiple words. For example, if you wanted to find information about Miami, Florida, type in the two words "Miami" and "Florida." If you just search for "Miami" or "Florida," the search engine might bombard you with websites about the Miami Dolphins football team or the Florida Marlins baseball team. In general, the more words you search for, the more likely the search engine will find exactly what you want.

Use Boolean operators

Many search engines allow you to focus your search by using two different Boolean operators: AND and OR.

If you wanted to search for all websites that contain both the words "hot" and "dog," you would simply type the following into the search field:

```
hot AND dog
```

This search would find websites devoted to hot dogs, but could also turn up websites that talk about ways to cool down a dog on a hot day.

If you wanted to search for all websites that contain either the word "hot" or "dog," you would type the following into the search field:

```
hot OR dog
```

This could turn up websites that talk about hot dogs along with sites that mention dogs, different ways air conditioning can cool you down on a hot day, hot chili sauces, or dog food.

Be wary of what you find

The order that a search engine ranks websites can influence which ones people may visit, so to increase the odds that people will visit a specific website, some websites pay search engines to put them first (or at least near the top) of any list of related websites. The better search engines identify which websites paid for greater exposure, but other search engines may not be so honest.

Also, because search engines scan websites for keywords that people are most likely to search for, many websites hide multiple copies of the same keyword on their web pages. This tricks a search engine into thinking the website contains more information about a particular keyword than it really does.

As with reading newspapers, listening to the radio, or watching the news on television, always be wary of the source of your information. Search engines can find information for you, but they can't verify the accuracy of the information. Anyone can put any information on a website.

REMEMBER THE LIMITATIONS OF SEARCH ENGINES

No search engine will find everything available on the Internet, so be sure to use several search engines to find websites that other search engines might not have found. The more search engines you use, the more information you'll find, and the more information you find, the more likely you'll have most of the facts you need to make an intelligent decision.

Sometimes the hardest part about finding an answer is knowing how to look for it in the first place. With so many different search engines available at your fingertips, there's no excuse for not finding the information you want on the Internet right away.

2

ALTERNATIVE SOURCES OF NEWS
AND INFORMATION

THINK YOU CAN BELIEVE EVERYTHING YOU READ IN THE PAPER, HEAR ON THE RADIO, OR SEE ON TV? Think again. Newspapers tend to contain detailed information about local events, but relatively little historical background or contextual information about international events. If you rely solely on local newspapers for information, your knowledge of national and international news is likely to be incomplete at best, and one-sided or completely wrong at worst.

Reading publications from other countries is one way to get a more balanced view of world events. Try looking at how newspapers from England and the United States cover a particular event, compared to how a newspaper from the Middle East or Asia covers that same event.

This chapter lists online newspapers, magazines, and other sources to get you started, but remember that these selections reflect the author's point of view. Be sure to spend some time searching for different newspapers and magazines on your own, as well.

NEWSPAPERS ONLINE

Newspapers don't report facts; they report information filtered through the eyes and opinions of the reporters, writers, editors, and news services that provide the information in the first place. Even worse, many newspapers find it more profitable and easier to tranquilize the public with shallow sensationalism, local stories, and trivia in order to capture the largest market share possible for their advertisers.

If you begin reading newspapers from different cities and countries, you may be surprised to find that African, European, and Asian newspapers report international events that American newspapers never bother to cover at all. Furthermore, even when foreign and American newspapers do cover the same event, the overseas newspapers often provide completely different points of view based on facts that American newspapers gloss over or completely ignore.

Browsing through multiple newspapers can give you a much wider exposure to news and a greater appreciation of a newspaper's inherent bias. Read an Iraqi newspaper to get a better understanding of how the Iraqi media portrays the feelings of their people toward America. Or read a Brazilian or Australian newspaper to learn

I trust the newspaper. The news people are very intelligent, and if they are giving the story, it must be true.

—SHOPKEEPER MOHAMMED IQBAL AFTER BEING TOLD THAT THE RUMOR ABOUT JEWS BEING FORE-WARNED ABOUT THE WORLD TRADE CENTER ATTACK WAS FALSE about events affecting the Southern Hemisphere that North American newspapers routinely ignore.

The following links point to some of the more prominent English-language newspapers (with the exception of *Le Monde*, which is French). Remember that English-language newspapers may offer information that differs slightly or dramatically from newspapers in other languages, and that the following links aren't the only newspapers available on the Internet.

Bahrain Tribune   News about the Middle East from Bahrain (http://www. bahraintribune.com/home.asp).

Bangkok Post   News from Thailand (http://www.bangkokpost.net).

Buenos Aires Herald   Get information about South America from an Argentinean newspaper that's been in business since 1876 (http://www.bueno-sairesherald.com).

China News   English-language website providing news about and from China (http://www.china.org.cn/english/index.htm).

Christian Science Monitor   A highly respected newspaper that maintains its own news bureaus in 13 countries, including Russia, Japan, Germany, France, the U.K., South Africa, and Mexico, as well as throughout the United States. (http://www.csmonitor.com).

Financial Times   Covers financial news from around the world (http://news.ft.com).

Gulf News   News from the United Arab Emirates (http://www.gulf-news.com).

Ha'aretz   Daily newspaper from Tel Aviv, Israel (http://www.haaretzdaily.com).

International Herald Tribune   A well-respected newspaper edited in Paris and published in conjunction with the *Washington Post* and the *New York Times* (http://www.iht.com).

Investor's Business Daily   A financial newspaper that covers international events, with an obvious emphasis on money and how the news affects different stock markets (http://www.investors.com).

Irish Times   Keep up with the latest business, sports, and politics of Ireland, and use this website as a search engine for Irish topics as well (http://www.ireland.com).

Japan Times   Provides the latest news of interest about Japan and Asia (http://www.japantimes.co.jp).

Los Angeles Independent Media Center   A news media that provides alternative viewpoints to the clone-like views offered by the more traditional news sources, which may be too timid to upset potential advertisers, government officials, or the status quo (http://la.indymedia.org).

Le Monde France's leading newspaper (written in French) covering world events from a uniquely French point of view (http://tout.lemonde.fr).

Moscow Times Read news from a Russian perspective in this English-language newspaper (http://www.themoscowtimes.com).

NetIran Provides links to five sources of news from Iran: IRNA (Islamic Republic News Agency), *Iran News*, IRIB (Islamic Republic of Iran Broadcasting), ISNA (Iranian Student News Agency), and the *Tehran Times* (http://www.netiran.com).

The New York Times and **The Los Angeles Times** Get the latest news from two of the largest cities in America (http://www.nytimes.com and http://www.latimes.com).

The New Zealand Herald News from New Zealand's major newspaper (http://www.nzherald.co.nz).

The Norway Post Get the latest news from Norway and the rest of Europe, as seen from Norway (http://www.norwaypost.com).

The Paperboy Provides links to the most popular international news-papers—see Figure 2-1 (http://www.thepaperboy.com).

Figure 2-1

The Paperboy website provides links to major newspapers from around the world.

Pravda   Once the political mouthpiece of the Soviet Union, *Pravda* is now a national newspaper covering all aspects of political and social life throughout Russia (http://www.pravda.ru).

Rwanda Post   Since news about Africa is often scarce, visit the *Rwanda Post* site to read the latest information about Rwanda and the rest of the African continent (http://www.rwandapost.com).

Russia Today   The Russian equivalent of *USA Today*, this newspaper provides information about daily activities in Russia (http://www.russiatoday.com).

South China Morning Post   The *South China Morning Post* is Hong Kong's English-language newspaper, covering financial, political, and technological news about Hong Kong, China, Thailand, Japan, and Singapore. Read this to get a better idea what the Asian public thinks about Europe, America, and the rest of the world (http://www.scmp.com).

The Sydney Morning Herald   Read the latest news from down under (http://www.smh.com.au).

The Telegraph (London)   Major British newspaper providing news about England, Europe, and the rest of the world (http://www.telegraph.co.uk).

The Times of India   One of India's major newspapers, covering national and world events (http://www.timesofindia.com).

The Times (London)   International news from a distinctly British point of view (http://www.the-times.co.uk).

Toronto Star   News from one of Canada's largest daily newspapers (http://www.thestar.com).

USA Today   An American newspaper that covers a broad range of news from around the United States. Best known for its colorful weather maps (http://www.usatoday.com).

The Wall Street Journal   Provides financial news from all over the world, emphasizing Europe, Asia, and North America (http://www.wsj.com).

The Washington Post   News from another well-respected American newspaper, most commonly known as the newspaper that helped break open the Watergate scandal in the early '70s (http://www.washingtonpost.com).

The Onion   A satirical American weekly newspaper (see Figure 2-2) that uses humor to reveal the truth behind the latest headline stories (http://www.theonion.com).

By opening your mind to the wealth of newspapers available through the Internet, you can be as fully informed (or ignorant) about world events as you wish to be. Once you start reading a British, Egyptian, or Japanese newspaper (or even just a newspaper from another city) on a regular basis, you may never look at your own world the same way again.

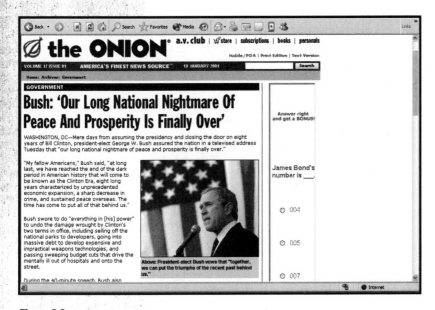

Figure 2-2

Sometimes the news can be funny if you just look at the hidden context behind the story.

MAGAZINES ONLINE

Whereas newspaper coverage is pretty much confined to stories that are deemed acceptable by a paper's corporate owners, magazines usually have more freedom to target specific audiences and advocate specific opinions and beliefs. As a result, two different magazines will often reach completely different conclusions about the same topic.

Although it's tempting to read only those magazines that support your own opinions, take some time to learn what people who have different political views or are from another country or continent might have to say. For foreign magazines, visit one of the websites listed below, or visit your favorite search engine and try to hunt up some magazines not listed in this book.

AlterNet.org   Online magazine that offers an alternative to mainstream investigative journalism. Regularly covers topics that the mainstream either ignores or glosses over, such as the drug war, sexual politics, and health issues (http://www.alternet.org).

The Economist   Comprehensive magazine that provides news about events from around the world, including places most American high school graduates can't find on a map (http://www.economist.com).

Federal Computer Week   Offers stories about how various U.S. government agencies are using computers to (hopefully) streamline their organization and improve efficiency (http://www.fcw.com).

Monday Morning   Lebanon's English-language weekly news magazine (http://www.mmorning.com).

The National Review   Conservative American magazine providing its own unique point of view on American politics and international events (http://www.nationalreview.com).

The New American   An ultra-conservative magazine that takes American patriotism to the extreme. Reading this magazine will certainly open your eyes to the way people can interpret world events (http://www. thenewamerican.com).

Philippine News Link   Links to an enormous range of newspapers and magazines that cover the Philippines, including *The Manila Times*, *Filipinas Magazine*, *Asiaweek*, and *The Manila Bulletin* (http://www.philnews.com).

ZMag   Available in English, French, Spanish, and Swedish, and billing itself as a magazine for people concerned about social change (http://www.zmag.org).

NEWS SERVICES ONLINE

Newspapers and magazines often get their information from national and international news services, which often get the information directly from people at the scene of the event itself. Local writers, unable to attend the news event in person, simply embellish, exaggerate, or expand on the information from these news services to create their own newspaper or magazine articles. So, rather than wait for news to appear in your favorite newspaper or magazine, go directly to the source by visiting a news service website.

21st Century Digest   Provides the latest news articles and links to several major news networks, including CNN and the BBC (http://www.21stcenturydigest.com).

ABC News, **CBS News**, and **MSNBC**   News from the three largest television news networks in North America (http://abcnews.go.com, http://cbsnews.cbs.com, http://www.msnbc.com).

Agence France-Presse   French news service that offers news in English, French, Spanish, German, and Portuguese (http://www.afp.com).

Associated Press   One of the most popular wire services, AP provides stories to newspapers throughout the United States, including the *Los Angeles Times*, the *Detroit News*, and the *Washington Times* (http://wire.ap.org).

Baltic News Service   The largest news agency in the Baltic states (http://www.bns.ee).

Business News Americas   Financial news about Latin America (http://www.bnamericas.com).

China Daily   News from mainland China covering Chinese and international news (http://www1.chinadaily.com.cn).

CNN   You can't ignore the only American news service that can get inside countries like Iraq and Cuba and interview world leaders like Saddam Hussein and Fidel Castro (http://www.cnn.com).

Federation of American Scientists   Information from the scientific community regarding various environmental, political, and technology stories (http://www.fas.org).

Fox News   News from the fast-growing Fox Network (http://www.foxnews.com).

Good News Agency   Unusual news service that only offers positive, uplifting news to counteract the deluge of pessimism so prevalent with most news services today (http://www.goodnewsagency.org).

Intelligence Online   This news service is especially designed for diplomats, military and political officials, heads of company security services, or academics interested in intelligence matters, business intelligence, and international political issues. Find news on money laundering, terrorist activities, weapons smuggling, and other types of crimes that are occurring at this very moment (http://www.intelligenceonline.com).

Inter Press Service   This non-governmental organization delivers daily news from around the world in English, Finnish, Dutch, German, Norwegian, Spanish, and Swedish (http://www.ips.org).

Korean Central News Agency   The official news service of North Korea. Learn about world events as seen from communist North Korea's point of view (http://www.kcna.co.jp).

Nando Times   Another news service providing information from around the world (http://www.nando.net).

One World   Provides news from over 150 global organizations, such as Save the Children, ActionAid, UNICEF, and Christian Aid. It is one of the few sites that presents news from a brutally honest point of view with headlines such as "Brazil to celebrate date that meant genocide for 5 million" (http://www.oneworld.net).

Reuters   Read information from one of the most popular and famous news services in the world (http://www.reuters.com).

Stratfor.com Analyzes global events to offer the general public information normally reserved for governments (http://www.stratfor.com).

Total Scoop Displays the tops stories of the day organized by categories such as Politics, Entertainment, Sports, Technology, and Travel (http://www.totalscoop.com).

Voice of America Voice of America offers the official United States government's view on the news. This is broadcast around the world, especially into countries that limit access to information (http://www.voa.gov).

Voice of Russia Voice of Russia broadcasts interviews, discussions, and historical information about Russia. Unlike the Voice of America, the Voice of Russia is primarily an entertainment and educational broadcast about life in Russia (http://www.vor.ru).

FINDING MORE NEWS SOURCES

Because space permits only a select listing of news sources, and since the number of newspapers, magazines, and news services present on the Internet keeps growing, you can get a more complete listing of sources by visiting the following websites, which list news services by region, continent, or country:

Aileena	http://www.aileena.ch
Discover	http://www.discover.co.uk/NET/NEWS/news.html
Editor & Publisher	http://www.mediainfo.com
MediaChannel	http://www.mediachannel.org/links/links-frameset.html
NewsDirectory	http://www.ecola.com
Newspapers.Com	http://www.newspapers.com

For a monthly fee, a service such as TracerLock (http://www.tracerlock.com) will scan through various news sites, magazines, and newspapers, and will email articles to you based on keywords that you give it. By using such a service, you can stay up-to-date on the latest news about a particular subject without having to search news sources yourself.

CORPORATE INFLUENCE ON THE NEWS

Most news media (newspapers, television and radio stations, and magazines) are owned by corporations that rely on other companies to place advertisements and help the media pay their bills. So what are the odds that a newspaper will run a story criticizing a major advertiser, or run a story exposing the media's corporate owner? More importantly, what news company is going to risk raising the ire of its own government, when doing so could jeopardize that company from attending any future government press conferences that their competitors will surely attend?

If you think that any of the news sources listed in this chapter are free from any bias, influence, or censorship, it's time to rethink your perception of how the news media really works. Every year, Project Censored (http://www.projectcensored.org) offers their top ten stories that the news media conveniently ignored, that inevitably turn out to be major environmental, political, or social disasters that make a prominent corporation or government look corrupt, exploitive, or just plain incompetent.

Some recent stories that Project Censored highlighted include a report by the U.S. National Academy of Sciences warning that catastrophic climate changes could be imminent due to global warming, the pesticide poisoning of 10,000 Ecuadoran farmers and Amazon Indians by DynCorp, and America's covert war in Macedonia to establish an oil pipeline to link the Black Sea with the Adriatic coast.

The Fairness & Accuracy in Reporting site (http://www.fair.org) reported that Dan Guthrie, a columnist for the *Grants Pass Daily Courier*, claims he was fired for criticizing President Bush as "hiding in a Nebraska hole" in the aftermath of the September 11 terrorist attacks. The column sparked angry letters to the editor, causing the newspaper to print an apology that stated, "Criticism of our chief executive and those around him needs to be responsible and appropriate. Labeling him and the nation's other top leaders as cowards as the United States tries to unite after its bloodiest terrorist attack ever isn't responsible or appropriate."

In another example, Tom Gutting was fired from the *Texas City Sun* for also criticizing President Bush on the day of the terrorist attacks. The newspaper later printed an editorial with the headline, "Bush's Leadership Has Been Superb."

Other corporate influences show up in the thinly disguised advertisements masquerading as news, such as stories urging Americans to get more calcium by drinking milk (indirectly promoting the dairy industry by ignoring other sources of calcium, medical information that suggests that milk is not a particularly healthy food after all, or listing the types of drugs that dairy farms use to force cows to produce more milk—drugs that can deform the cows and contaminate the milk itself).

Besides promoting a particular product, the news media may simply ignore information that puts the welfare and safety of individuals ahead of the liability and financial well-being of corporations. Common news stories offer tips about how parents can reduce the risk of sudden infant death syndrome (SIDS) while ignoring New Zealand research from 1994 (http://www.healthychild.com) that links SIDS to a fungus and toxic gases released by fire retardant chemicals in mattresses and blankets.

For more information about media bias and sources of alternative news, visit the following websites:

Chicago Media Watch	http://www.chicagomediawatch.org
Free Speech TV	http://www.freespeech.org
WebActive	http://www.webactive.com

THE NEWS MEDIA ONLY REPORTS THE FACTS— AND ANYTHING ELSE ANYONE WILL TELL THEM

No matter how much you may trust a particular news source, remember that they can always be wrong, and given enough time, they probably will be at one point or another. The news media gets its information from its own reporters, wire services, and anyone who faxes them what appears to be an interesting story. Slip some misleading information to the news media through any of these routes, and the media may not have the time to verify the facts and will simply report the information as "news" in the interest of higher ratings.

One self-proclaimed artist, Joey Skaggs (http://www.joeyskaggs.com), has turned misinformation into an art form, using the media itself as his canvas to demonstrate the media's unfailing gullibility to broadcast "news" without verifying the credibility of the source. Joey Skaggs has appeared on the television show *Good Morning America* and on CNN, as well as appearing in print in *The Philadelphia Inquirer* and *The Washington Post* for such outrageous "news," such as a vitamin pill made from cockroaches, a brothel for dogs, and an artificially intelligent computer program that could examine court evidence and spit out a verdict (it found O.J. Simpson guilty, by the way).

So the next time you form an opinion from something you've read, seen, or heard from your favorite trusted news source, it could be the truth, it could be partial information lacking crucial facts, or it could just be another media hoax perpetrated by someone like Joey Skaggs. Whatever the case, the odds are good that it won't be the whole truth, so read the news carefully and be aware that no matter how strongly you may hold an opinion, you could always be completely wrong.

THE NEWS AS HISTORY

There's no better way to learn about the past than by seeing what type of news people were reading and watching back when historical events actually occurred. For a trip back in time, visit the Internet Archive (http://www.archive.org) which provides early web pages from the fledgling days of the Internet to major events such as the September 11, 2001 terrorist attack on the World Trade Center. By browsing through these web pages, you can get a feel for the mood surrounding a particular newsworthy event, as shown in Figure 2-3.

The Internet Archive also stores old video clips of television reports about historical events, along with a library of old television commercials and U.S. government films distributed since the 1940s. By viewing these old government films, you can see how much (or how little) the American government has really changed.

Some classic government films to view include the infamous Duck and Cover film that teaches children how to survive a nuclear attack by holding a jacket over their head and a short film explaining the hazards of biowarfare, which warns that communist agents could attack the United States by pouring toxins in our water supply or

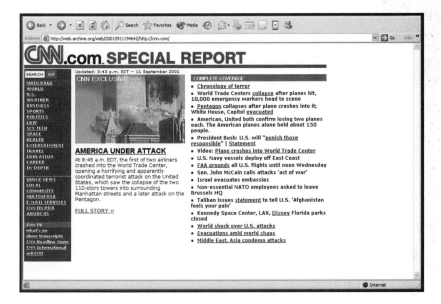

Figure 2-3

Viewing history through web pages from the past.

using crop dusters to spray an entire area with germs. Substitute the word "communist" with "terrorist" and you can see how relevant this particular film is today.

READING TO LEARN

Whatever your background, reading news from different countries and political viewpoints can open your eyes—especially if you've never previously gone beyond the information readily available around you. Reading something different every day will undoubtedly expose you to opposing, conflicting, and possibly confusing information. How you decide to react to any information that contradicts your own way of thinking is (of course) up to you.

3

CENSORING INFORMATION (WE KNOW WHAT'S BEST FOR YOU)

DECIDING WHAT SOMEONE ELSE CAN SEE, READ, AND HEAR IS A PERPET-
UAL DILEMMA. Parents, for example, want the right to control what their kids may
explore on the Internet, using their own ethical standards (which may be completely
different from another parent's ethical standards) as a guideline. One parent may feel
that children should freely explore any topic, such as homosexuality or Buddhism, in
an intelligent, rational manner, while a second parent may be horrified to find a child
learning anything that contradicts the parent's own beliefs, such as studying how
another religion worships God. In this situation, the ultimate authority must rest with
the parents, regardless of whether anyone believes they can make intelligent decisions or not.

> Censorship cannot
> eliminate evil, it can only
> kill freedom.
>
> —UNKNOWN

National governments face a similar dilemma. What should a government allow
its citizens to access on the Internet? Not surprisingly, many governments want to
prevent their citizens from viewing any information that may contradict or criticize the
government's official version of the news.

Some countries, like Saudi Arabia and China, funnel Internet access through
state-owned Internet service providers, which have filters that only allow users to
access government-approved websites. Prodigy filters Internet access for Chinese
citizens with the blessings of the Chinese government, while Saudi Arabia relies on
technology purchased from another American company, Secure Computing
(http://www.sctc.com), to filter Internet access for its citizens.

(The irony of any company knowingly accepting money from an oppressive
government to keep its citizens ignorant should not be lost on anyone. When Secure
Computing's Saudi Arabian contract expires, companies from America, Germany,
England, and the Netherlands plan to bid on the multimillion dollar contract, in the
hopes of supplying much of the Middle East with Internet filters. Apparently the
biggest problem with freedom of speech is that it's more profitable to suppress it
instead.)

While many people expect that communist governments and dictatorships will
readily embrace Internet censorship, they may be surprised to learn that many so-
called democratic governments eagerly view censorship as a way to tackle the twin
problems of pornography and terrorism (and also anti-government information) on the
Internet. Under the guise of protecting children from Internet pornography, Australia
has passed some of the most restrictive filtering laws in the world, holding Internet

service providers responsible for filtering Internet access. Essentially, Australia deems pornography illegal when it is online, but perfectly legal to buy offline.

The problem isn't that Internet filtering blocks pornography from both adults and children, but that the Internet filters themselves are highly unreliable and totally subject to the whims of the manufacturer, which are often foreign companies. So programmers in other countries are essentially in charge of deciding what Internet sites Australian citizens can access on their computers.

Another form of censorship has been considered by the Internet Service Providers Association of India—charging a tariff on overseas Internet websites. Under this system, if a company such as eBay or MSN wanted citizens from India to access their websites, the site would first need to pay a fee to the Indian government. Any website that refused to pay this tariff would simply be blocked from India's Internet market.

One potentially disturbing trend in the United States is the consolidation of Internet service providers, especially those that offer high-speed broadband Internet access. If only a handful of cable and telephone companies control high-speed Internet access, there's the chance that they (either alone or under the coercion of the government) could filter or block access to certain websites, and thus create a form of corporate censorship that might be more threatening than any government-sponsored censorship could ever be.

DEFEATING INTERNET FILTERS

While hackers can always circumvent any type of Internet filters, ordinary citizens aren't always as skillful. Rather than force everyone to develop hacking skills, programmers around the world have united to offer simpler solutions for defeating Internet filters. The oldest and simplest method is to retrieve web pages through email. A newer and more advanced method is to access websites through a neutral third-party site.

Accessing banned web pages by email

Blocking access to specific websites is easy. Scanning email to determine whether someone is sending or receiving banned information is more time-consuming and labor-intensive. To exploit this limitation in most Internet filters, programmers have developed a way to retrieve web pages by email through something called a *Webmail server*.

Basically, a Webmail server acts like a middleman between you and a banned website. You ask the Webmail server to access a banned website for you and it retrieves either the text or the entire web page (complete with text and graphics), which it then sends to you by email.

To use a Webmail server, you need to send an email to a Webmail server and list the URL address of the web page you want to see (such as http://www.cnn.com). Within a few minutes, hours, or days (depending on the server) the server will email your chosen web page as either plain text or HTML code so you can read information that your Internet filter doesn't want you to see.

For example, if you wanted to retrieve information from the CNN website using a Webmail server at webmail@www.ucc.ie, you would send the following email message:

```
To: webmail@www.ucc.ie
Subject: none
GO http://www.cnn.com
```

In the above example, you would type GO http://www.cnn.com in the body of your message where you would normally type your message. (Each Webmail server may use a slightly different syntax to retrieve web pages, so while the webmail@www.ucc.ie server uses the GO http://www.cnn.com, another Webmail server such as agora@capri.mi.mss.co.jp would require you to type SEND http://www.cnn.com instead.)

Here are some Webmail servers and the syntax to be used in the body of your message. Leave the subject line blank in all cases. Most of these Webmail servers will email you the complete HTML code for a particular website but a few only retrieve the text or require special commands to retrieve graphics too.

WEBMAIL ADDRESS	SYNTAX TO USE
agora@dna.affrc.go.jp	SEND <URL>
agora@kamakura.mss.co.jp	SEND <URL>
agora@capri.mi.mss.co.jp	SEND <URL> (To receive the page as an HTML attachment, omit the GET command.)
getweb@unganisha.idrc.ca	GET <URL>
www4mail@access.bellanet.org	GET <URL>
www4mail@wm.ictp.trieste.it	GET <URL>
www4mail@ftp.uni-stuttgart.de	GET <URL>
www4mail@collaborium.org	GET <URL>
www4mail@kabissa.org	GET <URL>
wwwmail@bnl.gov	GET <URL>
getweb@usa.healthnet.org	GET <URL>
text@pagegetter.com	GET <URL> (retrieves text)
web@pagegetter.com	GET <URL> (retrieves graphics)
webmail@www.ucc.ie	GO <URL>

NOTE: To learn more about accessing web pages through email, visit the Web-to-Email website at http://www.bellanet.org/email.html. For more detailed instructions about using a specific Webmail server, send an email message to the server of your choice with the word HELP in the body of the message (leave the subject line blank).

Accessing banned web pages through a third-party website

An Internet filter may keep you from accessing a specific website, such as http://www.playboy.com. However, an Internet filter won't always block you from accessing a website that appears harmless. Some programmers have taken advantage of this fact by letting you use a seemingly harmless website as a browser to access a banned website. The apparently harmless third-party website then conveniently encrypts any information you receive from the banned website, disguising it as an ordinary encrypted business transaction so that the filter can't recognize it.

One of the more popular projects designed to circumvent censorship is the Peekabooty Project (http://www.peek-a-booty.org). Anyone can run the Peekabooty program to link their individual computer to the Peekabooty network consisting of other computers scattered all over the world.

When somebody wants to access a banned website, they connect to the Peekabooty network, which selects a computer out of its network at random. This randomly selected computer then grabs the web pages from a website and sends them back to the user.

If you want to help people in other countries access information freely on the Internet, download and run the Peekabooty program today. Your computer just may help someone in an oppressed society find the banned information they need.

At one time, a CIA-sponsored company called SafeWeb (http://www.safeweb.com) offered a similar network called Triangle Boy. The CIA used Triangle Boy to allow Chinese citizens to circumvent the Chinese government's Internet filters. (Wouldn't it have been easier just to tell Prodigy not to filter the Internet for the Chinese government in the first place?) While the CIA used Triangle Boy ostensibly because the Chinese government restricts their citizens' right to information, they didn't use the same technology to help citizens in Saudi Arabia access websites that the Saudi government didn't want them to see—perhaps because China doesn't supply the United States with much of its oil, like Saudi Arabia does?

SafeWeb eventually licensed Triangle Boy to a company called PrivaSec (http://www.privasec.com) because they claimed it wasn't profitable enough to continue supporting. Researchers later discovered that Triangle Boy didn't mask a user's identity as much as it claimed. So the lesson is that, no matter how much a government might try to censor information, there will always be a way to circumvent those restrictions. Unfortunately, any attempts to circumvent censorship won't always be 100% successful either, so if you don't want to get caught violating your government's Internet restrictions, your best bet is to make sure you never support any government that endorses censorship in the first place.

BANNED WEB PAGES TO VISIT

While children (or even adults) could use email or programs like the Peekabooty software to slip pornography past any Internet filtering software that their parents or company may have installed, the intended purpose for circumventing Internet filters is to visit government-banned websites.

To learn what type of information may threaten certain governments, try looking at the following websites. Who knows? Maybe you'll find ideas to help you circumvent your own government's attempts to suppress any information it doesn't like.

Cuba

One of the more prominent anti-Castro groups is the Cuban American National Foundation (CANF, at http://www.canfnet.org). CANF provides firsthand reports of Cuban human rights violations (written by Cuban refugees), as well as reports of religious repression and debates about U.S. foreign policy toward Cuba.

CubaNet posts information it receives from Cuba's underground democracy movement to http://www.cubanet.org (which it hosts outside of Cuba), and regularly sends email back into Cuba so that Cuban dissidents there can spread their message to the rest of the world.

China

China regulates the use of the Internet by controlling the national telecommunications system, which all Chinese Internet providers must use. Thus, it can permanently block the websites of foreign newspapers (like *The New York Times*) and sites deemed pornographic (like *Playboy* magazine) from being accessed inside China.

Despite these restrictions, a few Chinese citizens still manage to access forbidden sites. A New York–based site, Human Rights in China (HRIC, at http://www.hrichina.org), claims dozens of hits each week from people inside China. Founded by Chinese scientists and scholars in March 1989, HRIC monitors the implementation of international human rights statutes in China. It also supports human rights and is an information source for Chinese people both inside China and abroad.

While the Chinese government can restrict access to particular sites from inside China, it can't screen the vast amount of email that crosses the Chinese borders every day. Exploiting this weakness, Chinese dissidents write and edit a weekly electronic magazine called Tunnel (http://www.geocities.com/SiliconValley/Bay/5598), sending their articles from inside China to a U.S. email account, from which the magazine is then distributed via email to readers in China. Using this method, the magazine hopes to prevent the Chinese government from identifying the writers and blocking the magazine's distribution in China.

Another newsletter, dubbed VIP Reference (http://www.bignews.org), provides information about human rights and pro-democracy movements inside China.

Saudi Arabia

The Movement for Islamic Reform in Arabia (MIRA, at http://www.islah.org/english-new.htm) has also managed to find its way onto the Saudi banned website list. MIRA's aim is to seek major reforms in Saudi Arabia, including freedom of expression and freedom of assembly. Saudi Arabia has a long history of oppressing women and foreigners and relies on a highly secretive justice system that denies fundamental due-process rights to suspected criminals. Prolonged solitary confinement, coerced confessions, torture, and secret trials are regular features of the Saudi justice system. For more information about the latest human rights violations of Saudi Arabia, visit the Human Rights Watch website (http://www.hrw.org) and read information about Saudi Arabia that its own citizens can't access freely.

Oppression and censorship everywhere else

To learn more about worldwide oppression, visit the Oppression.org website (http://www.oppression.org), shown in Figure 3-1. To learn more about worldwide censorship, visit the Index on Censorship website (http://www.indexonline.org).

If you're specifically interested in Eastern Europe, visit the Radio Free Europe website (http://www.rferl.org). By promoting free speech in any available form (Internet, newspapers, radio, etc.), Radio Free Europe hopes to create a well-informed citizenry that will act as a foundation for democracy in countries still struggling to shake off the destructive effects of communist rule.

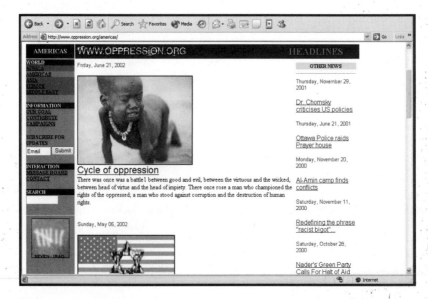

Figure 3-1

Oppression.org can show you how different countries around the world, including your own, are currently oppressing their own citizens.

For more information about censorship around the world, visit the following websites:

Electronic Frontier Foundation	http://www.eff.org/br
Electronic Privacy Information Center	http://www.epic.org/free_speech/ action
Global Internet Liberty Campaign	http://www.gilc.org
Internet Free Expression Alliance	http://www.ifea.net
Reporters Without Borders	http://www.rsf.org

PARENTAL CONTROL SOFTWARE

Just as national governments use filtering software to block certain websites, parents can use *parental control software* to monitor and filter their children's Internet use. These programs allow parents to block access to a list of URLs of their choosing, or to limit access to certain content by content scanning—blocking access to URLs or web pages that contain specific words.

When content scanning is in use, if your children enter a URL with a word like "love," "sex," or "nude" (such as www.love.com), or they try to access a page that contains similar words, the parental control program refuses to grant access. However, URL scanning does have limitations, since the program does not understand the context and cannot, for example, distinguish between scientific and pornographic use of the word "sex."

While few people argue that parents have the right to decide what their children can see, the debate about parental control software centers on the types of websites that parental control programs block. Most parental control programs block the obvious, such as Condom Country, Playboy, or Hustler. But since new pornographic websites appear every day, the publishers of parental control software must constantly update their lists of banned sites to maintain their programs' effectiveness, which presents a problem of time versus resources. Publishers of parental control software can't afford to hire enough people to visit and check suspect websites, so most publishers use programs that automatically scan websites and search for keywords.

When these programs determine that a site contains too many banned keywords, they store that site's address in their updated list of banned websites. The result is that parental control programs often block many innocent websites. Even worse, many blocked sites have no knowledge that they're being blocked by a particular parental control program.

Blocking political and educational sites

The biggest problem with parental control programs is the criteria they use to block specific websites. Besides blocking the obvious pornographic sites, many parental control programs also venture into the shady area of political censorship as well. Here are some examples:

Net Nanny (http://www.netnanny.com) has blocked the Banned Books page at the University of Pennsylvania (http://digital.library.upenn.edu/books/banned-books.html).

I-Gear (http://www.symantec.com) has blocked The Wisdom Fund (http://www.twf.org), an Islamic non-profit organization that provides information about Islam and opposes anti-Islamic bias in the media, and the Human Rights Campaign (http://www.hrcusa.org), an organization working to protect lesbian and gay rights.

CyberPatrol (http://www.cyberpatrol.com) has blocked such "dangerous" and "sexually explicit" sites as Envirolink (http://www.envirolink.org), an animal rights website; the Ontario Consultants on Religious Tolerance (http://www.religioustolerance.org), an organization devoted to promoting religious diversity and acceptance; Adoption Links Worldwide (http://www.alww.org); and the MIT Student Association for Freedom of Expression (http://www.mit.edu:8001/activities/safe/home.html).

SmartFilter (http://www.securecomputing.com), installed on computers in Utah schools and public libraries, blocked access to web pages that included the Holy Bible, the U.S. Constitution, the Declaration of Independence, anti-drug information, all of Shakespeare's plays, *The Adventures of Sherlock Holmes*, and the Koran.

Parental control software gone really bad: CYBERsitter

Perhaps the most controversial parental control program is CYBERsitter (http://www.cybersitter.com), which has blocked both NOW (National Organization for Women, at http://www.now.org) and the Human Awareness Institute site (http://www.hai.org), which promotes workshops for personal growth focusing on love, intimacy, and sexuality.

While most parental control programs allow sites to appeal a block, CYBERsitter seems to have constructed a wall of self-righteousness. For example, when NOW appealed its ban by CYBERsitter, Brian Milburn, the CEO of Solid Oak Software (CYBERsitter's publisher) replied, "If NOW doesn't like it, tough . . . We have not and will not bow to any pressure from any organization that disagrees with our philosophy."

CYBERsitter on the offensive

A heated battle has occurred between CYBERsitter and Bennett Haselton, cofounder of Peacefire (http://www.peacefire.org), an Internet anticensorship site. After Bennett posted information on the Peacefire site criticizing CYBERsitter, along with instructions for disabling various parental control programs including CYBERsitter, Peacefire was promptly added to the CYBERsitter banned website database.

Peacefire also claimed that during installation of the trial version, CYBERsitter scans the Internet Explorer cache and aborts the installation with a cryptic error message if it finds evidence of visits to the Peacefire site (such as the files peacefire.html or peacefire.gif).

Brian Milburn defended his software by saying, "We reserve the right to say who gets to install our software for free. It's our software—we own it, we publish it, we have an absolute legal right to protect our software from being hacked in any way, shape or form."

Cyber Patrol vs. cphack

In a dispute similar to the Peacefire versus CYBERsitter debate, Microsystems Software, the publisher of CyberPatrol, once filed a lawsuit against two computer programmers, Eddy L.O. Jansson and Matthew Skala, for creating the cphack program, which allows children to uncover their parents' passwords and view CyberPatrol's entire list of more than 100,000 banned websites.

"I oppose the use of Internet filtering software on philosophical grounds," Skala said. "The issue here was to see what does CyberPatrol actually block. Parents have a right to know what they're getting and without our work they wouldn't know."

To avoid a drawn-out legal debate, Microsystems Software announced that Jansson and Skala, the original authors of the cphack program, had settled with the company and granted them all rights to their cphack program. Microsystems then claimed that websites that posted the cphack program were violating the Microsystems Software copyright.

Project bait and switch: revealing the double standard of censorship

To show beyond a doubt that many parental control software publishers are using questionable tactics, Peacefire ran an experiment, dubbed Project Bait and Switch, to see if parental control programs would block certain content if it was hosted on a personal web page while not blocking the same content on the website of a large, well-funded, and well-known organization. (Read more about it on their site.)

They collected anti-gay quotes from the Family Research Council (http://www.frc.org), the Concerned Women for America (http://www.cwfa.org), Focus on the Family (http://www.family.org), and Dr. Laura's websites (http://www.drlaura.com). Then they posted these anti-gay quotes on free websites and submitted the pages anonymously to the publishers of SurfWatch, CyberPatrol, Net Nanny, Bess, SmartFilter, and Websense.

All of the companies agreed to block some or all of the "bait" pages (since they met their criteria for "denigrating people based on sexual orientation"), at which point Peacefire revealed the sites that were the source of these quotes. Surprisingly, none of the publishers agreed to block any of the four originating websites, yet they continued to block the "bait" pages, even though both sites contained identical homophobic quotes.

While this censorship may seem justified to protect children, there's still the question that always surrounds censorship in any form: Who decides what can and cannot be seen?

Defeating parental control software

To help people circumvent parental control programs, Peacefire offers a free program (http://www.peacefire.org/bypass) that can disable a variety of programs, including SurfWatch, CyberPatrol, CYBERsitter, Net Nanny, X-Stop, PureSight, and Cyber Snoop. (Unfortunately, the Peacefire bypass program only works under Windows 98.)

Although defeating parental control programs could allow children to access pornography, it also allows them to access a flood of other information at the same time. If you're going to use a parental control program, learn what type of websites they block (and why), and decide for yourself if you want to censor your children's access using someone else's criteria. If you don't want a stranger to tell you what you can and cannot let your children see and read, would you want a parental control program to do the same thing as well?

For more information that argues against censorship, visit Families Against Censorship (http://www.netfamilies.org). For more information about defeating censorware, visit The Censorware Project (http://censorware.net).

Child-safe browsers: the safe alternative to parental control programs

As an alternative to parental control programs, consider a *child-safe browser* instead, such as ChiBrow (http://www.chibrow.com) and SurfMonkey (http://www.surfmonkey.com). Unlike parental control programs that keep a proprietary list of banned websites that even parents can't see (let alone modify), child-safe browsers give parents complete control over which websites a child can access, while also offering the option to block Internet access during certain times of the day or after a specific amount of time has passed.

By offering complete control over the times and exact websites a child can visit, child-safe browsers protect your children while giving them access to educational, scientific, and intellectual websites that a parental control program might have blocked. While there's no substitute for parental supervision, a child-safe browser may be the next best alternative.

READING BANNED BOOKS ONLINE

In 1993, the school districts in Fairbanks, Alaska, and Harrisburg, Pennsylvania, came close to banning its students from reading the Bible, claiming that it contains "language and stories that are inappropriate for children of any age, including tales of incest and murder. . . . There are more than three hundred examples of 'obscenities' in the book."

In 1986, Gastonia, North Carolina, burned *The Living Bible*, by William C. Bower, claiming it was "a perverted commentary on the King James Version."

Harper Lee's novel *To Kill a Mockingbird* has been considered "dangerous" because of profanity. Parents throughout the years have claimed that the plot of a white lawyer defending a black man undermines race relations, at least according to school districts in Eden Valley, Minnesota, 1977; Warren, Indiana, 1981; Waukegan, Illinois, 1984; Kansas City, Missouri, 1985; and Park Hill, Missouri, 1985.

Despite persistent bans on classic literature and religious works, many parents, teachers, and government authorities still insist on the right to ban books that they consider harmful to someone else's intellectual, emotional, and spiritual development. To combat such governmental restrictions on books, Project Gutenberg offers famous works such as *The Adventures of Huckleberry Finn, Dracula*, and *A Tale of Two Cities* as plain ASCII text files that any computer can display and print. Their goal is to provide copies of famous and noteworthy works of literature so anyone can enjoy them for free.

To find banned books online, visit Banned Books Online (http://digital. library.upenn.edu/books/banned-books.html), MIT Press Bookstore (http://mit-press.mit.edu/bookstore/banned.html), The Online Books Page (http://digital. library.upenn.edu/books), or Project Gutenberg (http://www.promo.net/pg).

Of course, you still need to access the Internet to download a free e-book. But once you've downloaded it, you can share it with others. By copying and sharing, you can preserve your right to read certain books that other people (your parents, boss, or government) don't want you to see.

Secretly reading a banned book in broad daylight

Most websites that offer banned books as ASCII text files assume you're going to read the book using your computer. Of course, you could still get in trouble if someone catches you reading a banned book on your computer screen.

To disguise what you're reading, use a reading program like AceReader (http://www.stepware.com), which displays the entire text of an ASCII document across your screen in large letters, one word at a time, at speeds up to 1,000 words per minute, so that it's virtually impossible for anyone to see what you're reading at a glance. With this program, you can read the ASCII text of a book that your parents, school officials, or government authorities don't want you to read, right in front of their eyes without them ever knowing it.

IS ANYONE CENSORING THE CENSORS?

Despite the problems of censoring information, whether it's against religious, government, or sexual norms, many people continue to insist that censorship is necessary—just as long as they're the ones who get to pick and choose what others can and cannot see.

(Ironically, some foreign translations of this book had to delete certain chapters before some governments would allow the book to be published. If certain information is deemed too harmful for the public, shouldn't it also be too harmful for the censors to look at too?)

Fortunately, no matter what obstacles people may use to block your access to information, there will always be ways to defeat or avoid them if you just exercise a little bit of creativity. Perhaps the only form of censorship we have to worry about is self-censorship, when people are either too frightened to speak honestly and openly about anything they want, or so close-minded that they willingly shut their minds to any new ideas that disrupt their static way of thinking. Once that happens (usually under the guise of "political correctness"), censorship may finally succeed in stifling free speech.

4

HACKTIVISM: ONLINE ACTIVISM

GIVEN A CHOICE BETWEEN THE VOTE OF A SINGLE INDIVIDUAL OR THE WISHES OF A MAJOR CORPORATION THAT DONATED THOUSANDS OF DOL-LARS IN CAMPAIGN CONTRIBUTIONS, GUESS WHICH ONE WILL HAVE THE MOST INFLUENCE OVER A POLITICIAN? One solution for individuals who hope to have their voices heard by government officials is to band together with like-minded people and form a group too large for the politicians to ignore.

In the days before the Internet, such activists relied on meetings, newsletters, and mass mailings to keep their members organized and informed. However, the popularity of the Internet has given activists a new medium for spreading their ideas and making their goals known.

To learn more about using the Internet to form or improve an activist group, read The Virtual Activist training course offered by NetAction (http://www. netaction.org). If you want to find a protest rally near you, visit Protest.Net (http://www.protest.net), which lists protests around the world and offers an Activist's Handbook to help people get involved with a cause they believe in (see Figure 4-1).

> The state calls its own violence law, but that of the individual crime.
>
> —MAX STIRNER

GETTING THE WORD OUT WITH EMAIL AND WEBSITES

Email is one of the simplest, yet one of the more powerful, tools that activists use. The moment someone proposes a particularly interesting (or disturbing) bill, activists send out a flood of email, informing their members about the latest news and telling them what they can do to support or stop it.

Besides spreading news to members, activists also bombard the various news media with press releases by email. Since the press is always hungry for a story, a particularly interesting press release can spur them into giving a particular topic additional coverage, providing the activist group with greater exposure that could attract even more people to their cause.

Americans who want to find an email address for their particular representatives can visit e.thepeople.com (http://www.ethepeople.com). Besides listing American government representatives' email addresses, this website also lists various petitions you can support, or you can even start your own and post it on the site.

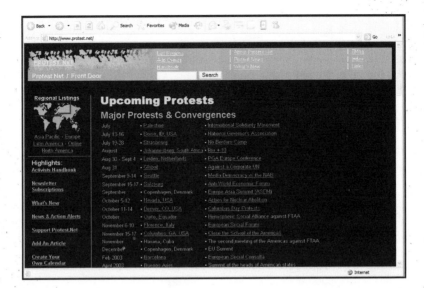

Figure 4-1

Protest.Net lists different types of protests by geographical location, date, and topic so that you can protest around the world at your convenience.

Another site, Progressive Secretary (http://www.progressivesecretary.org), allows anyone to start or join a letter-writing campaign to various American government officials, petitioning them on topics ranging from the environment and arms proliferation to the death penalty and the Cuban embargo. By combining forces with thousands of individuals, you can make your voice heard much faster than if you tried to write a single letter yourself.

Of course, email is simply a faster version of the mass mailings and faxing that activists relied on before the growth of the Internet. What gives activists greater visibility are websites that promote particular groups, their goals, and their philosophies to a worldwide audience. For greater influence, many activists have formed alliances with similar organizations. To learn more about networking over the Internet with other activist groups, visit the following sites:

Coalition for Networked Information	http://www.cni.org
Global Internet Liberty Campaign	http://www.gilc.org
Peoples' [*sic*] Global Action	http://www.nadir.org/nadir/initiativ/agp
Internet Free Expression Alliance	http://www.ifea.net
Internet Democracy Project	http://www.internetdemocracyproject.org

To find a particular activist group to join or form an alliance with, visit these sites:

Action Without Borders   http://www.idealist.org
GuideStar   http://www.guidestar.org
Activism.net   http://www.activism.net

Activism.net also provides more technical information about using a computer to promote your cause, including discussions of anonymous remailers and cryptography.

Of course, even activists need help once in a while, so visit Cause Communications (http://www.causecommunications.com) or Grassroots Enterprise (http://www.grassroots.com) to learn more about two consulting services that help activists achieve their goals. If you need facts to support your cause, visit Political Research Associates (http://www.publiceye.org), which offers its research on various antidemocratic, authoritarian, and oppressive movements, institutions, and trends.

In case you have information that your government doesn't want anyone to see, contact Cryptome (http://cryptome.org), which will post any secretive or banned information on their website for everyone to see.

USING THE INTERNET AS A MEDIUM

With so many activists using the Internet, it's only natural that many governments will try to outlaw or restrict Internet use for their citizens as a way to censor their speech. To counter this disturbing trend, activists such as the self-proclaimed Cypherpunks (http://www.csua.berkeley.edu/cypherpunks/Home.html) focus on using various technical tools like encryption to protect and ensure free speech on the Internet. Still other activists use the Internet itself as a medium for expressing and disseminating their beliefs. Combining hacking with activism, these "hacktivists" promote their ideas through computer viruses, web page defacements, and denial-of-service attacks.

Computer viruses as activist messages

Teaching people about a worthwhile cause can be the hardest job of any activist group. Ideally, activists need a way to deliver their messages for free that will spread to as many people as possible. Email may be free and have the potential to spread around the world, but an even more ideal communication medium is a computer virus.

Unlike email, which must be manually and intentionally transmitted from one person to another, a computer virus can act entirely on its own without any human intervention whatsoever. One of the earliest hacktivist viruses was an MS-DOS virus called the Fu Manchu virus, which buried itself in memory and waited for the user to type in the names of Ronald Reagan, Margaret Thatcher, or former South African President P.K. Botha. The moment the user typed in one of these names, the Fu Manchu virus changed the names into obscene words.

To protest French nuclear testing, someone wrote the Nuclear virus to infect Microsoft Word documents and insert the text, "STOP ALL FRENCH NUCLEAR TESTING IN THE PACIFIC!" at the end of every document.

Computer viruses can spread from one computer to another, but the speed of their infection can rarely match the speed of distribution that an email worm can achieve. Two hacktivist worms include the Mari@mm worm and the Staple worm, both of which can send a copy of themselves to every email address stored in a Microsoft Outlook address book. When the Mari@mm worm infects a computer, it puts a marijuana icon on the screen. If the user clicks on this icon, a dialog box appears, as shown in Figure 4-2, promoting the legalization of marijuana.

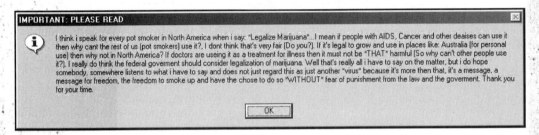

IMPORTANT: PLEASE READ

I think i speak for every pot smoker in North America when i say: "Legalize Marijuana"...I mean if people with AIDS, Cancer and other deaises can use it then why cant the rest of us (pot smokers) use it?, I dont think that's very fair (Do you?). If it's legal to grow and use in places like: Australia (for personal use) then why not in North America? If doctors are useing it as a treatment for illness then it must not be "THAT" harmful (So why can't other people use it?). I really do think the federal goverment should consider legalization of marijuana. Well that's really all i have to say on the matter, but i do hope somebody, somewhere listens to what i have to say and does not just regard this as just another "virus" because it's more then that, it's a message, a message for freedom, the freedom to smoke up and have the chose to do so "WITHOUT" fear of punishment from the law and the goverment. Thank you for your time.

OK

Figure 4-2

The Mari@mm worm promotes the legalization of marijuana.

The Staple worm emails itself to the first 50 email addresses stored in a Microsoft Outlook address book and displays the following message:

PLEASE ACCEPT MY APOLOGIES FOR DISTURBING YOU.

Remember that one day YOU may be in this situation.

We need every possible help.

Israeli soldiers killed in cold blood 12 year old Palestinian child

Mohammad Al-Durra, as his father tried to protect him in vain with

his own body. As a result of the indiscriminate and excessive use of

machine gun fire by Israeli soldiers, journalists and bystanders

watched helplessly as the child was savagely murdered.

Palestinian Red Crescent Society medic Bassam Balbeisi

attempted to intervene and spare the child's life but live

ammunition to his chest by Israeli fire took his life in the process.

The child and the medic were grotesquely murdered in cold blood.

Mohammad's father, Jamal, was critically injured and permanently paralyzed. Similarly, approximately 40 children were slain, without

the media taking notice or covering these tragedies.

THESE CRIMINAL ACTS CANNOT BE FORGIVEN OR

FORGOTTEN!!!! HELP US TO STOP THE BLOOD SHED!!

Unlike regular viruses or worms, hacktivist viruses or worms rarely destroy data deliberately, because their intent is to spread their message and not harm any users.

Defacing web pages with activist messages

Burying your activist message in a virus or a worm is like shoving a newsletter in a bottle and throwing it in the ocean with the hope that somebody will find it. Rather than risk letting their messages travel haphazardly around the world (and possibly appearing in front of people who can't even read that particular language), many hacktivists take a more assertive approach and deface web pages instead, as shown in Figure 4-3.

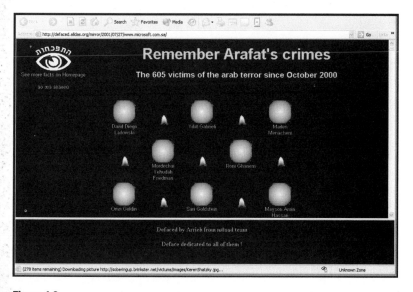

Figure 4-3

A defaced web page can publicize your message to a worldwide audience, such as this message defacing the website of Microsoft's office in Saudi Arabia.

Defacing a web page means sneaking past the website's security and modifying or replacing the home web page. Hacktivists would love to deface a highly visible website, such as http://www.whitehouse.gov or http://www.cnn.com, which would promote their message to thousands of people all over the world, but the more visible a website is, the more secure and closely watched it is likely to be. Deface the web page of a prominent newspaper, such as *USA Today*, and within minutes, someone will notice and contact the system administrators to shut it down and remove all your hard work.

As an alternative, many hacktivists target more obscure websites. Not only is security likely to be much weaker, but there's a greater chance that web page defacements will go unnoticed for several hours or even days, increasing the odds that more people will view the defaced web page, as shown in Figure 4-4. (Of course, although an obscure website that has been defaced may not be fixed as quickly, fewer people will likely see the defaced web pages no matter how long they may remain online.)

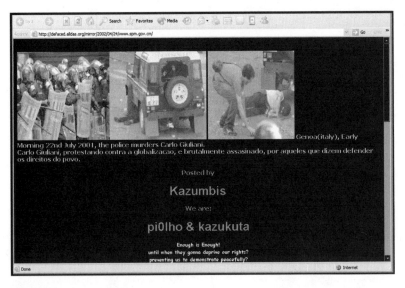

Figure 4-4

Defaced web pages often display graphic images to promote their messages, such as this web page that defaced the site of the Republic of Cameroon.

Web page defacements tend to increase during any period of conflict between opposing forces, such as during the bombing of Yugoslavia by NATO forces, the tension that occurred between China and the United States after an American spy plane made an emergency landing at a Chinese air base, and the never-ending battle between the Palestinians and the Israelis. Both sides tend to target the other side's websites with the goal being to deface as many web pages as possible, ideally targeting websites that have some direct relationship to the conflict in the first place.

Online monkey wrenching

Even web page defacements can be too timid for some hacktivists. Rather than simply publicize their ideas, some hacktivists would rather directly attack an enemy instead. This extreme form of hacktivism, similar to the monkey-wrenching tactics of environmentalists who spike trees or blow up bulldozing equipment, seeks to deny an enemy's ability to use their computers to promote their message to others.

To mimic the work-stopping abilities of sit-in protests, where hordes of people physically bring a factory, school, or government building to a standstill by getting in the way, a hacktivist group calling themselves the Electronic Disturbance Theater (http://www.thing.net/~rdom/ecd/ecd.html) decided to create software to help others stage virtual sit-ins that can disrupt an enemy's website or email access.

The Hacktivist (http://www.thehacktivist.com) offers the Electronic Disturbance Theater's tools, including Tribal Port Scan (written in Java) and FloodNet (a Java applet that tries to slow a targeted webserver to a standstill by continually requesting web pages). Also available from other sources are additional virtual sit-in tools with names like ClogScript, FloodScript, and WebScript, all of which allow multiple users to assault a target for a coordinated denial-of-service attack.

To help learn specific tactics involving hacktivism, you can even attend a training camp offered by the Ruckus Society (http://www.ruckus.org), which had previously trained protesters for disrupting the 1999 World Trade Organization (WTO) summit in Seattle. The Ruckus Society tends to attract all types of hacktivists, from those opposing Microsoft's monopoly on the operating system market to those fighting to allow free speech on the Internet by all citizens, regardless of nationality. For more information about the growing hacktivist movement, visit the Hacktivism site (http://infoshop.org/hacktivism.html).

Of course, some activists have no qualms about breaking the law or allying themselves with questionable organizations in order to further their agenda (which makes activists no more morally or ethically superior than the politicians, governments, and corporations they're attacking). For another look at different activist groups, visit the ActivistCash.com site (http://www.activistcash.com), which reveals information about activist groups that may not endear them to the general public.

For example, ActivistCash.com reports that PETA (People for Ethical Treatment of Animals) once gave $70,500 to Rodney Coronado, a convicted arsonist who served a five-year prison sentence for a 1992 animal-rights-related firebombing at Michigan State University. ActivistCash.com also reports that the founder of Mothers Against Drunk Drivers (MADD), Candy Lightner, recently broke ties with the group, believing "that the movement I helped create has lost direction." Rather than focus on eliminating drunk drivers, many believe that MADD has unnecessarily expanded their aims to prohibit any alcohol use at all.

THE THREAT OF CYBERTERRORISM

Back in the 1950s, the American government blamed nearly every social, economic, and political problem on communists. Nowadays, every possible social, economic, and political problem is being blamed on terrorists. With the possible threat that terrorists could use the Internet to communicate with each other, many governments want to limit their citizens' privacy, free speech, and access to the Internet. (Of course, terrorists can also communicate using paper and pencil, but so far no government has tried to ban writing instruments or office supplies.)

At the simplest level, terrorist groups can simply post information about themselves and their goals on websites located in other countries, as shown in Figure 4-5. For a peek at what a terrorist's website looks like, visit two of Hizbullah's websites:

http://www.hizbollah.org	Provides basic information about Hizbullah
http://www.moqawama.tv	Describes Israeli aggression and Hizbullah's attacks against Israeli targets

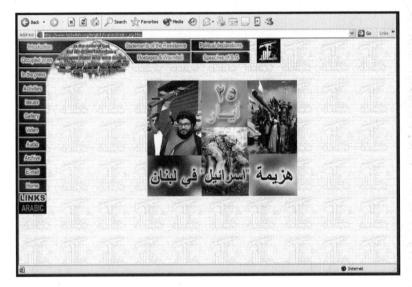

Figure 4-5

The Hizbullah website, offering information about their goals.

Even Sri Lanka has their own terrorists, known as the Liberation Tigers of Tamil Eelam (http://www.eelam.com). For more information about terrorist groups around the world (at least according to the United States), visit the Terrorist Groups Profiles site (http://library.nps.navy.mil/home/tgp/tgp2.htm).

The real danger is that cyberterrorism can evolve from the hacktivist denial-of-service and virus attacks to outright destruction of property and loss of lives. Some possible examples of what cyberterrorists could accomplish range from the frightening to the bizarre. One possible cyberterrorist scenario involves hacking into an air traffic control system and redirecting civilian aircraft to collide. A more unusual study warned that hackers could break into the processing control system of a cereal manufacturer and change the level of iron supplement in the cereal, causing children to get sick and die.

A third scenario envisioned cyberterrorists disrupting the computers controlling international financial transactions, causing banks to fail and stock markets to crash (which means that corrupt politicians and CEOs of major corporations could be classified as cyberterrorists if they only used a computer).

While the threat of terrorism is real and cyberterrorism is a possibility, there's still a fine line separating terror from the law. From the British point of view, the Boston Tea Party was an act of terrorism, but from the American point of view, it was an act of valid protest. So the next time you hear about the latest act of terrorism or activism, find out the motives and beliefs of each side of the conflict, and then decide for yourself who is right and who is wrong (if you can).

5

PLEDGING ALLEGIANCE: HATRED AS PATRIOTISM

WHILE NEWSPAPERS AND MAGAZINES HERALD THE INTERNET AS THE CURRENT REVOLUTION IN COMMUNICATIONS, THEY OFTEN IGNORE ANOTHER ASPECT OF ITS LOW-COST, WORLDWIDE AVAILABILITY: HATE GROUPS HAVE FLOCKED TO THE INTERNET TO USE IT AS AN INEXPENSIVE AND EASY WAY TO RECRUIT NEW MEMBERS AND COMMUNICATE WITH EXISTING ONES.

If we believe absurdities we shall commit atrocities.

—VOLTAIRE

As early as 1995, Don Black, the ex-Grand Dragon of the Ku Klux Klan and owner of the white supremacist Stormfront website (http://www.stormfront.org), said that the "... Internet has had a pretty profound influence on [the white supremacist] movement whose resources are limited. The access is anonymous and there is unlimited ability to communicate with others of a like mind" (*New York Times*, March 13, 1995).

MONITORING HATE GROUPS

Because so many hate groups use the Internet to spread their messages, the organizations Positive-Youth Foundation (http://www.antiracistaction.net), Tolerance.org (http://www.hatewatch.org), and the Southern Poverty Law Center (http://www.splcenter.org) were founded to keep track of the different hate groups and their activities. The more people learn about different hate groups, the more concerned individuals, academics, organizations, and media can study and fight back against the activities of these hate groups.

After browsing through the various links in this chapter to the sites of hate-mongering white supremacists, skinheads, black radicals, neo-Nazis, Holocaust deniers, Christian nationalists, antigay activists, anti-Christian groups, and anti-Arab groups, you may wonder whether people will ever learn to live together in peace.

While there are people who might use these links to find the nearest hate group to join, existing hate groups can also browse through these same links to find groups that hate them just as much as they hate others.

White supremacy

Perhaps the most well-known white supremacy group in the United States is the Ku Klux Klan (http://www.kukluxklan.org), an organization that promotes the idea of "an America in which our borders are secure and non-whites who don't share our concepts of liberty find entrance impossible." (Missing from this proclamation is whether whites who don't share the Klan's concepts of liberty will also find entrance impossible.)

The vision of the Klan further emphasizes their desire to see "an America in which our children are not confronted by anti-white and anti-Christian propaganda, where they are not confronted with the 'joys' of homosexuality or race mixing, but rather the condemnation of these behaviors by God. We envision an America in which these anti-Christian behaviors are punished and serve as additional deterrents to anyone toying with the satanic notion of race mixing or homosexuality."

Like other groups that promote apartheid, the Klan claims that it does not hate non-whites. For example, it claims that "We envision an America in which all races are given the opportunity to return to their native lands, to govern themselves and to choose their own destiny. We envision an America where those non-whites choosing to stay to enjoy the benefits of Christian living are respected, protected, and given the opportunity to prosper to the best of their ability while recognizing the lawful authority of White Christians to rule over America. A guest in your home is always expected to respect your authority. Likewise non-whites who reside in America should be expected to conduct themselves according to Christian principles and must recognize that race mixing is definitely wrong and out of the question. It will be a privilege to live under the authority of a compassionate White Christian government." One can only question how "compassionate" such a White Christian government really would be in achieving their goal of promoting racial separation.

Another group working for the advancement of the white race is The Creativity Movement (http://www.creator.org), which offers the following insights into their philosophy:

The World Church of the Creator is often described with words like "hatemonger," "hate organization," "hate speech." Is this fair?

No, it isn't fair since every organization—whatever it may be—hates something or someone. Since other organizations aren't labeled "hate" groups, etc., why should we be singled out like this? We don't exist out of hatred for the other races but out of love for our own Race.

But isn't it part and parcel of your religion to hate the Jews, blacks and other colored people?

True, but if you love and want to defend those whom you love, your own family, your own White Race; then hate for your enemies comes natural and is inevitable. Love and hate are two sides of the same coin. Only a *hypocrite and a liar will go into battle against his enemies proclaiming love.*

What then is CREATIVITY'S final position on love and hate?

We follow the eternal wisdom of Nature's laws, which are completely opposite to the suicidal teachings of Christianity. Whereas Christianity says to "love your enemies" and to hate your own kind (see, e.g., Luke 14:26), we say just the opposite. We say that in order to survive, we must overcome and destroy those that are a threat to our existence; namely, our deadly enemies. At the same time, we advocate love and protection for those that are near and dear to us: our family and our own race, which is an extension of the family.

If you think that all white racists are men, visit SIGRDRIFA Publications (http://www.sigrdrifa.com) or Women for Aryan Unity (http://www.stormfront.org/crusader/texts/wau/), two groups that promote the woman's role in the white pride movement.

One of the more devious tricks of white supremacy groups is to snatch up domain names that appear to belong to legitimate organizations. For example, the domain names MartinLutherKing.org and MLKing.org are actually owned by the two white supremacy groups Stormfront and National Alliance. Both domain names point to the same website, which deride Martin Luther King as "Just a sexual degenerate, an America-hating Communist, and a criminal betrayer of even the interests of his own people." Ironically, much of the negative information about Martin Luther King comes from declassified FBI documents from the 1960s when the FBI organized a smear campaign against King. Although the FBI's propaganda has been largely discredited, it does show how the FBI, at one time, discriminated against blacks and by today's standards would have been considered a hate group in its own right.

You can even buy pro-white merchandise from Resistance Records (http://www.resistance.com), which sells a wide variety of pro-white T-shirts, CDs, and even video games such as "Ethnic Cleansing," a first-person shooter game where players wander through urban streets and subway tunnels in search of African-American, Hispanic, and Jewish characters to gun down.

For more exposure to white supremacy ideas, visit these websites:

Heritage Front	http://www.freedomsite.org/hf
National Alliance	http://www.natvan.com
White Aryan Resistance	http://www.resist.com

Or browse these select Usenet newsgroups: alt.politics.white-power, alt.skinheads, alt.politics.nationalism.white, alt.music.white-power, or alt.flame.niggers.

Neo-Nazis

Unlike the white racists who claim they aren't necessarily enemies of non-whites, neo-Nazis advocate violence against non-whites in support of Adolf Hitler's Third Reich. One of these organizations is the American Nazi Party (http://www.american-naziparty.com), based in Michigan. After reading their message of hate, blaming non-whites for all the problems of society, you have to wonder why so many neo-Nazis live in countries that their leader, Adolf Hitler, tried to bomb during World War Two.

To get the inside scoop on two more American organizations that probably didn't know which side to root for in *Saving Private Ryan*, visit the National Socialist Movement (http://www.nsm88.com—see Figure 5-1) or The New Order (http://www.theneworder.org). The New Order site proclaims:

> *We are the Movement of Adolf Hitler. We are His heirs. He has given us a commission, which it is our duty to discharge. For it was Adolf Hitler who came into the world to remind modern man of Nature's eternal laws, and to make them the basis for a miraculous regeneration in human affairs. That is why we proudly recognize Him as the greatest figure of the age, and why we regard His cause as the one great hope of Aryan mankind on this Earth.*

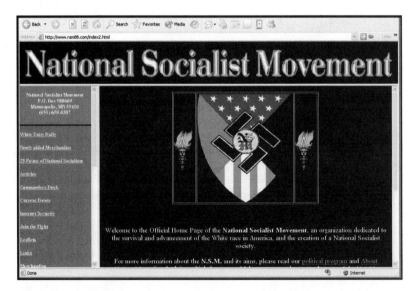

Figure 5-1

The National Socialist Movement can help Americans become Nazis.

To learn about other groups that combine white supremacy attitudes with a socialist political twist, visit American Nationalist Union (http://www.anu.org) or try the alt.flame.jews or alt.fan.ernst-zundel Usenet newsgroups.

Holocaust deniers

While many Holocaust deniers do not claim to be Nazis (or neo-Nazis, if there's any difference), they still upset many people by their persistent denial that the slaughter of six million Jews ever took place. The Adelaide Institute (http://www.adelaideinstitute.org), for example, asks for proof of the Holocaust:

> Anyone who claims that homicidal gas chambers existed at the Auschwitz concentration camp, makes the terrible allegation against Germans, and those of German descent, that during World War Two Germans exterminated European Jewry, et al, therein.

> Individuals who make such an allegation owe it to the world to answer Dr Robert Faurisson's challenge:

> "Show me or draw me the Auschwitz homicidal gas chambers!"

> To date not a single person has produced evidence that proves these huge chemical slaughterhouses ever existed.

For another denial of the Holocaust, visit the Air Photo Evidence website (http://www.air-photo.com), which claims that aerial and ground-based photographs prove that the Holocaust could not have happened, even to the point of stating that "ground photos show happy well-fed inmates" at the Plaszow Camp, but fails to include any supporting testimonials from all these happy, well-fed inmates.

To probe further into the bizarre and dangerous world of Holocaust deniers, try visiting the following sites:

Institute for Historical Review	http://www.ihr.org
Campaign for Radical Truth in History	http://www.hoffman-info.com
The Zundelsite	http://www.zundelsite.org

Or share your thoughts with others in the alt.revisionism Usenet newsgroup.

Black racists

Not all racists are white. Blacks can be racists too, and their favorite targets are usually whites and Jewish people. If you visit the Blacks and Jews Newspage website (http://www.blacksandjews.com), you'll find the following, which attempts to justify hatred of an entire group of people based on the actions of a few:

The following passages are from Dr. Raphael's book Jews and Judaism in the United States a Documentary History (New York: Behrman House, Inc., Pub, 1983), pp. 14, 23-25.

"Jews also took an active part in the Dutch colonial slave trade; indeed, the bylaws of the Recife and Mauricia congregations (1648) included an imposta (Jewish tax) of five soldos for each Negro slave a Brazilian Jew purchased from the West Indies Company. Slave auctions were postponed if they fell on a Jewish holiday. In Curacao in the seventeenth century, as well as in the British colonies of Barbados and Jamaica in the eighteenth century, Jewish merchants played a major role in the slave trade. In fact, in all the American colonies, whether French (Martinique), British, or Dutch, Jewish merchants frequently dominated.

Using this same logic against the Blacks and Jews Newspage, white racists can justifiably claim that blacks should be held accountable for the actions of a few—since some blacks have committed crimes, then all blacks must be criminals.

While black racists attack whites and Jews for profiting from the slave trade, they ignore any evidence that many black Africans sold their own people into slavery for profits too.

To learn more about how blacks can be just as racist as whites, visit the alt.politics.nationalism.black or alt.flame.whites newsgroups. As an extra challenge, ignore all references to skin color and try to determine the difference between a white racist and a black racist.

Anti-Semitism

While you might expect neo-Nazis to be anti-Jewish, it is surprising how many other groups also have no qualms about attacking the Jews, usually accusing them of conspiring to control world governments. The Holy War website (http://holywar.org, shown in Figure 5-2) claims:

The only Nazi country in the world is the satanic State of Israel! All of their leaders are wanted for crimes against humanity. They are wanted for 50 years of ethnic cleansing in Palestine, and the Palestinian Holocaust of six (6) million. They are also responsible for the Jewish Communist Holocaust that cost the lives of 300 million Christians.

If you want to explore the minds of people who believe that all Jewish people are secretly conspiring to control the world and all non-Jews in the process, you might find the following websites interesting:

First Amendment Exercise Machine	http://www.faem.com
The Tangled Web	http://www.codoh.com/zionweb/ zionweb.html

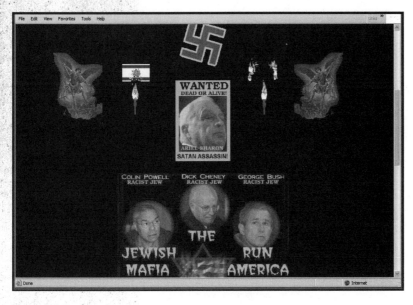

Figure 5-2

The Holy War site claims that the Bush administration is part of the Jewish Mafia.

Anti-Arab groups

The radical Jewish Defense League (JDL, at http://www.jdl.org) has taken what it calls self-defense to the extreme in the following statement: "It has always been a JDL priority to encourage as many Arabs as possible to leave Israel to make new homes in America or wherever they wish to live." Hmmm. Sounds strangely similar to the Ku Klux Klan's belief that non-whites can live anywhere they want, just as long as they get out of America.

The Kahane web page (http://kahane.org), another extreme Jewish group, toes a similar line:

> It is a central tenet of Judaism that G-d wished the Jew to create a unique, total, pure and complete Jewish life, society and state in Eretz Israel. This being so, who can honestly believe that He then sanctioned the democratic right of a non-Jew, who is totally alien and outside the Jewish society and who is free of its religious obligation, to have the slightest say in its workings?

To see that there is little unique or new in the rhetoric of hate groups, try this exercise: The next time you read or hear anything from radical Jewish groups or the Ku Klux Klan, substitute the name of a new villain in the diatribe, such as the word "Arab" for "black" (or vice versa). Then see if you can still tell which group is talking.

Anti-Christians

While Muslims and Jews take the brunt of most anti-religious attacks, a few people have decided that Christians shouldn't be exempt from hatred. Some anti-Christian groups target Christianity as the source of everything wrong in society, as shown in this message found on the Black Plague website (http://www.blackplague.org):

> The Christian Holocaust movement founds its kinetic potential upon the simple discovery of how language, culture, and social inculcation dictate individual human intellectual precepts, forming the filter which the individual uses to process the world. Christianity believes heavily in that filter with its duty-centric justification-based system of moral logic and its karmic work ethic, the primary elements of control in society today.
>
> For this reason there came about a movement which realized that the shared cultural understanding of this filter permits the brutal abuse of environment, human rights, and human value as we are abused in jobs designed to leave us four waking hours of free time. Society has brought us many good things and the addiction of their continued expense; Christianity believes this is progress and conveniently denies the importance of death with its explanation of the afterlife.

If you want to learn more from another anti-Christian group, try The Altar of Unholy Blasphemy (http://www.anus.com/altar) or the Judeo-Christian Holocaust (http://www.fuckchrist.com) websites.

Antigay activists

When people use the Bible to rationalize attacks on homosexuals, they ignore that same Bible that tells people to practice forgiveness. One of the most prominent anti-gay hate websites is God Hates Fags (http://www.godhatesfags.com), run by the Westboro Baptist Church in Topeka, Kansas. Its FAQ web page offers insight into their way of thinking:

> **Why do you preach hate?**
>
> Because the Bible preaches hate. For every one verse about God's mercy, love, compassion, etc., there are two verses about His vengeance, hatred, wrath, etc. The maudlin, kissy-pooh, feel-good, touchy-feely preachers of today's society are damning this nation and this world to hell. They are telling you what you want to hear rather than what you need to hear, just like what happened in the days of Isaiah and Jeremiah.

*Do you ever pray for the salvation of those who you feel are con-
demned?*

*Of course not! For, if we follow (as we ought) the example of our Saviour
and the clear commandment of God, we would not dare to do so.*

And here's more from the antigay sermon of the Westboro Baptist Church:

*The only true Nazis in this world are fags. They want to force you by law
to support their filth, and they want to shut you up by law when they hate
what you say. They would be perfectly happy to make it a crime to preach
that "God hates fags" under the guise of "hate speech legislation."
Likewise, baby-killers support the genocide of millions of innocent
babies, and then act indignant that Hitler killed a few million innocent
Jews.*

*The only true Jews are Christians. The rest of the people who claim to be
Jews aren't, and they are nothing more than typical, impenitent sinners,
who have no Lamb. As evidence of their apostacy [sic], the vast majority
of Jews support fags. Of course, there are Jews who still believe God's
law, but most of them have even departed from that.*

In case this website hasn't opened your eyes to the way people can turn religion into a forum of hatred, there's even more evidence in the God Hates America
(http://www.godhatesamerica.com—see Figure 5-3) and Bob Enyart Live
(http://www.enyart.com) sites. Or try joining the alt.flame.fucking.faggots Usenet
newsgroup and share your thoughts with others.

LEARNING FROM HATE GROUPS

Anytime you join an organization based on race, religion, or nationality, it's easy to target people outside your organization as enemies. What an insider might call "a
patriot," an outsider might call "a hate monger." Hatred can come in all colors, religions, and nationalities, so rather than blindly condemn entire groups of people, ask
yourself what you really fear or what you're angry about, and then decide if the
destruction of an entire group of people will really help you solve your problem.

After browsing through various hate group websites, you may notice a common
denominator: Hate groups want the freedom to prevent others from exercising the
same rights that they enjoy. If you look beyond the surface distinctions (skin color,
national citizenship, religious affiliation, etc.) that hate groups use to identify their
members, you'll see that hate groups are often more similar to each other than they
are to the people they're trying to recruit.

While people like to believe that hate groups only represent the extreme fringe
elements of society, every individual or group is susceptible to prejudice and revision-
ism. Many churches hold the unspoken belief that other religions are blasphemous,

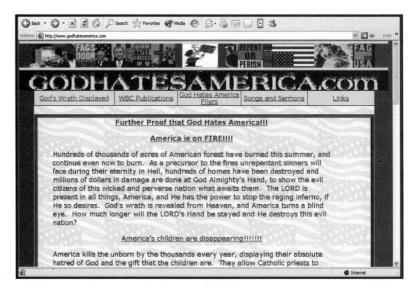

Figure 5-3

The God Hates America website is an example of a site that uses religion to justify its hatred of others.

and national governments regularly extol their innocence while carefully shunting aside any mention of atrocities they may have committed in the past.

To learn what other governments want to hide, look in the history textbooks that they give to their school children. Japanese history books portray Japan as a victim of World War Two, culminating with the atom bomb attacks on Hiroshima and Nagasaki (while avoiding any mention about the Bataan Death March that killed 10,000 American and Filipino soldiers, or the fact that Japan was also trying to develop an atom bomb as well). American history books gloss over the fact that they consistently broke treaties with the Native Americans and deliberately gave them small pox–infected blankets in an effort to wipe them out.

So the next time you pledge allegiance to any group, organization, or nation, take some time to think. While you may be pledging allegiance to some noble idea, don't let that blind you to the fact that your cherished group, organization, or country may also have a questionable and immoral history as well. If you blindly support any cause using any means necessary to advance it, other people may see you as part of a hate group, and you won't even know it.

6

WHERE THE HACKERS ARE

PERHAPS THE MOST UNUSUAL SOURCE OF ALTERNATIVE INFORMATION COMES FROM COMPUTER HACKERS THEMSELVES. Although the term *hacker* often conveys an air of mystery and intrigue, hackers are simply people who are very skilled at using technology. To differentiate between "good" and "bad" hackers, the media has created a variety of terms such as *white hat hackers* (the "good" ones) and *black hat hackers* (the "bad" ones). Other terms for a "bad" hacker include *malicious hacker* and *cracker*.

Whatever you call them, the fact is that hackers are people, and, like any group of people (Americans, police officers, teachers, accountants, Christians), some will be good and some will be bad. But unlike most other groups, hackers rely exclusively on computers and the Internet to communicate with each other.

Finding a hacker on the Internet is fairly easy if you know where to look. Just as you can quickly find a drug dealer or policeman if you know where to look in a city, you can also find good and bad hackers if you know where to look on the Internet.

WARNING: Hacker sites tend to appear and disappear with disturbing regularity. When a hacker site disappears, a pornographic site inevitably takes over the domain name. If any of the websites listed in this chapter suddenly disappear, you may find an X-rated site appearing when you type in the domain address, instead of the expected hacker site.

HACKER WEBSITES

Many hackers have banded together to post and advertise their own websites. Most hacker sites provide information about the hacker world told from the hacker's point of view, which mainstream media typically ignores. On hacker websites you'll find the latest security holes found in the more popular operating systems, and even hacker programs for invading other computers.

To learn more about hacking from the hacker's point of view, take a look at any of the following sites:

Attrition.org News and archives of hacker text and program files (http://www.attrition.org).

BlackCode Full-service hacker site selling merchandise, offering free downloads of hacker tools, and providing a proxy server to strip away your identity so you can surf the Internet anonymously (http://www.blackcode.com).

Cipherwar Provides news about hacking and the political debates surrounding the government's efforts to legislate, regulate, and otherwise control the Internet (http://www.cipherwar.com).

Cult of the Dead Cow Infamous hacker group responsible for releasing the Back Orifice remote administration tool that can also be used as a Trojan horse to hijack another computer (http://www.cultdeadcow.com).

Hack Canada Unique website focusing on hacking, phone phreaking, and anarchy from a Canadian point of view (http://www.hackcanada.com).

Hackers.com A hacker site that pledges to uphold the "old school" of hacking, which provides information to the curious, but avoids destructive and malicious hacking tools such as computer viruses or Trojan horses (http://www.hackers.com).

Hideaway.Net Specializes in covering news about computer security so that you can see the latest flaws in various firewalls, servers, and browsers (http://www.hideaway.net).

Insecure.org Lists plenty of security flaws and "exploits" in all your favorite operating systems, including Windows, Solaris, and Linux (http://www.insecure.org).

New Order Provides plenty of links to various hacker resources, such as anonymous remailers, encryption software, ICQ exploits, Novell network hacking, and hacker e-zines (http://neworder.box.sk).

Sys-Security Group dedicated to computer security research, offering plenty of information about port scanning (http://www.sys-security.com).

Underground News Offers hacker tools and news, and sells backpacks and messenger bags as well (http://www.undergroundnews.com).

Wiretapped Website specializing in intrusion detection software and cryptography (http://www.wiretapped.net).

COMPUTER SECURITY WEBSITES

On the other side of the hacker world are the professional computer security people, who include many former hackers and many so-called white hat hackers. By browsing through different computer security websites, you can read about the latest flaws and vulnerabilities that hackers could use to break into your computer.

@stake Once known as L0pht Industries, this hacker group decided there was more money to be made as a security consulting firm than as a renegade hacker group (http://www.atstake.com).

AntiOnline Offers hacker news, virus source code, and Trojan horse programs, along with a comprehensive profile of hackers for use by law enforcement agencies (http://www.antionline.com).

InfoSysSec Yahoo-like portal (see Figure 6-1) providing links to various computer security resources (http://www.infosyssec.net).

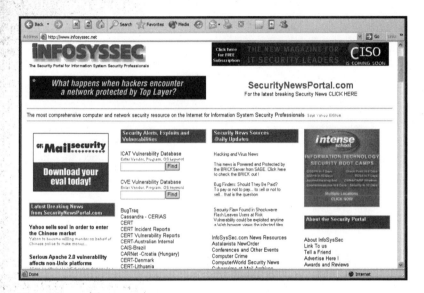

Figure 6-1

The InfoSysSec site lists the top ten ports that hackers use to break into a computer.

SecurityFocus Tries to offer news about the latest computer security flaws before they are known by the rest of the computer security field (http://www.securityfocus.com).

SecurityNewsPortal Provides the latest headlines covering hacking, information warfare, and virus outbreaks (http://www.securitynewsportal.com).

WindowsSecurity.com Offers articles and white papers covering anti-virus software, firewalls, intrusion detection systems, and network auditing (http://www.securitysearch.net).

HACKER MAGAZINES

One of the best ways to keep up with the ever-changing underground culture of computer hackers is to read hacker magazines. Because you probably won't find a hacker magazine at your favorite newsstand (with the exception of *2600* magazine), your best bet is to read some hacker magazines online. Hacker magazines tend to have an irregular publishing schedule, so don't be surprised if the latest issue is several months old.

2600 The home of the quarterly hacker magazine, *2600*. While its website doesn't offer any articles from the magazine, it does provide the latest hacker news along with an archive of defaced web pages (http://www.2600.com).

Computer Underground Digest A journal carrying news, research, and discussion of legal, social, and ethical issues concerning computer culture. Publication has since ceased, but this site can still be a rich source of hacker history (http://sun.soci.niu.edu/~cudigest).

Crypt Newsletter An online publication that pokes fun at the latest media hype surrounding computer viruses, hacker attacks, or encryption regulations. Covers computer crime, viruses, and the comical attempts of governments and corporations to control hackers for their own profit (http://sun.soci.niu.edu/~crypt).

Phrack The online version of one of the oldest hacker magazines, in operation since 1985. Phrack focuses on networking, telephony, and phone phreaking, and occasionally delves into other computer hacking topics as well (http://www.phrack.com).

TelecomWriting An unusual website specializing in the telephone system. At one time, this site published a magazine called Private Line, but when that magazine failed, the publisher focused on creating a comprehensive site covering all aspects of the telephone network (http://www.privateline.com).

FINDING MORE HACKER WEBSITES

Only a handful of hacker sites stay up for longer than a year. The majority of them appear with a flurry of activity, and then disappear when the founders lose interest and move on to other hobbies. Because hacker website life spans are so short, finding these sites can be difficult. Fortunately, there are ways to find them.

Hacker search engines

There are a variety of specialized search engines for finding hacker websites (see Figure 6-2). These hacker search engines can help you quickly find anything from source code to the latest dreaded virus to the current version of an online harassment program that attacks America Online or ICQ users. If none of the hacker sites listed earlier in this chapter have what you need, try one of the following specialized search engines instead:

Astalavista	http://astalavista.box.sk
Cyberarmy HakSearch	http://www.cyberarmy.com
Secureroot	http://www.secureroot.com
Startplaza.nu	http://www.startplaza.nu

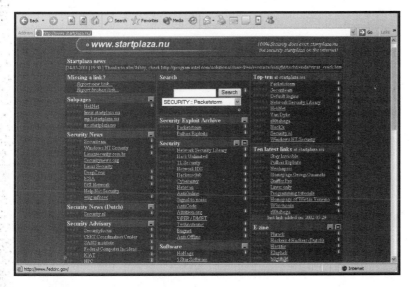

Figure 6-2
Use a hacker search engine like Startplaza.nu to find the hacking tool you need.

Hacker website lists

Many hackers like to claim that their website is the best, most comprehensive source of hacker information on the Internet. Since so many websites make this claim, hackers have put together lists that arrange competing hacker sites according to the number of votes each one gets from users. So, if you want to find the most popular hacker sites at the moment, browse through these lists and vote for your favorite:

Elite Toplist	http://www.elitetoplist.com
Secureroot	http://www.secureroot.com
Sub-List.Com	http://underground.sub-list.com

Web rings

Instead of blindly groping around the Internet with a search engine, you might want to try using a web ring instead. Web rings provide links to websites that focus on a specific topic. If you're interested in, say, computer virus writing, harassing America Online, or defacing web pages, visit the Web Ring site (http://www.webring.org), click on the Computers & Internet section, and then on the Cyberculture category and finally on the Hacking category for a list of additional hacker websites.

HACKER USENET NEWSGROUPS

Hackers often communicate with each other through Usenet newsgroups. Unlike ordinary newsgroups where people share information and answer questions, hacker newsgroups more often resemble shouting matches full of insults, sprinkled between ads for get-rich-quick schemes or pornography websites.

Still, if you don't mind wading through these types of messages cluttering hacker newsgroups, you can learn about the newest hacker websites and share source code and hacker programs with others on the newsgroup.

General hacking newsgroups

To start learning about hacking in general, try a general-purpose hacking newsgroups. Unlike other types of newsgroups that focus on stamp collecting or photography, hacker newsgroups tend to stray from their topics. For example, the alt.binaries.hacking.beginner newsgroup, which says it is about helping new hackers find and use hacking programs, is often filled with discussions about virus programming and encryption or, if you're lucky, vicious insult wars. Here are some more hacking newsgroups: alt.hacker, alt.hacking, alt.binaries.hacking.beginner, alt.binaries.hacking.websites, alt.2600.hackers, and comp.hackers.

Computer virus newsgroups

Computer virus writers often publish their latest creations in newsgroups (or post URLs where you can download their latest virus creations). If you want to find the latest live virus (or the source code to a virus), visit one of the following newsgroups: alt.comp.virus, alt.comp.virus.source, alt.comp.virus.source.code, or comp.virus.

Encryption newsgroups

Since hackers often skirt the legal boundaries of their nation's laws, they wisely hide their identity or messages using encryption, the same technology that government agencies use to protect national secrets. To learn the latest about using and writing encryption (which you'll learn more about in Chapter 15) to protect your sensitive data, visit one of the following newsgroups: alt.cypherpunks, alt.security, alt.sources.crypto, misc.security, sci.crypt, or sci.crypt.research.

Cracking newsgroups

Most games and applications are copy-protected to keep people from sharing them with their friends. Likewise, many shareware programs provide limited features until the user pays for a code or key to unlock the additional features.

Some hackers try to circumvent, or crack, copy-protected and "locked" shareware programs. Cracking methods include sharing serial numbers, unlocking codes, or using programs designed to unlock or copy copy-protected games. To read about these programs and techniques, visit any of the following newsgroups: alt.2600.crack, alt.2600.crackz, alt.binaries.cracked, or alt.cracks. To learn more about how programmers try to protect their software from crackers, pick up Pavol Cerven's *Crackproof Your Software*, published by No Starch Press.

FINDING HACKERS ON IRC

You can chat with a hacker in real time in one of the many hacker chat rooms that pop up on nearly every Internet Relay Chat (IRC) network.

To do so, you need a special IRC program, such as mIRC (available at http://www.mirc.co.uk). Once you have an IRC program, you'll need to pick an IRC network to join. Some of the more popular networks are EFnet, DALnet, Undernet, and 2600 net (run by the hacker magazine *2600*).

Once you're connected to an IRC network server, you can create a new chat room or join an existing one. While the 2600 network is specifically designed for hackers, you may have to search other networks for chat rooms containing hackers. To find a hacker chat room, look for rooms with names like #2600, #phreak, #carding, #cracks, #anarchy, or any other phrase that sounds hackerish.

Using IRC is a special skill in itself, and many hackers may get upset if you intrude on their chat rooms, so use care when exploring the different networks and chat rooms. With enough patience, you can eventually meet and make friends in the various chat rooms. Soon, you too can become a regular and experienced IRC user and you'll be able to chat with hackers all over the world. To learn more about how to use IRC, pick up Alex Charalabidis' *The Book of IRC*, published by No Starch Press.

HACKER CONVENTIONS

A hacker convention is a good place to meet people you may have only met in a chat room or through a newsgroup; it's also a good place for meeting new friends from both the hacker side of the computer underground as well as the law enforcement side, including FBI and Secret Service agents who may be attending the conference. Anyone can attend a hacker convention; you don't need credentials! Whether you're a hacker, a law enforcement agent, or just someone curious to see what life looks like in the computer hacking world, you might find something of interest at these top hacker conventions.

DefCon   Annual hacker convention held in Las Vegas, often attended by hackers, media, and government officials. One popular contest is "Spot the Fed," where attendees attempt to locate FBI agents keeping an eye on the conference (http://www.defcon.org).

HOPE (Hackers On Planet Earth)   An annual convention run by *2600* magazine, focusing on all aspects of hacking, including phone phreaking, virus writing, social engineering, and information warfare (http://www.h2k2.net).

SummerCon   One of the oldest hacker conventions, it focuses on hacking, phone phreaking, and computer security (http://www.summercon.org).

ToorCon   One of the newer computer security conferences run by another group of talented hackers who wish to spread their knowledge to others (http://www.toorcon.org).

DON'T PANIC: HACKERS ARE PEOPLE, TOO

As you meet more and more hackers, whether through newsgroups, websites, or in person at a hacker convention, your perception of hackers may well change. Some hackers you meet might fit into the hacker stereotype, but others will vary dramatically from any preconceived notions you may have about them.

Of course, like any group of people, there will always be some that you would do well to avoid. Some of these malicious hackers may try to snare your credit card number, use your identity online, or just harass you by routing a 900 sex hotline to your home phone.

Rather than openly harass you, many hackers may just ignore you and label you a *newbie*, a derogatory term for "newcomer" that is meant to intimidate you, in the hopes that you'll go away and stop wasting their time. Don't let them frighten you away! You have the right to learn whatever you want, and even the most seasoned hacker was once a novice too. Just keep learning on your own and from others who are willing to help you, and soon you too can be as knowledgeable as the rest of them.

PART 2

DANGEROUS THREATS ON THE INTERNET

7

VIRUSES AND WORMS

TWO OF THE GREATEST THREATS TO EVERY COMPUTER ARE VIRUSES AND WORMS, WHICH ARE NOTHING MORE THAN COMPUTER PROGRAMS THAT SOMEONE EITHER WROTE FOR "FUN," OUT OF CURIOSITY, OR AS A CHALLENGE TO CREATE THE MOST DESTRUCTIVE VIRUS OR WORM POSSIBLE. Although some viruses and worms are completely harmless, the majority of viruses and worms cause a wide range of trouble, from displaying nonsensical messages on the screen, to making the keyboard work erratically, to deleting files or entire hard disks.

While a virus or a worm won't always cause any damage, it is always unwanted on any computer. Table 7-1 lists some of the more infamous viruses, worms, and Trojan horses throughout history:

> Freedom is the most contagious virus known to man.
>
> — HUBERT H. HUMPHREY

Table 7-1: Virus, Worm, and Trojan Horse "Milestones"

1986	Brain virus: First computer virus released in Pakistan.
1986	PC-Write Trojan: First Trojan horse disguised as a major shareware program, the PC-Write word processor.
1988	MacMag virus: First Macintosh virus released.
1988	Scores virus: First major Macintosh virus outbreak.
1988	Internet worm: First worm to cause widespread havoc on the Internet, shutting down computers all over the country and making worldwide headlines.
1989	AIDS Trojan: First Trojan horse that held the user's data hostage by encrypting the hard disk and demanding that the user pay for an encryption key that would prevent the Trojan horse from deleting data.
1990	First Virus Exchange Bulletin Board System (VX BBS) appears in Bulgaria where callers could trade live viruses and virus source code.
1990	The Little Black Book of Computer Viruses published by Mark Ludwig. This was one of the first books to provide detailed instructions and accompanying source code to teach people how to write computer viruses.
1991	Tequila virus: First polymorphic virus capable of changing its appearance to avoid detection by antivirus programs.
1992	Michelangelo virus: First computer virus that caused a major media alert. Despite claims that millions of computers were in danger, the Michelangelo virus actually caused relatively little damage.

Table 7-1: Virus, Worm, and Trojan Horse "Milestones" *(continued)*

1992	Dark Avenger Mutation Engine (DAME): First toolkit designed to turn any computer virus into a polymorphic virus. Despite its threatening appearance, its wide-scale use was prevented by the toolkit's complexity and program bugs.
1992	Virus Creation Laboratory (VCL): First toolkit for creating a virus using pull-down menus.
1996	Boza: First Windows 95 virus released.
1996	Concept virus: First macro virus released that infects Word documents.
1996	Laroux virus: First macro virus released that infects Excel spreadsheet files.
1996	Staog virus: First Linux virus released.
1998	Strange Brew virus: First Java virus released.
1998	Back Orifice: First remote access Trojan horse (RAT) that allows others to completely take over a target computer through the Internet.
1999	Melissa virus: First virus to spread by email through Microsoft Outlook and Outlook Express address books.
1999	Tristate virus: First macro virus capable of infecting Word, Excel, and PowerPoint files.
2000	First large-scale denial of service attacks to shut down major websites, including Yahoo, Amazon.com, CNN, and eBay.
2000	Love Bug worm: The fastest spreading worm in history, causing an estimated $2 to $15 billion in damages.
2000	Timofonica worm: First worm to attack mobile phones using calls generated from an infected computer.
2000	Life Stages worm: First worm to spread as an SHS (Microsoft Scrap Object) file that appears as a harmless text file.
2000	Phage: First virus to infect the Palm operating system.
2000	Liberty: First Trojan horse for the Palm operating system. It claims to be a cracking tool for the Liberty Gameboy emulator program.
2000	WebTV/Flood: First virus to affect WebTV users by infecting through Usenet newsgroups messages.
2000	Hybris: First worm that can automatically update itself by connecting to the alt.comp.virus newsgroup and looking for new plug-in components to install.
2001	Klez: A fast-spreading worm that mass mails itself and infects computers with a polymorphic virus named ElKern even if users just preview the infected email message using Microsoft Outlook or Outlook Express.
2001	Rans: First virus to infect Perl files.
2001	Peachy: First worm to infect Adobe Acrobat PDF files.
2001	MTX: First combination worm/virus/Trojan horse. The worm component mass mails itself to infect computers. The virus component attempts to block the infected computer from accessing popular antivirus websites. The Trojan horse component attempts to open a back door allowing access into an infected computer.
2002	SWF.LFM: First virus to infect Shockwave Flash animation files.

Table 7-1: Virus, Worm, and Trojan Horse "Milestones" *(continued)*

2002	Myparty: Mass mailing worm that installs a Trojan horse back door and contacts the worm author so he can break in to all infected computers.
2002	Scalper: First worm to infect Apache webservers.

HOW DIFFERENT VIRUSES INFECT A COMPUTER

Viruses use one or more of the following methods to infect a computer:

- → Infecting program files
- → Infecting the boot sectors of floppy disks
- → Infecting documents using the macro capabilities of a word processor or spreadsheet

Spreading a file-infecting virus

File infectors only infect programs, such as WordPerfect or Microsoft Excel. A file-infecting virus spreads whenever you run an infected program. The two most common ways to spread a file-infecting virus is through a removable disk (such as a floppy disk, a Zip disk, or even a CD) or by email.

Parasitic program infectors

When a virus infects a file, it has three choices: It can attach itself to the front or back of a file, or it can plant itself in the middle. (If the virus deletes part of the file it's infecting, it's known as an *overwriting virus*.)

When a virus attaches itself to the front or back of a file, it changes the file's size and usually doesn't harm the infected file. This virus is known as a *parasitic program infector* and can easily be spotted by the change in file size (see Figure 7-1). While it's possible to notice a change in file size by browsing through your files, you're more likely to detect an infected virus by running an antivirus program instead.

Overwriting file infectors

Overwriting viruses are a bit more dangerous. Because they physically alter any files they infect by replacing some of the program's code with their own, they can damage or destroy files. If you run a program infected by an overwriting virus, the program usually won't work. Overwriting viruses can often escape detection because they infect a file without changing its size (see Figure 7-2).

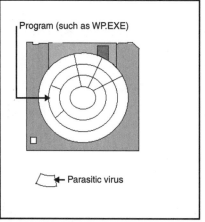

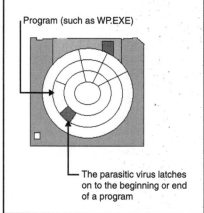

Figure 7-1

How a parasitic program infector works.

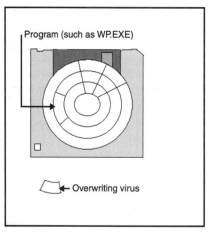

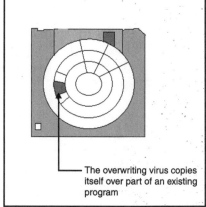

Figure 7-2

How an overwriting file infector works.

Chernobyl virus

On April 26, 1999, a virus struck in Korea and infected as many as one million computers, resulting in more than $250 million in damages. Dubbed the Chernobyl virus (or the CIH virus), this virus was written by 24-year-old Chen Ing-hau and is considered one of the most destructive viruses ever written.

The virus can infect 32-bit Windows 95 and higher executable files but can only run under Windows 95/98/ME. If you run an infected program, the virus resides in your computer's memory and infects every file that your computer accesses.

To avoid detection, the CIH virus never alters the size of any files it infects. Instead, it searches for empty space in the infected file, breaks itself up into smaller pieces, and inserts those pieces in the unused spaces.

There are three known variants of the CIH virus. Version 1.2 and Version 1.3 attack on April 26 (the date of the Chernobyl Soviet nuclear disaster) and Version 1.4 attacks on the 26th of every month.

When the CIH virus triggers, it launches two separate attacks. The first attack overwrites the hard disk with random data until the computer crashes, ultimately preventing the computer from booting up from the hard disk or floppy disk, and making the overwritten data on your hard disk nearly impossible to recover. The second attack targets the data stored in your computer's Flash *BIOS* (the Basic Input Output System, which is the part of your computer that controls all system devices, including the hard drive, serial and parallel ports, and the keyboard). Fixing this problem requires replacing or reprogramming the BIOS.

While every antivirus program can protect against the CIH virus, the 26th of every month still finds some companies getting their data wiped out.

Spreading a boot virus

Boot viruses only infect the boot sector of a disk, which is the part of every disk that tells the computer how to use that particular disk. A boot virus spreads whenever you boot from (or access) an infected hard or removable disk (floppy, Zip, CD, etc.). Since every disk has a boot sector with instructions that tell the computer how to use that particular disk, it's possible for a boot virus to infect any removable storage device as well.

When you turn on your computer, it first checks to see if there's a floppy disk in the disk drive. If a disk is present, the computer reads the boot sector of that floppy disk. If the floppy disk in your drive has been infected by a boot virus, that boot virus now infects your hard disk and could spread to every floppy disk you insert in your computer from this point on (see Figure 7-3). If no floppy disk is present, the computer uses the boot sector on the hard disk, called the *Master Boot Record* (MBR).

You can also boot from a CD, which means if a boot sector virus has managed to infect your CD when you created it, it's possible for that boot sector virus to spread each time you boot up from the infected CD.

Michelangelo virus

The Michelangelo virus became, in 1992, the first virus to warrant worldwide media coverage. The virus scare began when Leading Edge, a major computer manufacturer, accidentally shipped several hundred computers infected with the Michelangelo virus, and it was another boot virus. Within a month, two software publishers, DaVinci

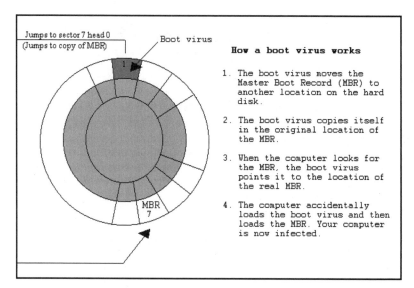

Figure 7-3

How a boot virus works.

Systems and Access Software, also shipped disks infected with the Michelangelo virus.

For some odd reason, the media quickly latched on to the Michelangelo virus story and spread hysteria far and wide, warning computer users that the Michelangelo virus would destroy their hard disks on March 6, Michelangelo's birthday. The *Houston Chronicle* called the virus "a master of disaster." *USA Today* warned that "Thousands of PCs could crash Friday." The *Washington Post* displayed its own scare tactic headline, "Deadly Virus Set to Wreak Havoc Tomorrow."

Estimates about the number of infected computers ranged wildly, from a low of five thousand to a high of five million. In the meantime, antivirus software publishers sold thousands of antivirus programs to a hysterical public. When March 6 arrived, computer users around the world braced themselves for the impending attack—and nothing happened.

Although the Michelangelo virus is real and did attack a few computers, the danger was nowhere near what the media proclaimed. Some experts say that if the media had failed to warn the public of the virus, the Michelangelo virus would have proven more disastrous. Others claim that the Michelangelo virus was never widespread to begin with, and that the media hype simply made antivirus program publishers wealthier.

Whatever the case, the great Michelangelo virus scare of 1992 did make the general public aware of the virus threat for the first time. And every year, around March 6, software publishers report that sales of their antivirus programs increase dramatically, much to the delight of their stockholders.

Spreading a multipartite virus

Both file infectors and boot viruses have their strengths and weaknesses. File-infecting viruses can only spread if you run an infected program. If the virus happens to infect a seldom-used file, then the program may be infected, but the virus may never spread and do any damage. Some computers can be infected for years without ever having any problems.

Similarly, boot viruses spread only when you boot up from an infected floppy or hard disk. If you don't boot up or use an infected disk, the virus can't spread.

To increase their chances of spreading, some viruses combine the features of both file infectors and boot viruses. Called *multipartite viruses*, these viruses can infect either (or both) files and boot sectors. Although this increases their chances of infecting a computer, multipartite viruses also make themselves more vulnerable to detection by increasing the places an antivirus program can find them. They're also more complicated to write, so there are fewer multipartite viruses in the wild to worry about.

Natas virus

The Natas (Satan spelled backward) virus is one of the more common multipartite viruses, originally discovered running rampant in Mexico. Natas can infect both files and boot sectors on both hard disks and floppies while also changing its appearance in an attempt to hide from antivirus programs.

Besides being one of the more common and destructive viruses in the wild, Natas also has the odd distinction of being written by a hacker, dubbed Priest, who later accepted a consulting job at Norman Data Defense Systems, an antivirus company. The company later decided they could not trust a known virus writer and let him go, but not before the entire antivirus community screamed in protest and vowed that they would never stoop so low as to hire virus writers to help write antivirus software.

Spreading a macro virus

Macro viruses only infect files created by a specific program, such as documents created in Microsoft Word or spreadsheets created in Microsoft Excel. Macro viruses spread when you load an infected file, such as an infected Word document.

Unlike other types of viruses that are written using assembly language, C/C++, BASIC, or Pascal, macro viruses are written using the macro programming language in a specific program. Most macro viruses are written using Microsoft's macro language, called Visual Basic for Applications (VBA), although a few older macro viruses are written in WordBasic, an older macro programming language for Microsoft Word.

Macro viruses infect the templates that define the margins, font, and general formatting for documents. Every time you create a new document from a template infected by a macro virus, the macro virus tries to infect another template and your new document.

Because most people share document files instead of template files, macro viruses cleverly convert infected documents into template files, while maintaining their appearance of ordinary document files. So while you think you're opening up a document for editing, you're actually opening up a template instead.

Despite their prevalence in the wild, macro viruses (at least at the time of this writing) have been limited to infecting documents created by Microsoft products such as Word, Excel, or PowerPoint. Although some people have tried writing macro viruses to infect WordPro or WordPerfect documents, these don't spread as easily because WordPro and WordPerfect documents store their macros in a separate file. In contrast, when you copy a Word or Excel document file onto a floppy disk, through a network, or over the Internet, you're automatically copying both your document and any macros in a single file, which gives the macro virus a chance to spread.

The Concept macro virus

The world's first macro virus, dubbed the Concept virus, can infect Microsoft Word documents on both Windows and the Macintosh. This virus was written in the macro language found in Microsoft Word version 6.0, although it can also infect Word documents created by other versions.

The Concept macro virus appears to have been written to prove that viruses really could be written using a macro programming language. As a result, Concept simply displays a dialog box announcing its existence, but it won't deliberately wreck any files on your disk.

Melissa

Taking macro virus programming one step further was the Melissa virus, which made headlines in early 1999 by becoming the fastest spreading virus in history. This virus infects Word documents and then uses VBA macro commands to read the address book of Microsoft Outlook, a common email program that comes with Microsoft Office.

The Melissa virus then creates an email message and sends it to the first 50 names in the Outlook address book, where each message appears with the subject "Important Message From" (followed by your name), with a body text that states, "Here is that document you asked for . . . don't show anyone else ;-)." The virus then attaches a copy of the infected Word document to the email message.

As soon as the recipient opens the infected Word document, the virus spreads to that computer and repeats the process of emailing itself to another 50 people stored in that person's Microsoft Outlook address book.

If you peek inside the macro virus source code, you'll find the following message:

```
'WORD/Melissa written by Kwyjibo
'Works in both Word 2000 and Word 97
'Worm? Macro Virus? Word 97 Virus? Word 2000 Virus? You Decide!
'Word —> Email | Word 97 <—> Word 2000 . . . it's a new age!
```

The original Melissa virus didn't do anything destructive, but variants do cause damage by erasing files.

HOW VIRUSES AVOID DETECTION

Viruses can survive only if they remain undetected long enough to give them time to spread to other computers. To increase a virus's chance of surviving, virus programmers have used a variety of tactics.

Infection methods

Antivirus programs can spot a virus in one of two ways. First, the antivirus program may recognize a particular virus's *signature*, which is nothing more than the specific instructions embedded in the virus that tell it how to behave and act. A virus's signature is like a criminal's fingerprint—each one is unique and distinct.

A second way antivirus programs can detect a virus is through its behavior. Antivirus programs can often detect the presence of a previously unknown virus by catching a virus as it tries to infect another file or disk.

To sneak past an antivirus program, many viruses use a variety of methods to spread:

→ Direct infection

→ Fast infection

→ Slow infection

→ Sparse infection

→ RAM-resident infection

Direct infection means that the virus infects a disk, or one or more files, each time you run the infected program or open the infected document. If you don't do either, the virus can't spread at all. Direct infection is the simplest but also the most noticeable way of infecting a computer and can often be detected by antivirus programs fairly easily.

Fast infection means that the virus infects any file accessed by an infected program. For example, if a virus infects your antivirus program, watch out! Each time an infected antivirus program examines a file, it can actually infect that file immediately after certifying that the file is virus-free.

Slow infection means that the virus only infects newly created files or files modified by a legitimate program. By doing this, viruses attempt to further mask their presence from antivirus programs.

Sparse infection means that the virus takes its time infecting files. Sometimes it infects a file, and sometimes it doesn't. By infecting a computer slowly, viruses reduce their chance of being detected.

RAM-resident infection means that the virus buries itself in your computer's memory, and each time you run a program or insert a floppy disk, the virus infects that program or disk. RAM-resident infection is the only way that boot viruses can spread. Boot viruses can never spread across a network or the Internet since they can only spread by physically inserting an infected floppy disk into a computer, although they can still infect individual computers attached to a network.

Stealth

Viruses normally reveal their presence during infection. For example, a file-infecting virus typically changes the size, time, and date stamp of the file that it infects. However, file-infecting viruses that use stealth techniques may infect a program without modifying the program's size, time, or date, thus remaining hidden.

Boot viruses always use stealth techniques. When the computer reads a disk's boot sector, the boot virus quickly loads the real boot sector (which it has safely stashed away in another location on the disk) and hides behind it. This is like having your parents call you at home to make sure you're behaving yourself, but you really answer the phone at the neighborhood pool hall by using call forwarding. As far as your parents are concerned, they called your home number and you answered. But in reality, their call got routed from your home phone to the pool hall phone. Such misdirection is how boot viruses use stealth techniques to hide their presence from the computer.

In most cases, stealth techniques mask the virus's presence from users but cannot always fool an antivirus program. For further protection against an antivirus program, viruses may use polymorphism.

Polymorphism

To keep from infecting the same file or boot sector over and over again (and revealing itself), viruses must first check to see whether they have already infected a particular file or boot sector. To do so, viruses look for their own signature—the set of instructions that make up that particular virus. Of course, antivirus programs can also find viruses by looking for these signatures, as long as the virus has been caught and examined—if that hasn't happened, an antivirus program will never know the virus's signature.

If convicted criminals could modify their fingerprints each time they committed a crime, they would be harder to catch. That's the idea behind polymorphism.

Theoretically, a *polymorphic virus* changes its signature each time it infects a file, which means that an antivirus program can never find it. However, because polymorphic viruses need to make sure they don't infect the same file over and over again, polymorphic viruses still leave a small distinct signature that they (and an antivirus program) can still find.

Retaliators

The best defense is a good offense. Rather than passively hiding from an antivirus program, many viruses actively search out and attack them. When you use your favorite antivirus program, these *retaliating viruses* either modify the antivirus program so that it can't detect the virus, or they infect the antivirus program so that the antivirus program actually helps spread the virus. In both cases, the attacked antivirus program cheerfully displays a "Your computer is virus-free" message while the virus is happily spreading throughout your computer.

WORM INFECTION METHODS

Unlike viruses that need to infect a file, a boot sector, or a document, worms can spread all by themselves. The two most common ways a worm can spread are through email and security flaws in computers connected to a network or the Internet.

Worms that use email to spread are known as *mass-mailing worms*, are typically written in a variant of the Visual Basic programming language, and usually exploit the Microsoft Outlook or Outlook Express emailing programs on Windows. Typically, the worm checks a user's Outlook or Outlook Express address book for a list of stored email addresses and then the worm sends a copy of itself to each address.

Mass-mailing worms can spread particularly quickly since they tend to come from someone that the victim knows. The recipient is likely to read the email and accidentally help the worm spread to their own address book of email addresses.

Mass-mailing worms most often target Microsoft Windows users running Microsoft Outlook or Outlook Express, because those are the most common operating systems and email programs. Thus, one way to protect yourself against a mass-mailing worm is to either use a different operating system (such as Linux or the Mac OS) or use a different email program (such as Eudora or Pegasus).

Internet worms, in contrast, spread by searching the Internet for a computer running a specific type of operating system or webserver with a known flaw in it. Once the worm finds a vulnerable computer, the worm copies itself to that computer through the known flaw and then proceeds to use that computer to look for other targets to attack.

Sometimes the mere existence of a worm mass mailing or copying itself across the Internet can cause your computer to slow down or even crash without the worm deliberately trying to harm your computer. Other times the worm may include a payload that wipes out data, infects your computer with a virus, or retrieves documents at random from your hard disk (which could include sensitive business or highly personal documents) before mass mailing them to everyone listed in your Microsoft Outlook or Outlook Express address book.

Like mass-mailing worms, Internet worms often target the most popular operating systems (such as Microsoft Windows or Unix) or webserver programs (such as Apache or Microsoft IIS). To reduce the risk that an Internet worm will target your computer, you can either use less popular operating systems or webserver programs, or constantly install software "patches" to your operating system or webserver program, which essentially close all known flaws that Internet worms use to spread themselves.

NOTE: Many antivirus programs can now detect worms as well, so make sure you keep your antivirus program updated regularly for maximum protection against both viruses and worms.

VIRUS MYTHS AND HOAXES

Since each new outbreak of a virus causes hysteria and panic among computer users, you can cause nearly as much trouble by inventing a fictional virus rather than creating a real one. By visiting the Vmyths.com page (http://www.vmyths.com), you can learn about the latest virus hoaxes. The following are examples of some more common virus hoaxes.

The chain-letter virus hoax

Some of the more annoying virus hoaxes are those that encourage you to email copies of the hoax to your friends. Not only does this spread the virus hoax, but it creates undue panic and confusion.

To convince people to propagate the hoax, virus hoaxes often contain information that sounds valid and threatening. One virus hoax, dubbed the Disney hoax, consists of this message:

Hello Disney fans,

And thank you for signing up for Bill Gates' Beta Email Tracking. My name is Walt Disney Jr. Here at Disney we are working with Microsoft which has just compiled an email tracing program that tracks everyone to whom this message is forwarded to. It does this through an unique IP (Internet Protocol) address log book database. We are experimenting with this and need your help. Forward this to everyone you know and if it reaches 13,000 people, 1,300 of the people on the list will receive $5,000, and the rest will receive a free trip for two to Disney World for one week during the summer of 1999 at our expense.   Enjoy.

Note: Duplicate entries will not be counted. You will be notified by email with further instructions once this email has reached 13,000 people.

Your friends,

Walt Disney Jr., Disney, Bill Gates

& The Microsoft Development Team.

The publicity stunt virus hoax

Since warnings of a new virus almost always grab someone's attention, many people have deliberately created virus hoaxes for publicity. A pornographic website once issued a virus hoax purportedly from a "Dave Norton, VirusCenter@CNN.com" with a message claiming, "CNN Brings you information on the new devastating computer virus known as the 'Lions Den' virus. This virus is reported to be costing internet providers such as AOL, MSN, Yahoo, and Earthlink millions of dollars due to loss of members." The end of the message provided a link where readers could find more details about protecting their computer, but clicking on that link led directly to the porn site.

A struggling rock band named Disturbing The Peace, concocted a phony virus dubbed the New Ice Age virus, which they used to promote their new CD. The hoax warned that terrorists had stolen the New Ice Age virus from a top secret government information warfare program and provided a link to the band's website for additional details.

LEARNING MORE ABOUT VIRUSES AND WORMS

Whenever you hear of a possible new virus, check with one of the following websites for additional information:

AVP Virus Encyclopedia	http://www.avp.ch/avpve
F-Secure Security **Information Center**	http://www.europe.f-secure.com/vir-info
Sophos	http://www.sophos.com
Symantec	http://www.symantec.com/avcenter
McAfee Security	http://www.mcafee.com/anti-virus
Trend Micro	http://www.trendmicro.com/vinfo

These websites list all known viruses (and virus hoaxes), their characteristics, what damage (if any) they cause, and how to detect them. To exchange messages about computer viruses, visit the comp.virus or alt.comp.virus Usenet newsgroups.

Whether you're a beginner or advanced computer user, expect that your computer will be attacked by a virus or worm at some time or another. The best way to protect your computer is to buy an antivirus program and update it regularly. Then take care to limit the chances that a virus or worm may infect your computer by doing the following:

→ Never open suspicious email (stops macro viruses and mass-mailing worms)

→ Install a firewall (stops Internet worms)

→ Never run a program for the first time without scanning it with an antivirus program (stops file-infecting viruses)

→ Never boot up your computer with a disk in the floppy drive (stops boot viruses)

→ Buy an antivirus program and update it regularly (detects and removes all types of viruses and worms)

→ Download any patches for your operating system, browser, and email program regularly (stops viruses or worms from exploiting known flaws in your programs)

Remember, the time to learn about viruses and worms is now, before you lose any data. Tomorrow may be too late.

8

TROJAN HORSES: BEWARE OF GEEKS BEARING GIFTS

TROJAN HORSES ARE NAMED AFTER THE FAMOUS RUSE IN WHICH THE ANCIENT GREEKS LEFT A GIANT WOODEN HORSE BY THE GATES OF TROY AND SAILED AWAY AS IF THEY HAD GIVEN UP AFTER TEN LONG AND GRUEL-ING YEARS OF WAR. Thinking the Trojan horse was a gift to the gods and a symbol of the Greek defeat, the people of Troy pulled the horse into their city. Later that night, Greek soldiers—who had been hiding inside the wooden horse—snuck out, attacked the Trojan guards, and opened the gates of the city to their returning army.

In the computer world, a *Trojan horse* is any program that masquerades as something else while concealing its true purpose. The main difference between a virus, a worm, and a Trojan horse is that a Trojan horse cannot spread by itself, but instead relies on unwary users to spread it far and wide.

HOW TROJAN HORSES SPREAD

Before a Trojan horse program can attack, it must first find a way to entice the victim to copy, download, and run it. Since few people knowingly run a malicious program, Trojan horses must disguise themselves as other programs that the victim believes to be harmless (such as games, utilities, or popular applications).

Besides disguising themselves as harmless programs, Trojan horses can also disguise themselves inside a legitimate program, such as Adobe Photoshop or Microsoft Excel. To do this, malicious hackers have created special wrapper or binder programs with names like Saran Wrap, Silk Rope, or The Joiner, which can package any Trojan horse inside another program, thereby reducing the likelihood that some-one will discover it. Since most users won't suspect that a program from a large, well-known publisher would contain a Trojan horse, the victim is likely to run the linked program containing the Trojan horse.

Once someone has written a Trojan horse, the next step is to spread it by copy-ing it onto a victim's computer, posting it on a website for others to download, sending it as a file attachment via email, distributing it through IRC and online service chat rooms, or sending it through ICQ and other instant messaging services.

Physically copying a Trojan horse to a computer

If someone has physical access to your computer, he can simply copy a Trojan horse to your hard disk. If the attacker is particularly skilled, he can create a custom Trojan horse that mimics the appearance of a program that is unique to that particular computer, such as a corporate log-in screen or a company database program. Not only would such a Trojan horse be more likely to trick its victim, but the Trojan horse could also perform an action specific to that particular computer, such as stealing a company's list of credit card numbers or copying the source code of a game company's unreleased products and posting them on the Internet.

Downloading software from a website

Trojan horses are commonly found on websites that offer free software, such as shareware programs. These communal gathering spots on the Web give Trojan horse writers a degree of anonymity along with the chance of attacking as many random victims as possible. Since website operators rarely have time to thoroughly examine every file posted, an occasional Trojan horse can slip through the checking procedures unnoticed.

Of course, as soon as the website administrator discovers the existence of the Trojan horse, she can delete it to prevent others from downloading it. However, between the time that the Trojan horse was posted and the time the website administrator deletes it, many people could have downloaded the Trojan horse and passed it along to others. So, even though deleting a Trojan horse may be easy, finding and deleting all copies of that Trojan horse will be time-consuming, difficult, and nearly impossible.

Rather than post a Trojan horse to somebody else's website, some people set up their own websites and pretend to offer hacker tools or pornographic files for others to download. Naturally, some of these files will be Trojan horses, so the moment an unwary user downloads and runs them, the programs are free to cause whatever damage their writer intended.

Receiving a Trojan horse as an email attachment

Another common way to spread a Trojan horse is to attach the program file to an email message. To get you to open the file attachment, it may be disguised as a message from a legitimate organization (such as Microsoft or America Online); as a tempting program, such as a hacker tool for gaining illegal access or privileges to a well-known computer; or as a contest announcement, pornographic file, or similar message designed to pique your curiosity.

Catching a Trojan horse from a chat room or instant messaging service

Many people send Trojan horses to people visiting online chat rooms because they can do so without having to find an email address. The hacker typically strikes up a friendly conversation with a potential victim and then offers to send the person a hacker program or pornographic file. When the victim accepts the file and tries to open it, the Trojan horse attacks.

Hackers also send Trojan horses to people who use an instant messaging service such as ICQ or AOL Instant Messenger. Like email, instant messaging services allow an attacker to send a Trojan horse directly to a particular person, based on the person's instant messaging ID, which is readily available through member directories.

TYPES OF TROJAN HORSES

Once a Trojan horse has found a way onto your computer, it can unleash a variety of different payloads, much like a computer virus. These attacks range from harmless to destructive, including

- → Displaying taunting or annoying messages
- → Wiping out data
- → Stealing information, such as a password
- → Placing a virus or another Trojan horse on your computer
- → Allowing remote access to your computer

To help Trojan horses avoid detection, many hackers simply rename the Trojan horse file. While this won't fool an antivirus program or a Trojan horse detector, a simple name change is often enough to trick an unsuspecting user into running the Trojan horse.

Joke Trojans

A *joke Trojan* causes no damage but may play an annoying sound from your computer's speaker, warp the appearance of your computer screen, or display a taunting message on the screen, such as "Now formatting hard drive!" Although irritating and unwanted, joke Trojan horses are harmless and easily deleted.

NVP Trojan

NVP Trojan is a Macintosh Trojan horse that modifies the system file so that when the user types any text, the vowels (*a, e, i, o,* and *u*) fail to appear. To entice victims to run this Trojan horse, the NVP Trojan masquerades as a utility program that can customize the look of the computer display.

IconDance Trojan

The IconDance Trojan minimizes all application windows and then starts rapidly scrambling all the desktop icons. Beyond scrambling your desktop icons, it does nothing more than make you take the time to reorganize your Windows desktop.

Destructive Trojans

A *destructive Trojan* can either wipe out your hard drive or selectively delete or modify certain files. Although these are the most dangerous Trojans, their very nature tends to limit their spread: In the process of attacking your computer, they reveal their presence, often by displaying a taunting message on the screen. And, if they reformat your hard drive, they also wipe themselves out.

   The only warning you may have that you've been hit by a destructive Trojan may be a blinking light or grinding noise from your hard disk. By the time you notice this suspicious sound, at least some of your files will likely already be wiped out.

Feliz Trojan

When the Feliz Trojan runs, it displays the image shown in Figure 8-1. If the victim clicks the Exit button, a series of message boxes appears, warning the user not to run programs. At the end, the program displays a message wishing the user a Happy New Year.

Figure 8-1
The Feliz Trojan horse displays a threatening image to warn users that the program is about to attack.

   While the program displays its message boxes, it deletes the core Windows files, thus preventing the computer from rebooting.

AOL4Free Trojan

In 1995, a Yale student named Nicholas Ryan wrote a program called AOL4FREE, which allowed users access to America Online without having to pay the normal sub- scriber fee. Immediately following news of the AOL4FREE program, someone started a hoax, warning that the AOL4FREE program was actually a Trojan horse:

> Anyone who receives this [warning] must send it to as many people as you can. It is essential that this problem be reconciled as soon as pos- sible. A few hours ago, someone opened an Email that had the subject heading of "AOL4FREE.COM". Within seconds of opening it, a window appeared and began to display all his files that were being deleted. He immediately shut down his computer, but it was too late. This virus wiped him out.

Inevitably, someone actually wrote a Trojan horse, called it AOL4FREE, and on March 1997, began distributing it to America Online users by email. Attached to the email message was the archive file named AOL4FREE.COM, which claimed to pro- vide the original AOL4FREE program for allowing access to America Online for free.

Once executed, the Trojan wipes out every file from your hard drive and then displays "Bad Command or file name" along with an obscene message.

Trojans that steal passwords and other sensitive information

One of the most common uses for a Trojan horse is to steal passwords. Hackers often build custom Trojans to gain unauthorized access to a computer. For example, if a school computer requires a password before anyone can use it, a hacker can install a program that looks like the log-in screen, asking the user to type in a password.

When an unsuspecting victim comes along and types a password, the Trojan stores the password and displays a message like "Computer down" to convince this person to go away or try another machine. The hacker can then retrieve the saved passwords and use them to access other people's accounts.

If hackers can't physically access a targeted computer, they can sometimes trick a victim into loading the Trojan under the guise of a game or utility program. Once loaded, the Trojan can steal files stored on the hard disk, and it can then transmit them back to the hacker. Because you may not even be aware that the Trojan is on your computer, it can steal information every time you use your computer.

Once someone has stolen your password or other vital information (like a credit card number), guess what? The thief can now access your account and masquerade as you without your knowledge, using the account to harass others online in your guise or your credit card information to run up huge charges.

Hey You! AOL Trojan

The Hey You! AOL Trojan often arrives in an unsolicited email with "hey you" in the subject line and the following text:

> hey i finally got my pics scanned..theres like 5 or 6 of them..so just
> download it and unzip it..and for you people who dont know how to then
> scroll down..tell me what you think of my pics ok?
> if you dont know how to unzip then follow these steps
> When you sign off, AOL will automatically unzip the file, unless you have
> turned this feature off in your download preferences.
> If you want to do it manually then
> On the My Files menu on the AOL toolbar, click Download Manager.
> In the Download Manager window, click Show Files Downloaded.
> Select my file and click Decompress.

If the victim downloads and runs the attached file, the Trojan horse hides in memory and tries to send your ID and password by email to the waiting hacker. Armed with your America Online ID and password, anyone can access America Online using your account and even change your password, locking you out of your own account.

ProMail Trojan

In 1998, a programmer named Michael Haller developed an email program dubbed Phoenix Mail. Eventually, he tired of maintaining the program and released it as free-ware, even to the point of providing the Delphi language source code so that anyone could modify it. Unfortunately, someone took the Phoenix Mail source code and used it to create a Trojan horse dubbed ProMail v1.21.

Like Phoenix Mail, ProMail claims to be a freeware email program, and has been distributed by several freeware and shareware websites including SimTel.net and Shareware.com as the compressed file, proml121.zip.

When a victim runs ProMail, the program asks for a whole bunch of information about the user's Internet account—similar to the information you'd enter when setting up email software to download your email:

→ User's email address and real name

→ Organization

→ Reply-to email address

→ Reply-to real name

→ POP3 username and password

→ POP3 server name and port

→ SMTP server name and port

Once the user provides this information, ProMail encrypts it and attempts to send it to an account (naggamanteh@usa.net) on NetAddress (http://www.netaddress.com), a free email provider.

Since ProMail allows users to manage multiple email accounts, it's possible that this Trojan horse can send information about each account to the waiting hacker, allowing that person complete access to every email account the victim may use.

Remote access Trojans

Remote access programs are legitimate tools that people use to access another computer through the telephone or the Internet. For example, a salesman might need to access files stored on a corporate computer, or a technician might need to troubleshoot a computer online without physically accessing that computer. Some popular remote access programs are pcAnywhere, Carbon Copy, LapLink, and even the remote assistance feature built into Windows XP. *Remote access Trojans* (RATs) are simply remote access programs that sneak onto a victim's computer. While people knowingly install remote access programs like pcAnywhere on their computer, RATs trick a victim into installing the Trojan on their computer first. Once installed, the RAT allows an unseen user (who may be anywhere in the world) complete access to that computer as if he were physically sitting in front of its keyboard—he can see everything that you do and see on your computer.

Using a RAT, a hacker could erase files on your hard disk, copy files (including viruses or other Trojan horses) to your machine, type messages in a program that the user is currently running, rearrange your folders, change your log-in password, open your CD-ROM drive door, play strange noises through the speaker, reboot the computer, or watch and record every keystroke that you type, including credit card numbers, Internet account passwords, or email messages.

RATs come in two parts: a *server file* and a *client file*. The server file runs on the victim's computer and the client file runs on the hacker's computer. As long as a hacker has the right client file, he can connect to any computer that has inadvertently installed the server file of that particular Trojan horse.

To fool someone into installing the server file of a Trojan horse, hackers often disguise this file as a game or utility program, as shown in Figure 8-2. When the victim runs the Trojan, the server file installs itself and waits for anyone with the right client file to access that computer.

Once the server file has been successfully installed, it opens a port on your computer that allows your computer to send and receive data. Many hackers methodically probe a network of computers (such as those connected to cable or DSL modems) and try client files from different Trojan horses. The hope is that if they or another hacker has managed to infect a computer with a server file, they'll be able to connect to it using the right client file.

Some Trojans will even secretly email the hacker once they're installed and notify him that the server file has successfully been installed on a target computer and give that target computer's IP address. Once a hacker knows the IP address of an infected computer, he can access that computer through the Trojan horse. Or if he's

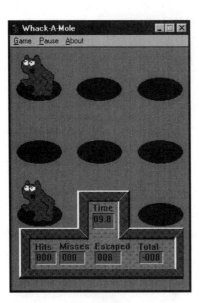

Figure 8-2

To trick a victim, many hackers disguise the server file of a Trojan horse as a game for the victim to play.

particularly devious, he can publicize his find and let any hacker with the right Trojan horse keep returning to that computer again and again and again. . . .

Back Orifice (BO)

The most famous remote access Trojan is Back Orifice (dubbed BO), named to mock Microsoft's own Back Office program. Back Orifice is one of the few Trojan horse programs with its own website (http://www.cultdeadcow.com/tools/bo.html).

An underground computer group, called the Cult of the Dead Cow (http://www.cultdeadcow.com), originally wrote Back Orifice as a Trojan and released it in 1998. The program caused an immediate uproar as hackers around the world began infecting computers with the Back Orifice server file and accessing other people's computers.

In 1999, the Cult of the Dead Cow released the updated version of Back Orifice called Back Orifice 2000 (or BO2K). Unlike the previous release, Back Orifice 2000 came with complete C/C++ source code so that anyone could examine how the program worked. In addition, Back Orifice 2000 provided a plug-in feature so programmers around the world could extend its features by writing their own plug-ins.

With the release of Back Orifice 2000, the Cult of the Dead Cow moved the program away from its hacker roots and promoted BO2K as a remote administration tool for Windows, putting it in the same class of remote access programs as pcAnywhere and Carbon Copy. Besides giving away Back Orifice 2000 for free along with its source code, the Cult of the Dead Cow further embarrassed the commercial vendors by comparing the features of BO2K with commercial remote access tools.

Besides costing you money, commercial remote access programs hog more disk space and memory than BO2K. While BO2K requires just over 1MB of disk space and 2MB of RAM, Carbon Copy requires about 20MB of disk space and 8MB of RAM, and pcAnywhere requires about 32MB of disk space and 16MB of RAM. Perhaps more surprising is that both BO2K and Carbon Copy offer a stealth remote installation feature, which means that both programs could be used to remotely access a computer without the user's knowledge!

Although the computer community shuns Back Orifice 2000 as a cheap hacker tool, it's really no more a hacker tool than Carbon Copy. Yet considering the group that made it and its original intent, Back Orifice treads the fine line between a Trojan and a legitimate remote access tool for administrators. Used carefully, Back Orifice can be an invaluable program. But used recklessly, it can become a dangerous weapon.

SubSeven

SubSeven (see Figure 8-3) is another Trojan that has been growing in popularity. Besides the standard features of remote access (deleting, modifying, or copying files and folders), SubSeven can also steal ICQ identification numbers and passwords, take over an instant messaging program such as AOL Instant Messenger, and make the victim's computer read text out loud in a computer-generated voice.

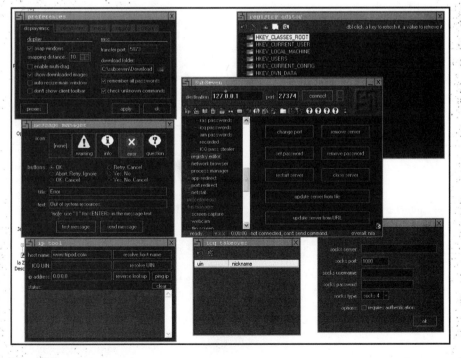

Figure 8-3

The SubSeven client program lists all the Trojan horse features in a user-friendly interface.

The Thing

The server files for RATs such as BO2K or SubSeven can range in size from 300KB up to 1.2MB or more. Trying to hide such a large file may be difficult, so hackers sometimes use smaller Trojans like The Thing.

The Thing takes up only 40KB of space, thus ensuring that it won't be detected when linked or bound to another program. Unlike other RATs, The Thing won't give you complete access to a victim's computer. Instead, it only opens a single port so a hacker can later upload a larger RAT, like Back Orifice or SubSeven, which does provide complete control over a victim's computer. Once a hacker has uploaded and installed one of the more sophisticated RATs, he can erase The Thing from the victim's computer and use the other RAT to wreak havoc.

HOW HACKERS WRITE A TROJAN HORSE

Hackers have written Trojan horses in practically every programming language, including MS-DOS batch files and BASIC. The choice of programming language isn't as important as creating a Trojan that can avoid detection, install itself without the victim's knowledge, and do its work. Still, the two most popular programming languages for writing RATs are C/C++ (Back Orifice, for example) and Delphi (NetBus), because both languages can create small programs that can be stored in a single executable file.

While it's possible to write a RAT in a language like Visual Basic, the chances of such a Trojan running are much lower, since Visual Basic programs require special, large run-time files, while C/C++ and Delphi programs do not. If a computer lacks the correct run-time files, Visual Basic programs won't run.

Some Trojans are easier to write than others. A Trojan horse that mimics a login screen to steal passwords will be much easier to write than a remote access Trojan. To help each other out, many hackers provide the source code for their Trojans on hacker sites. Hackers can then study the source code and try to write a new Trojan from scratch or modify the source code to create a new variant instead.

Another way to get source code to create a Trojan horse is to copy the code from any open source project. (Linux is the most famous open source project, but there are other ones as well, such as Phoenix Mail, which was used to create the ProMail Trojan horse.) Once hackers have the source code to a legitimate program, they can add their own code to turn the program into a Trojan horse.

STOPPING A TROJAN HORSE

To protect yourself against Trojan horses, use a combination of different protective tools and a little common sense.

First of all, make sure you know who has access to your computer. Lock it up, password protect it, or disconnect it from a network if you're not using it.

Second, be careful where you get your software. Anytime someone tries to give you a program through email, a chat room, or an instant message, watch out! That program could be infected with a Trojan horse, either with or without the sender's knowledge.

When downloading software, download only from the software publisher's official website. If you download a program from another website, someone could have inserted a Trojan horse into that program. Many hacker websites even post pirated software and hacker tools for others to download, and some of those files could also be infected with a Trojan horse.

But no matter how careful you may be with your computer, someone could also slip a Trojan horse on your computer in your absence. To further protect yourself, consider installing a rollback program, an antivirus program, a firewall, and an anti–Trojan horse program.

Rollback programs

One of the biggest problems with today's software is that much of it, once installed, seems to muck up even perfectly fine computers. *Rollback programs* guard against these problems by tracking changes made to your hard disk and taking periodic "snapshots" of the contents of your hard disk. That way, if a newly installed program crashes your computer, you can run the rollback program to undo the changes you made to your hard disk and return your computer to its prior condition.

Although originally designed to protect against software conflicts, rollback programs can also protect your computer against viruses or Trojans. The moment a Trojan wipes out your data, run your rollback program to return your computer to the state it was in before the Trojan horse wiped out your hard disk.

While rollback programs can recover your computer from damage caused by a Trojan horse, virus, or even hard disk crash, they can't prevent problems from happening in the first place. But when used together with frequent backups, a rollback program can provide valuable insurance for your important data and reduce the chance that a Trojan horse attack will prove catastrophic.

Some of the more popular rollback programs that you can buy include ConfigSafe (http://www.imagine-lan.com), FlashBack (http://www.aladdinsys.com), GoBack (http://www.roxio.com), EasyRestore (http://www.powerquest.com), and Undelete (http://www.execsoft.com).

Antivirus programs

Although *antivirus programs* are designed to detect and remove computer viruses, many can also detect and remove the client files of the more common RATs. However, antivirus programs may only recognize the most popular Trojans, so they may not protect you against lesser-known, destructive Trojans, RATs, or custom Trojans. Consider an antivirus program a supplement to the defense of your computer, but not your sole defense against Trojan horses.

Firewalls

A *firewall* can isolate your computer network from any outside threats (see Figure 8-4). While a firewall can't remove a Trojan horse, it can monitor and shut down external traffic flowing through any open ports on your computer. By shutting down a port, a firewall prevents hackers from accessing your computer through a RAT. Firewalls can also track and log all attempts to access your computer, trace an intruder probing your computer for openings, and sound an alarm whenever someone tries to access your computer without your permission.

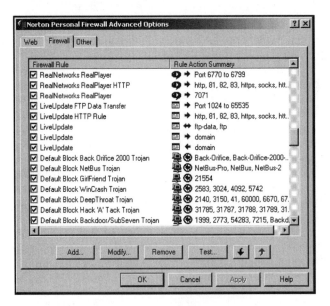

Figure 8-4

A firewall can monitor specific ports and notify you if any are being used without your knowledge.

Some of the more popular firewalls include: BlackICE PC Protection (http://www.iss.net), Personal Firewall (http://www.mcafee.com), Norton Internet Security (http://www.symantec.com), Outpost and Jammer (http://www.agnitum.com), and ZoneAlarm (http://www.zonelabs.com).

Anti–Trojan horse programs

Your best defense against a Trojan horse is to install a program specifically designed to scan and remove any Trojans from your computer. *Anti–Trojan horse programs* contain a database of Trojan horse signatures that are unique to particular Trojan horses (see Figure 8-5). The program scans the hard disk and checks whether the content of any file matches a known Trojan horse signature stored in its database. If the program finds a match, it knows it has found a Trojan horse, and it can then remove the offending program and fix any changes it might have made to other parts of the hard disk, like the Windows registry.

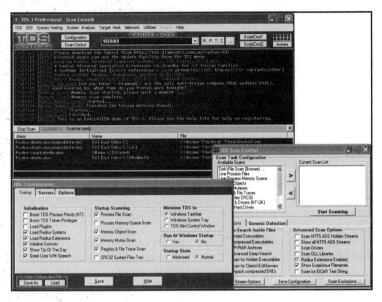

Figure 8-5
An anti–Trojan horse program knows how to detect and remove dangerous Trojan horses before they have a chance to attack your computer.

Unlike firewalls that can block ports that would allow access to your computer through a network or the Internet, anti–Trojan horse programs can monitor open ports for suspicious behavior associated with Trojan horse activity. The moment a RAT tries to access or open a port on your computer, an anti–Trojan horse program can detect the activity, find the Trojan horse, and kill it.

Like antivirus programs, anti–Trojan horse programs must be constantly updated to protect against the latest Trojans. Some popular anti–Trojan horse programs include: Hacker Eliminator (http://hacker-eliminator.com), Tauscan (http://www.agnitum.com), TDS-3: Trojan Defence Suite (http://tds.diamondcs.com.au), NetSpyHunter (http://www.netspyhunter.com), Anti-Trojan (http://www.anti-trojan.net), and The Cleaner (http://www.moosoft.com).

Hacker anti-Trojan tools

Since hackers often target each other, many hackers have written their own tools to remove specific Trojan horses from their computers. Unlike general purpose anti–Trojan horse programs that scan for all known Trojan horses, hacker Trojan horse—removing programs are meant to detect and remove a specific Trojan horse. (Just be careful that some malicious hacker doesn't infect an anti–Trojan horse program with a real Trojan horse and trick you into downloading it.)

To find a hacker anti–Trojan horse program, look for programs with names such as Back Orifice Eradicator, Busjack, NetBus Remover, Nemesis, Anti Socket, Anti BD, Backfire, BO2K Server Sniper, TW-Trojan Scanner, or Toilet Paper.

LEARNING MORE ABOUT TROJAN HORSES

To protect yourself against Trojan horses, use a combination of different protective tools and a little common sense.

The best way to stop a Trojan horse is to make sure you block all possible ways it could infect your computer, such as installing a firewall, taking care not to run unknown programs, and physically blocking access to your computer so some stranger doesn't purposely or accidentally install a Trojan horse on your computer when you're not looking. For more information about Trojan horses, visit HackFix (http://www.hackfix.org), which offers information about Trojan horses, or TL Security (http://www.tlsecurity.net), which provides Trojan horses and source code for you to examine.

Trojan horses may be dangerous, but by avoiding unknown programs and protecting yourself with a handful of defensive programs, you should be able to keep your computer free from any Trojan horses that might threaten your data. Now you just have to worry about the people around you.

9

CON GAMES ON THE INTERNET

COMBINE LAZINESS WITH GULLIBILITY AND GREED, AND YOU HAVE THE PRIME INGREDIENTS FOR LOSING YOUR MONEY TO ONE OF THE MANY SCAMS CIRCULATING AROUND THE INTERNET. In addition to unparalleled opportunities for mass communication on a worldwide scale, the Internet has created global opportunities for cheating people, as well. Of course, the Internet itself isn't to blame for con games. The Internet simply provides a new medium for con artists to lure new victims.

Con games always involve three elements:

→ Exploiting the victim's trust

→ Enticing the victim to pay money in advance

→ Promising a fantastic reward in return for little or no effort

Because nearly everyone would love to make a lot of money without doing anything to earn it (which may explain why so many people go into politics), all of us risk becoming potential con game victims. To keep yourself from falling prey to a con game, take some time to educate yourself on the different types of cons that have been fleecing people for years.

You can't cheat an honest man.

— CON MAN'S SAYING

THE AREA CODE SCAM

Area code scams play off people's ignorance of the growing proliferation of different telephone area codes. The con artist starts by contacting you, either by leaving a message on your answering machine, by sending you email, or by paging you. The goal of the message is to get you to call a telephone number in another area code by claiming that you won a fabulous prize in a contest, that your credit card was wrongly charged so you need to call and correct the matter, or that one of your relatives has died, been arrested, or fallen ill.

The moment you call the phone number, you may be put on hold, directed to a long-winded recorded message, or put in touch with someone who claims to speak broken English. In any event, the person on the other end simply tries to keep you on the phone as long as possible because (surprise!) the phone number has a "pay-per-call" area code (much like 900 numbers) where you (the caller) ring up astronomical charges, which can amount to as much as $25 per minute!

The most common area code used in the scam is the 809 area code, which is actually located in the Caribbean, so the scammer can avoid any American laws warning you of the charge, the rate involved, and a time period during which you may terminate the call without being charged. And, since you don't need to dial an international code to reach the number (you simply dial 1-809 and the number), most people won't realize that they're making an international call.

Area code scams are extremely hard to prosecute. Because you actually did make the call, neither your local phone company nor your long distance carrier will likely help you or drop the charges, because they are simply providing the billing for the foreign phone company.

To avoid this scam, be careful when returning unknown phone calls with a different area code. To help you locate other area codes located in the Caribbean, visit the LincMad website (http://www.lincmad.com/caribbean.html). To learn about all the area codes around the world, visit the North American Numbering Plan Administration website (http://www.nanpa.com/area_codes/index.html). To learn more about the 809 scam, visit your favorite search engine and look for the phrase "809 fraud" or "809 scam."

THE NIGERIAN SCAM

Many people in other countries hate Americans, which may seem natural because the only contact most overseas countries have with Americans is through the actions of American tourists (whom they don't like) and American politicians (whom we don't like).

Other countries also get their information about Americans through American television shows. So after watching shows like *Baywatch* or *Sex and the City*, most countries believe that Americans are not only rich and beautiful, but lousy actors as well.

But no matter how people in other countries perceive Americans, the fact remains that America is one of the wealthiest countries on the planet. Given the wide disparity between the average American's income and that of people in other countries, it's no surprise that other countries feel no guilt or shame in conning Americans out of their money at every available opportunity.

For some odd reason, not only have many of these scams originated in Nigeria, but the Nigerian government has often been involved to the point where many people believe that international scams make up the third-largest industry in Nigeria. The general view in Nigeria is that if you can cheat an American out of her money, it's the American's fault for being gullible in the first place.

Nigerian scams are often called "Advance Fee Fraud," "419 Fraud" (four-one-nine, after the relevant section of the Criminal Code of Nigeria), or "The Fax Scam." The scam works as follows: The victim receives an unsolicited email, fax, or letter from Nigeria containing a money-laundering proposal, a seemingly legitimate business proposal involving crude oil, or a proposal about a bequest left in a will.

The fax or letter usually asks the victim to facilitate the transfer of a large sum of money to the victim's own bank and promises that the recipient will receive a share of the money if he (or she) will pay an "advance fee," "transfer tax," "performance bond," or government bribe of some sort. If the victim pays this fee, complications mysteriously occur that require the victim to send more money until the victim either quits, runs out of money, or both.

With the growing popularity of the Internet, Nigerian con artists have been very busy, so don't be surprised if you receive email from Nigeria asking for your help. The following is a sample letter sent from Nigeria offering the lure of fantastic wealth in exchange for little work on your part:

Dear Sir

I am working with the Federal Ministry of Health in Nigeria. It happens that five months ago my father who was the Chairman of the Task Force Committee created by the present Military Government to monitor the selling, distribution and revenue generation from crude oil sales before and after the gulf war crisis died in a motor accident on his way home from Lagos after attending a National conference. He was admitted in the hospital for eight (8) days before he finally died. While I was with him in the hospital, he disclosed all his confidential documents to me one of which is the business I want to introduce to you right now.

Before my father finally died in the hospital, he told me that he has $21.5M (twenty one million five hundred thousand U.S. Dollars) cash in a trunk box coded and deposited in a security company. He told me that the security company is not aware of its contents. That on producing a document which, he gave to me, that I will only pay for the demurrage after which the box will be released to me.

He further advised me that I should not collect the money without the assistance of a foreigner who will open a local account in favor of his company for onward transfer to his nominated overseas account where the money will be invested.

This is because as a civil servant I am not supposed to own such money. This will bring many questions in the bank if I go without a foreigner.

It is at this juncture that I decided to contact you for assistance but with the following conditions:

1. That this transaction is treated with Utmost confidence, cooperation and absolute secrecy which it demands.

2. That the money is being transferred to an account where the incidence of taxation would not take much toll.

3. That all financial matters for the success of this transfer will be tackled by both parties.

4. That a promissory letter signed and sealed by you stating the amount US $21.5M (twenty-one million five hundred thousand US Dollars) will be given to me by you on your account and that only 20% of the total money is for your assistance.

Please contact me on the above fax number for more details. Please quote (QS) in all your correspondence.

Yours faithfully,

DR. AN UZOAMAKA

To learn more about scams originating from Nigeria, visit one of your favorite search engines (see Chapter 1) and use one or more of the following keywords: 419 fraud or Nigerian scam.

Since the United States sent troops to Afghanistan, a new variation of the Nigerian scam has emerged where potential victims receive an email supposedly from an American soldier who has discovered a large stash of money and needs the help of an American citizen to sneak the money back to the United States. Other than using the name of an American soldier instead of a Nigerian official, the scam is the same.

(For an entertaining analysis of various Nigerian scam letters, visit http://archive.salon.com/people/feature/2001/08/07/419scams/index.html.)

PYRAMID SCHEMES

The idea behind a *pyramid scheme* is to get two or more people to give you money. In exchange, you give them nothing but the hope that they can get rich too—as long as they can convince two or more people to give them money. The most common incarnation of a pyramid scheme is a *chain letter*.

A typical chain letter lists five addresses and urges you to send money ($1 or more) to each of the addresses. You then copy the chain letter, remove the top name from the list of addresses, and put your own name and address at the bottom of the list. Then, mail five copies of the chain letter to other people and wait for fabulous riches to come pouring into your mailbox within a few weeks.

To avoid the stigma of the chain-letter label, many chain letters claim that you must sign a letter stating that you are offering the money as a gift or that you are buying the five addresses as a mailing list. In this way, the chain letter claims you will not be breaking any laws.

Multilevel marketing (MLM) business opportunities are similar to chain letters. Valid MLM businesses offer two ways to make money: by selling a product or by recruiting new distributors. Most people get rich within an MLM business by recruiting new distributors. Unfortunately, many scams masquerade as legitimate MLM businesses with the key difference that, as a phony MLM business, you can only make money by recruiting others and that the only product being sold is a nebulous "business opportunity."

Pyramid schemes often make a few people very wealthy, but at the expense of nearly everyone else at the bottom of the pyramid. Most pyramid schemes attempt to recruit new members through Usenet newsgroups or by spamming (see Chapter 16) multiple email accounts. As long as you realize that pyramid schemes need your money to make other people rich, you can learn to ignore pyramid scheme offers that come your way, no matter how tempting. (And if you want to con others out of money, there's no faster way than by starting your own chain letter with your name at the top.)

Beware of Mega$Nets

The prevalence of computers and the Internet has brought with it an electronic version of the chain-letter pyramid scheme known as Mega$Nets (see Figure 9-1). Unlike paper chain letters that require each person to be honest (and not put their own name at the top of the chain-letter list), Mega$Nets uses software to track a list of names and keep people from cheating. You often buy the Mega$Nets software for about $20 (although many people just give it away for free).

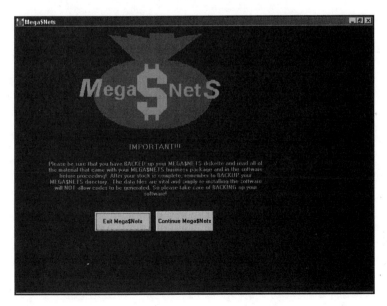

Figure 9-1
The Mega$Nets program is simply a chain letter in the form of a freely distributable program.

Once you have the Mega$Nets software installed on your own computer, a list of five names and addresses appears. You're supposed to send each person $20 and, in return, each person sends you a six-character computer code. After you have paid for computer codes from all five people, the program adds your name to its list. From this point on, you can sell (or give away) copies of the Mega$Nets program to others, who will have to pay you $20 for your special computer code so that they can put their names on the Mega$Nets list, and so on.

The Mega$Nets program prevents people from cheating in two ways. First, people can't erase someone else's name, because Mega$Nets stores the names in an encrypted file. Second, the only way you can put your own name on the Mega$Nets list (so others will send you $20) is to first pay all five people on your list $20 for their codes.

To avoid the appearance of being a chain letter (which it is), the Mega$Nets "business opportunity" claims that you are selling both the Mega$Nets program (for $20) and computer codes (for another $20) that only the Mega$Nets program can generate. Unlike valid MLM plans where people get a usable product (like vitamins or food supplements), the Mega$Nets plan simply sells everyone the Mega$Nets program itself, which you can only sell to other suckers who think they can make money by selling the Mega$Nets program too.

To view various websites created by people who got suckered into the Mega$Nets scam (as shown in Figure 9-2), visit your favorite search engine and look for the "mega$nets" string.

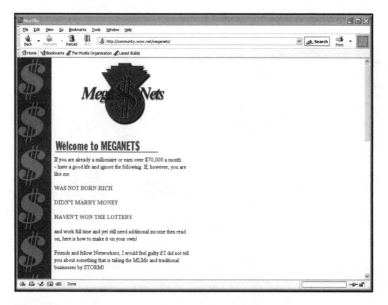

Figure 9-2
Many deluded souls have put up websites in an effort to convince others to download the Mega$Nets software and join in on the online scam.

Cracking Mega$Nets

Mega$Nets can be cracked by using a Visual Basic program that is whimsically dubbed Mega$Hack (as shown in Figure 9-3). Mega$Hack can edit the Mega$Nets encrypted data file so you can erase other people's names and add your name to the list without paying anyone $20 for their codes. By cheating, you can either convince others of the futility of relying on Mega$Nets to make money, or you can con others into paying you money because they think you legitimately joined Mega$Nets.

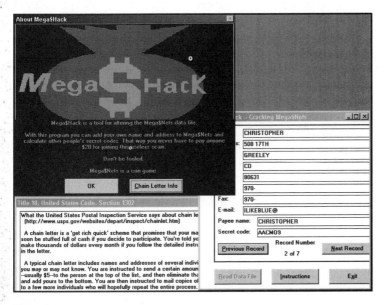

Figure 9-3
Mega$Hack allows you to crack the Mega$Nets database.

WORK-AT-HOME BUSINESSES

Besides pyramid schemes, many people receive messages offering them fabulous moneymaking opportunities that can be done at home. Here are some typical scams.

Stuffing envelopes

The most common work-at-home business scam claims that you can earn hundreds of dollars stuffing envelopes in your spare time.

First of all, who in their right mind would want to spend their life stuffing envelopes for a living? If this logic still escapes you, and you actually send money for information on how you can earn money by stuffing envelopes, you need to seriously examine your dreams in life. If you do send money, you'll probably receive the following:

→ A letter stating that if you want to make money, just place your own ad in a magazine or newspaper offering to sell information on how others can make money by stuffing envelopes. In this case, stuffing envelopes is just a pretense to get you to send the company your money in the first place.

→ Information about contacting mail-order companies and offering to stuff their envelopes for them. Unfortunately, the money you can make stuffing envelopes is so trivial, you'll soon find that stuffing envelopes pays less than making Third World wages. See? They tricked you into thinking that you could actually make money doing mindless work without getting a government job.

Make-it-yourself kits

Another work-at-home business scam offers to sell you a kit (like a greeting card kit) at some outrageous price. You're supposed to follow the kit's instructions to make custom greeting cards, Christmas wreaths, flyers, or other useless products that people are supposed to buy. The business may sound legitimate, but the kit is usually worthless, and the products that it claims you can sell will rarely earn you enough money to recoup the cost of your original investment.

Work as an independent contractor

If you don't want to stuff envelopes or make custom greeting cards, why not pay to work as an independent contractor (once again, at a phenomenally inflated wage)? This scam typically claims that a company is willing to pay people thousands of dollars a month to help the company build something, like toy dolls or baby shoes. All you have to do is manufacture these items and sell them to the company.

What usually happens is that the work is so boring that most people give up before they even have a chance to sell one product. For those stubborn enough to actually manufacture the products, the company may claim that the workmanship is of poor quality and thus refuse to pay you for your work. Either way, someone else now has your money.

Fraudulent sales

People have been fooled into buying shoddy or nonexistent products for years. The Internet just provides one more avenue for con artists to peddle their snake oil. Two popular types of fraudulent sales involve "miracle" health products and investments.

Miracle health products have been around for centuries, claiming to cure everything from cancer and impotence to AIDS and indigestion. Of course, once you buy one of these products, your malady doesn't get any better—and may actually get worse. In the meantime, you're stuck with a worthless product that may consist of nothing more than corn syrup and food coloring.

Investment swindles are nothing new either. The typical stock swindler dangles the promise of large profits and low risk, but only if you act right away (so the con artist can get your money sooner). Many stock swindlers are frequent visitors to investment forums or chat rooms on America Online or CompuServe, and they scout these areas for people willing to believe that the stock swindler possesses "ground-floor" opportunities, which entices people to hand money to complete strangers.

Like worthless miracle health products, investment scams may sell you stock certificates or bonds that have no value whatsoever. Typically these investments focus on gold mines, oil wells, real estate, ostrich farms, or other exotic investments that seem exciting and interesting but prove to be nonexistent or worthless.

The Ponzi scheme

One of the oldest and more common investment scams is a variation on a pyramid scheme known as the *Ponzi scheme*, named after post–World War I financier Charles Ponzi, who simply took money from new investors and used it to pay off early investors. Because the early investors received tremendous returns on their investments, they quickly spread the news that Charles Ponzi was an investment genius.

Naturally, as this news quickly spread, new investors rushed forward with wads of cash, hoping to get rich too. At this point, Charles Ponzi took the new investors' money and disappeared.

Ponzi schemes can usually be spotted by the promise of unbelievably high returns on your investment within an extremely short period of time. If anyone claims that they can double or triple your money with no risk in a week or two, be careful. You may be about to lose your money in a Ponzi scheme.

The infallible forecaster

Any time you receive a letter or email from a stranger who wishes to help you for no apparent reason, watch out. Many con games start by offering a victim something for nothing, which immediately plays off the victim's greed and willingness to cut corners (proving the adage "You can't cheat an honest man").

In this investment scam, a "broker" may contact you and offer you an investment prediction at no charge whatsoever. The purpose is simply to demonstrate the broker's skill in forecasting the market. The broker may tell you to watch a particular stock or commodity—and sure enough, the price goes up, just like the broker claimed.

Soon you may see another message from the same broker, offering still another prediction that a stock price or commodity is about to drop. Once again, the broker simply wants to convince you of his infallible forecasting abilities—and once again, the price does exactly what the broker predicted.

Finally you may receive a message offering a third prediction, but this time giving you a chance to invest. Because the broker's previous two predictions seemed accurate, most people are likely to jump at this chance for a "sure thing," often by giving the broker as much money as possible. At this point the broker takes the money and disappears.

What really happened was that in the first letter, the broker contacted 100 people. In half of those letters, the broker claimed a stock or commodity price would go up; in the other half, that the price would go down. No matter what the market does, at least 50 people will believe that the broker accurately predicted the market.

Out of these remaining 50 people, the broker repeats the process, telling 25 of these people that the price will go up and 25 people that the price will go down. Once more, at least 25 of these people will receive an accurate forecast.

So now the con artist has 25 people (out of the original 100) who believe that the broker can accurately predict the market. These remaining 25 people send the broker their money—and never hear from the broker again.

THE LONELY HEARTS SCAM

The lonely hearts scam involves fleecing a rich victim by dangling the promise of love and affection. In the old days, the con artist had to physically meet and talk with the potential victim, but nowadays, con artists can use the Internet to fleece victims from afar.

The con artist simply contacts potential victims and claims to be a beautiful woman currently living in another country, such as Russia or the Philippines. After sending a potential victim a photograph (which is usually a picture of someone else), the con artist steadily gains the trust and confidence of the victim through email, faxes, or letters.

When the con artist believes he has gained the victim's trust, the con artist makes a simple request for money to get a visa so the woman can leave the country and meet the victim. Inevitably, if the victim sends the con artist money, complications arise, and the victim needs to send more money for bribes or additional fees.

Sometimes the victim realizes he's been fleeced and stops sending money, but other times the victim honestly believes that the con artist is a woman trying to get out of another country, and keeps sending the con artist money in hopes of eventually meeting the beautiful woman in the photograph. The longer the con artist can maintain this illusion, the more money he can fleece from the victim.

PACKET SNIFFERS, WEB SPOOFING, PHISHERS, AND KEYSTROKE LOGGERS

Many con games have been around for years; others are brand new to the Internet. The prime con game on the Internet involves stealing your credit card number so the con artist can rack up charges without your knowledge. Con artists have several ways to steal your credit card number: packet sniffers, web spoofing, phishing, and keystroke loggers.

Packet sniffers

When you type anything on the Internet (such as your name, phone number, or credit card number), the information doesn't go directly from your computer to the website you're viewing. Instead, the Internet breaks this information into "packets" of information and routes it from one computer to another, like a bucket brigade, until the information reaches the actual computer hosting the website you're viewing.

Packet sniffers search for credit card numbers by intercepting these packets of information. Typically, someone will plant a packet sniffer on the computer hosting a shopping website. That way a majority of packets that are intercepted will contain credit card numbers or other information that a thief might find useful.

Packet sniffers intercept information on the Internet in much the same way that a thief can intercept calls made with cordless or cellular phones. If you order merchandise over a cordless or cellular phone, a thief could intercept your call and steal your credit card number as you recite it over the phone for the order taker. After the packet sniffer intercepts a credit card number, it copies it and sends the credit card number to its final destination. Consequently, you may not know your credit card number has been stolen until you find unusual charges on your next bill.

To protect yourself against packet sniffers, never send your credit card information over the Internet. If you still wish to order merchandise online, only trust websites that encrypt your credit card number (a tiny lock icon appears in the bottom of the screen when you're connected to a supposedly secure online shopping site).

While the threat of someone intercepting your credit card number through a packet sniffer is fairly remote, the biggest threat to your credit card is actually a company storing it on their (usually insecure) computer. Hackers can break into that computer and steal all the credit card information stored there, and there's nothing you can do about it.

Web spoofing

Web spoofing is quite similar to packet sniffing, but instead of secretly installing a packet sniffer on a computer host, web spoofing involves setting up a fake website that either looks like a legitimate online shopping website or masquerades as an existing, legitimate website (see Figure 9-4).

Fake websites often have URLs similar to the website they're spoofing, such as http://www.micrsoft.com (misspelling Microsoft), so victims will believe they're actually connected to the legitimate site. When you think you're sending your credit card number to a legitimate firm to order merchandise, you're actually handing the thieves your credit card number.

To protect yourself against web spoofing, make sure you can always see the website address in your browser. If you think you're accessing Microsoft's website (http://www.microsoft.com), but your browser claims that you're actually accessing a website address in another country, you might be a victim of web spoofing.

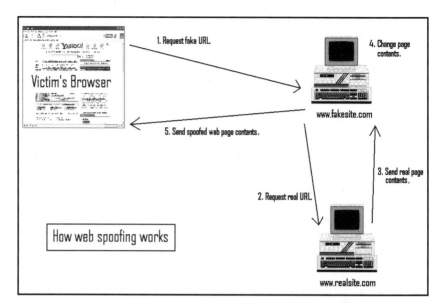

1. Request fake URL.

4. Change page contents.

Victim's Browser

www.fakesite.com

5. Send spoofed web page contents.

3. Send real page contents.

2. Request real URL.

How web spoofing works

www.realsite.com

Figure 9-4

Web spoofing tricks you into visiting a phony website masquerading as a legitimate website.

Phishing

The boldest way to get someone's credit card number is just to ask for it. Naturally most people won't hand over their credit card numbers without a good reason, so con artists make up seemingly valid reasons.

Phishing involves contacting a victim by email or through a chat room. The con artist may claim that the billing records of the victim's Internet service provider or online service need updating, so would the victim be kind enough to type their credit card number to verify their account? (See Figure 9-5.) Phishing is especially popular in the chat rooms of America Online or CompuServe.

Obviously, no legitimate business has any reason to ask for your credit card number through a chat room or by email. To protect yourself from these scams, make sure you never give out your credit card number to strangers through the Internet or any online service.

Keystroke loggers

A *keystroke logger* is a special program or piece of equipment that secretly records a user's keystrokes, such as the keystrokes that person uses to type a password or credit card number. If a con artist has access to your computer, he or she can secretly install a keystroke logger on your computer to record everything you type. Then when you're gone, the hacker can return to retrieve your captured keystrokes.

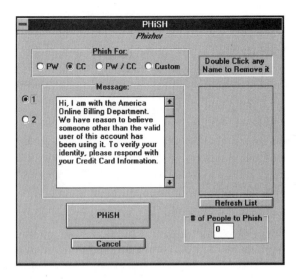

Figure 9-5
Phishing means sending potential victims seemingly legitimate messages, asking for passwords, credit card numbers, or other confidential information.

Software keystroke loggers hide in memory, while hardware keystroke loggers either connect between the computer and the keyboard or hide inside specially disguised keyboards. Visit KeyGhost (http://www.keyghost.com) to view examples of both types of keystroke loggers.

If a hacker doesn't have access to your computer, he or she can still install a keystroke logger on your computer remotely by using a remote access Trojan horse or RAT (see Chapter 8.) The con artist simply contacts potential victims through email or chat rooms and convinces them to download and run the Trojan horse. Once the victim runs the Trojan horse, it opens a port and contacts the hacker. From this point on, the hacker can read any files or watch the keystrokes on the victim's computer without the victim's knowledge.

REROUTING YOUR INTERNET CONNECTION

Along with web spoofing, sniffers, and phishers, another Internet-only scam involves rerouting your Internet connection. This scam begins by inviting you to view pornographic graphic files. The catch is that if you want to view these files, you need to download a "free" program.

Once you have downloaded this "free" program, it takes control of your modem, turns off your computer's speakers, cuts off your local Internet connection, and then secretly dials a number in the former Soviet republic of Moldova.

The more time that people view the pornographic files, the longer they stay connected to this foreign Internet service provider, which may ring up toll charges of

$2 to $3 a minute. The customers don't realize they have been scammed until they receive their phone bills.

Although the Federal Trade Commission (FTC) shut down the original scam shortly after it appeared, watch out for copycat scams. Anytime a website requires that you download "free" software before you can continue browsing their web pages, watch out. If you have an external modem, watch the status lights to make sure your modem doesn't disconnect and then mysteriously reconnect all by itself. If you have an internal modem, your only defense is to be careful whenever a website lures you into downloading "free" software as a prelude to spending more time browsing the Internet.

ONLINE AUCTION FRAUDS

One of the more recent crazes on the Internet is *online auctions*, where people can offer junk, antiques, or collector's items for sale to anyone who wants to bid on them. But be careful! Besides having to deal with fraudulent bids from people who have no money or intention of buying an item up for auction, consumers have to watch out for con artists selling their own fraudulent items.

The simplest con game is to offer an item for auction that doesn't even exist. For example, every Christmas there is always a must-have toy that normally costs $10 to purchase, but because of its scarcity in stores, it can cost up to several thousand dollars if purchased from a private seller. Many con artists will claim to offer such a product, and when you send them the money, the con artist simply disappears.

Other online auction frauds include misrepresentation. For example, selling counterfeit collector's items such as autographed baseballs or sports jerseys. To protect yourself against online auction fraud, follow these guidelines:

→ Identify the seller and check the seller's rating. Online auction sites, such as eBay, allow buyers and sellers to leave comments about one another. By browsing through these comments, you can see if anyone else has had a bad experience with a particular seller.

→ Check to see if your online auction site offers insurance. eBay will reimburse buyers up to $200, less a $25 deductible.

→ Make sure you clearly understand what you're bidding on, its relative value, and all terms and conditions of the sale, such as the seller's return policies and who pays for shipping.

→ Consider using an escrow service, which will hold your money until your merchandise safely arrives.

→ Never buy items advertised through spam. Con artists use spam because they know that the more email offers they send out, the more likely it is they'll run across a gullible victim who will send them money. If someone's selling a legitimate item, they're more likely to go through an online auction site instead.

The ScamBusters website (http://www.scambusters.org/Scambusters31.
html) offers additional sage advice:

→ Don't conduct business with an anonymous user. Get the person's real
  name, business name (if applicable), address, and phone number, and verify
  this information before buying. Never send money to a post office box.

→ Be more cautious if the seller uses a free email service, such as Hotmail,
  Yahoo!, etc. Of course, most people who use these services are honest, but
  most problems occur when a free service is used. After all, with a free email
  service, it is very easy for the seller to keep his or her real identity and information hidden.

→ Always use a credit card to purchase online so that if there's any dispute, you
  can have the credit card company remove the charges or help you fight for
  your product.

→ Save copies of any email and other documents involved in the transaction.

THE FALLACY OF INTERNET MALLS

You may receive email or junk mail urging you to start your own business by offering
products or services through an Internet Mall. By selling your products through an
Internet Mall (so the mall owner claims), you can realize the benefits of an actual
shopping mall with the convenience of the Internet.

Although the cost to set up a "storefront" through an Internet Mall may not
always be extravagant, the real con is that Internet Malls fail to provide the same benefits that a physical shopping mall offers. In a real shopping mall, people often browse
neighboring stores. But in an Internet Mall, the customer has to click on a store to see
it. So even though your store is "only a click away," the chances of a customer seeing it
are quite slim.

Given the choice between setting up your own website or paying someone
extra money to set up a storefront in an Internet Mall, you're better off just creating
your own website. Not only will it be less expensive in the long run, but you'll be able
to choose your own easy-to-remember domain name as well. In general, the only
people who get rich off Internet Malls are the ones selling the concept to unsuspecting merchants.

URBAN LEGENDS

An *urban legend* is a story that everyone swears is really true but that nobody seems
able to find any proof of actually happening. Common urban legend stories include
free (but non-existent) promotional offers from major companies like Microsoft or
Hewlett-Packard, horror stories about insect parts or other unsavory items found in
meals served by popular fast-food restaurants, or terrifying killings or mutilations

occurring in certain parts of the world. Urban legends are not only false and potentially libelous, but highly annoying. If you email someone one of these urban legends, it can be as unwelcome as unsolicited email (spam) from advertisers.

To learn more about the various urban legends, both past and present, visit these sites:

About	http://urbanlegends.about.com/science/urbanlegends
ScamBusters	http://www.scambusters.org/legends.html
Urban Legends Reference Pages	http://www.snopes.com

CREDIT CARD FRAUD

While many people worry about typing and sending credit card numbers over the Internet, the reality is that few credit card numbers are stolen off the Net. Not only would a potential thief need to tap into your Internet account at the exact moment you're sending your credit card number to a website, but he or she would have to break the encryption scheme that many websites use to protect your credit card numbers online.

If someone's going to steal your credit card number, they're more likely to get it by breaking into the computers of a large organization, such as Amazon.com or CD Universe, and stealing the credit card numbers stored there. Such companies may also have the odd untrustworthy employee who has access to the company's list of customer credit card numbers, and who can steal a number simply by copying it off the computer screen.

Credit card fraud is actually much more troublesome for merchants, because merchants are responsible for verifying credit card orders. If a thief steals someone's credit card and orders thousands of dollars worth of merchandise, the merchant pays for the loss, not the owner of the stolen credit card.

So if you're a merchant, be extra careful when accepting credit card orders. To help protect your business, follow these guidelines:

→ Validate the full name, address, and phone number for every order. Be especially vigilant with orders that list different "bill to" and "ship to" addresses.

→ Watch out for any orders that come from free email services (hotmail.com, juno.com, usa.net, etc.). Free email accounts are easy to set up with phony identities, which means most credit card thieves will list a free email account when asked for an email address. When accepting an order from a free email account, request additional information before processing the order, such as asking for a non-free email address, the name and phone number of the bank that issued the credit card, the exact name on the credit card, and the exact billing address. Most credit card thieves will avoid such requests for additional information and look for a less vigilant merchant to con.

→ Be especially careful of extremely large orders that request next-day delivery. Thieves usually want their merchandise as quickly as possible, before they can be discovered.

→ Likewise, be careful when shipping products to an international address. Validate as much information as possible by email or preferably by phone.

For more information about protecting yourself from credit card frauds and other online thievery, visit the AntiFraud website at http://www.antifraud.com.

PROTECTING YOURSELF

To protect yourself, watch out for the following signs of a scam:

→ Promises of receiving large quantities of money with little or no work.

→ Requirements of large payments in advance, before you have a chance to examine a product or business.

→ Guarantees that you can never lose your money.

→ Assurances that "This is not a scam!" along with specific laws cited to prove the legality of an offer. When was the last time you walked into K-Mart or McDonald's and the business owner had to convince you that you weren't going to be cheated?

→ Ads that have LOTS OF CAPITAL LETTERS and punctuation!!! or that shout "MIRACLE CURE!!!" or "Make BIG $$$$$ MONEY FAST!!!!!" should be viewed with healthy skepticism.

→ Hidden costs. Many scams offer free information, and then quietly charge you an "entrance" or "administrative" fee.

→ Any investment ideas that appear unsolicited in your email account.

Just remember: You can't get something for nothing (unless you're the one running a con game on others).

To learn more about scams (whether to protect yourself or to get ideas on how to fleece others), visit your favorite search engine and look for the following terms: scam, fraud, pyramid scheme, Ponzi, and packet sniffer. Or contact one of the following agencies:

Cagey Consumer   Offers updated information about the latest promotions, offers, and con games (http://cageyconsumer.com).

Council of Better Business Bureaus   Check out a U.S. business to see if it has any past history of fraud, deception, or consumer complaints filed against it (http://www.bbb.org).

Federal Trade Commission   Lists consumer protection rules and guidelines that all U.S. businesses must follow; also provides news on the latest scams (http://www.ftc.gov).

Fraud Bureau   A free service established to alert online consumers and investors of prior complaints relating to online vendors, including sellers at online auctions, and to provide consumers, investors, and users with information and news on how to safely surf, shop, and invest on the Net (http://www.fraudbureau.com).

International Web Police   The International Web Police provide law enforcement services for Internet users. Many International Web Police officers are also land-based law enforcement officers who can help resolve crime through the Internet (http://www.web-police.org).

National Fraud Information Center   Issues timely news on the latest scams and the status of ongoing and past investigations. The site allows you to lodge your own complaint against a business and read information to help avoid scams (http://www.fraud.org).

ScamBusters   Provides information regarding all sorts of online threats, ranging from live and hoax computer viruses to con games and credit card fraud. By visiting this website periodically, you can make sure you don't fall victim to the latest Internet con game (http://www.scambusters.org).

Scams on the Net   Provides multiple links to various scams circulating around the Internet. Search through here to make sure any offer you receive doesn't fall under the scam category that has tricked others (http://www.advocacy-net.com/scammks.htm).

ScamWatch   ScamWatch assists victims of web fraud and scams. Their website allows anyone to post suspected scams for other web users to read and post their comments or suggestions concerning these scams. If ScamWatch determines that a scam exists, they'll work to help resolve the problem (http://www.scamwatch.com).

Securities and Exchange Commission   The U.S. SEC regulates security markets and provides investing advice, information on publicly traded companies, warnings about investment scams, assistance to investors who believe they may have been conned, and links to other federal and state enforcement agencies. If you're one of those boomers flinging money into the stock market, check it out (http://www.sec.gov).

10

ONLINE STALKERS

EVERY TIME YOU USE A CREDIT CARD, APPLY FOR A JOB, OR FILL OUT A SURVEY, YOU ARE GIVING AWAY YOUR PRIVACY. Even worse, your information will likely be stored on a computer where any government, company, or individual may be able to access it 24 hours a day, seven days a week. If you're worried that others can access your personal information without your knowledge or consent, your fears are completely justified.

I have always believed that to have true justice we must have equal harassment under the law.

—PAUL KRASSNER

Of course, information works both ways. Even though others may be able to retrieve your personal information, you can retrieve personal information about them as well. You can find an old roommate, track down a family member, even stalk someone you are obsessed with. With the help of the Internet and this chapter, you can find names, addresses, and phone numbers of others and minimize the spread of your own personal information to others.

If you think your private life is private, visit any of the websites listed in this chapter and search for your own name. You may be surprised to find out how much information is available about you on these websites—information available to anyone, anytime.

FINDING PHONE NUMBERS, STREET ADDRESSES, AND EMAIL ADDRESSES

People may join the ranks of the "missing" for many reasons. Some may appear missing to you because they change addresses and phone numbers so often that eventually you lose touch with them. Others may have deliberately erased their trail by adopting a false name and disguising their appearance. Still others seem to simply disappear.

Yet no matter how people wind up missing, they almost always leave behind some form of paper trail you can use to find them—phone book directory listings, tax records, or utility bills. Even when people deliberately "disappear" to avoid arrest, lawsuits, or other legal responsibilities, they usually leave behind at least a clue about where they've gone.

The first step to finding someone is to gather up as much personal data about your target as possible, details like his or her full name, Social Security number, date of birth, age, and last known address. Useful information sources include marriage, medical, and military records, property transfers, and vehicle registrations. The more you know about your target, the quicker your search will be.

People finders

Since you probably know at least the person's name, use a people-finding website (like the one shown in Figure 10-1) to search for a recent mailing address or home phone number. These websites get their information from publicly available sources like telephone books, and while some charge for their services, many others are free.

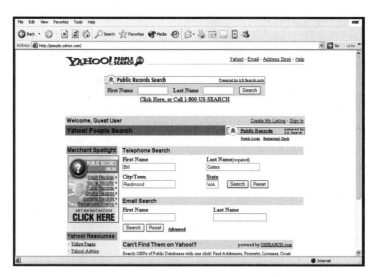

Figure 10-1

The Yahoo! search engine can help you find the phone number and city of someone you know.

You can also use the following people-finding sites to track down your target's relatives, friends, or former neighbors. Although the person you're trying to find may be erasing his or her paper trail, chances are good that ex-colleagues or neighbors are not.

555-1212.com   Provides Yellow Pages directory to search for businesses, White Pages directory to search for individuals, and reverse lookups to find someone based on their telephone number, email address, or street address (http://www.555-1212.com).

Freeality   Look for individuals based on name, city, and state using a variety of the most popular people-finding search engines, such as Switchboard, WorldPages, and Four11 (http://www.freeality.com/find.htm).

InfoSpace   Search businesses by name, category, or city, or search for individuals by name or city (http://www.infospace.com).

Switchboard   Search for businesses and individuals by name, city, and state (http://www.switchboard.com).

Telephone Directories on the Web   Search for businesses and individuals using telephone directories published all over the world, including North America, Europe, Asia, and Africa. They also sell CDs containing names and addresses of businesses all over Europe (http://www.teldir.com).

USSearch.com   Fee-based search service that offers a variety of results ranging from basic street address and phone numbers to property records, friends and relatives, and marriage and divorce records of a specific person (http://www.ussearch.com).

WhoWhere   Search for people by name to find their email address, phone number, or any web pages that contain their name (http://www.whowhere. lycos.com).

Yahoo! People Search   Search for individuals by name, city, state, or email address (http://people.yahoo.com).

If you'd rather not dig through the Internet to look up somebody's name, you might find it more convenient to use a CD containing information scanned in from the White Pages of telephone directories from around the country instead. (Just remember that by the time a company scans in and saves names and addresses on a CD, packages the whole thing in a fancy box, and ships the package to a store, that data may well be out-of-date.) To locate a CD containing a database of names, visit InfoUSA (http://www.phonedisc.com).

If all else fails, visit your local public library. Many libraries keep old phone directories and criss-cross directories (from city censuses) indexed by year. Old phone directories can help you verify the correct spelling, middle initial, and previous address of a person. City census directories often contain unlisted phone numbers, names of a spouse or children, occupation information, and mailing addresses.

If your local library doesn't store old census directories, check with the Chamber of Commerce or the Better Business Bureau in the city where you think your target may be living. You can also request information from the public libraries in the other cities by phone or letter, if it is impractical to visit them yourself.

Reverse searches

Telephone numbers are another great way of tracing someone. If you have a phone number scribbled on an envelope or cocktail napkin but can't figure out who the number belongs to, use a reverse phone search. This searches through publicly avail-able phone books to match a name and address to a given phone number.

Just be aware that reverse phone searches can only search through phone books, so if someone has an unlisted number, a reverse phone search may not turn up anything. Some reverse search engines can also work with someone's email or street address. To do a reverse search, try one of the following websites:

AnyWho	http://www.anywho.com
InfoUSA	http://adp.infousa.com
InfoSpace	http://www.infospace.com/info/reverse.htm
WhitePages.com	http://whitepages.com

Track down someone using a Social Security number

The fastest way to track someone down in America is through a Social Security num-ber. Because it is required by employers, the Internal Revenue Service, and banks, a Social Security number can be the quickest tracking device for pinpointing where someone lives and works.

Finding the Social Security number may be difficult unless you once employed or were married to that person; then your search may not be too difficult. For example, if you're trying to track down a former spouse, try to find your former spouse's Social Security number on an old joint tax return. If you don't have a copy, you can order old copies of your joint tax returns from the IRS or your local State Tax Commission.

Joint applications for credit cards, loans, and bank accounts almost always list both partners' Social Security numbers, and you can ask the credit agency or bank for a copy of these old applications. Take a look at your divorce papers, because many states require both parties to list their Social Security numbers.

If you're trying to track down a former employee, you can find Social Security numbers on old employment applications or tax forms.

Once you have your target's Social Security number, a number of websites can help you track down that person for a small fee. Here are a few:

Computrace	http://www.amerifind.com
Fast-Track	http://www.usatrace.com
USSearch	http://www.ussearch.com
Find A Friend	http://findafriend.com

The Social Security Administration's location service can also help you find a person if you have the person's Social Security number. Although they won't give out addresses, they will forward a letter for you, and you might get a reply. You might increase the chance of getting a reply by making up a phony letter offering a prize, inheritance, or similar incentive to trick your target into replying and revealing his or her current address.

To forward a letter through the Social Security Administration, write to:

Social Security Location Services
6401 Security Blvd.
Baltimore, MD 21235

Using a Social Security number is the fastest and most accurate way to track a person down. If the person is still alive, the Social Security number can lead you to a current mailing or work address. If that person is dead, the Social Security Administration will verify this information too.

Finding people in the military

The military maintains a vast database of everyone who has served in it. If you're looking for someone currently on active duty in the armed forces, the military should be able to help you track a person down, no matter where in the world he or she might be stationed.

To find someone on active duty, call or write to the appropriate address below and include as many of the following personal details as possible:

→ Name

→ Service serial number

→ Last known address

→ Date of birth

→ Social Security number

You'll need to pay a fee for this search. Here's some contact information for the different branches of service:

Air Force: Directorate of Administrative Services
Department of the Air Force
Attn: Military Personnel Records Division
Randolph AFB, TX 78148
(210) 565-2660

Army Personnel World Wide Locator:
(703) 325-3732

Coast Guard (Enlisted Personnel) Commandant (PO)
U.S. Coast Guard
1300 East St. NW
Washington, DC 20591

Marine Corps
Commandant of the Marine Corps
Attn: MSRB-10
Washington, DC 20591
(703) 784-3942

Chief of Naval Personnel
Department of the Navy
Washington, DC 20270
(901) 874-3070

If you're searching for someone no longer on active duty (such as an old military buddy), try the Department of Veterans Affairs website (http://www.va.gov) or GISearch (http://www.gisearch.com).

Searching public records

Public records are another good source of names and addresses. If you know the general vicinity in which the person last lived, check with the utility companies and services (garbage collection, cable television) in that area. Also check with that state's motor vehicles department and search its voter registrations. Marriage records can be especially helpful in discovering a woman's married name, because they contain the wife's maiden name and address along with witnesses' and parents' names. Look also for the marriage license application, which may include each partner's Social Security number.

Here are some more ideas:

→ Tax records can provide another clue to someone's location. Every homeowner pays a property tax, which the government records. These records list the person's name, current address, and sometimes a forwarding address.

→ Licensing and certification boards in many states regulate certain professionals, such as real estate and insurance agents, attorneys, and doctors. If your target needs a license to run a business, the state licensing agency can give you a business address and phone number.

→ Try the county or state fishing and hunting license department. License applications contain the applicant's full name, date of birth, and address.

→ Dog licenses, building permits, and boat, car, or airplane registrations are other sources. Check with the Federal Aviation Agency for both aircraft registration and pilot certification by contacting Aircraft Registration (post email to http://www.faa.gov) or Pilot Certification (405-954-3205).

→ The FAA can provide you with a copy of someone's pilot's license, which includes an address. To get this information, you need a name and birth date or Social Security number. To use this service, contact:

FAA Airman Certification Branch VN-460
P.O. Box 25082
Oklahoma City, OK 73125

→ Because almost everyone gets a traffic ticket at one time or another, check the county court records. Traffic tickets will not only list someone's name and address, but also date of birth and driver's license number.

→ If you're trying to find someone who once worked for the federal government, you can obtain records with a Freedom of Information Act request. This information won't give you that person's home address, but it will include present and past positions (and maybe locations) that person held in the federal government. For more information write to:

National Personnel Records Center
111 Winnebago Street
St. Louis, MO 63118

→ To check a person's driving record, credit history, voter registration information, criminal record, or birth and death certificates, have your credit card ready to pay a fee and visit the National Credit Information Network (http://www.wdia.com).

→ If you're looking for someone who has committed a major crime, visit The World's Most Wanted website (http://www.mostwanted.org). Who knows? If you find a criminal before the police do, you could get yourself a reward (see Figure 10-2).

Figure 10-2

You can check to see if a friend, loved one, or enemy's name appears on The World's Most Wanted website.

Searching driver's license and automobile registration records

If the person you're looking for owns a car, try searching state vehicle registration records. To search the vehicle registration records, you just need your target's full name and (in case of duplicate names) date of birth. The vehicle registration records can give you the last known address of the person you're looking for. If that person sold the vehicle, you can use these records to find the address of the buyer, who might be able to provide some information to help you further track down your wanted person.

You can also order the driver's license records from the state motor vehicle department. These records provide a wealth of information about a person, including his or her current or last known address; height, weight, eye, and hair color; previous names, if any; and the numbers and types of currently owned vehicles. If your target has moved, driver's license records will also show the state where the person surrendered his or her driver's license. Even if a person uses phony names, you may recognize one of the aliases.

For a list of every state's driver's license bureau, visit the Foundation for American Communications (FACS) website (http://www.facsnet.org). The FACS organization provides tips and resources to help journalists track down information for their news stories.

Searching death records

If the above methods fail, try searching the death records of the person's relatives. Death records often reveal the names and addresses of a dead person's survivors and heirs. Every state provides a bureau that tracks births, deaths, and marriages. To find the state bureau near you, visit the FACS website.

If state records don't provide you with what you need, try the Social Security Administration's Master Death Files. These records contain more than 43 million names, and the details of everyone who has died in the United States since 1962, the year the system was automated. The Master Death Files provide the following information about each dead person:

→ Social Security number

→ First and last name

→ Date of birth

→ Date of death

→ Zip code where the death occurred

→ Zip code where the lump sum death payment was made

To access the Master Death File, contact the Social Security Administration. For faster access, visit a large city library, particularly a federal depository library, which will likely have the Master Death File available on a compact disc that you can access for free.

To use the Master Death File, follow these steps:

1. Search the Master Death File for the missing person's parents. If one of them has died, the search will reveal the ZIP code where they died.

2. Using this ZIP code, determine the town where the parent died and order a death certificate from the local county clerk or health department. The death certificate will identify the funeral home that performed the burial or cremation.

3. Contact the funeral home and examine their records to determine the names and possible addresses and phone numbers of the dead parent's next of kin.

Finding relatives

When you're looking for someone, always check the public records at the county courthouse or other state government building. If you're looking for a relative, this search can be quite easy because either you or other family members are likely to know specific information about a missing person, such as full name, birth date, and birthplace.

To find a birth parent, start by examining the Birth Index Records—an index of all births in a particular state, indexed by name or date. The Birth Index is usually available as a public record, whereas most birth certificates are not.

If you know someone's birth date, scan the Birth Index for a list of all children born on that date. Then, eliminate all children of the wrong gender. Finally, to narrow the search to a few names, eliminate all children born in cities other than the one you're looking for. Scan through this remaining list, and you should be able to find the names of that person's birth parents.

To track down brothers or sisters, start with school records. High schools hold regular reunions, and these reunion committees can often lead you directly to a brother or sister. Colleges also keep records of students and often solicit donations from alumni. If you know what college your target attended, you might be able to find his or her address. Even if the address is old, you can use it as a starting point.

If you're adopted and would like to find your birth parents, or if you gave up your child for adoption and would like to see what became of him or her, visit one of the following websites, which can help reunite parents and children:

AdoptionRegistry.com	http://www.adoption.com/reunion
Find-Me	http://www.findme-registry.com
International Soundex Reunion Registry	http://www.plumsite.com/isrr
Reunion Registry	http://www.reunionregistry.com

| Seekers of the Lost | http://www.seeklost.com |
| WhereAbouts, Inc. | http://www.whereabouts.org |

Also try browsing your county civil court records for information about lawsuits, divorces, name changes, adoptions, and other litigation. Divorce records can be particularly revealing, because they contain property settlement agreements (listing vehicles, houses, boats, real estate, bank accounts, and so on) and child custody agreements (including detailed information about the children—their names, ages, and Social Security numbers).

Finding email addresses

With so many people flocking to the Internet, the odds are getting better that the person you want to find could have an email address. To track down somebody's email address, you need his or her name and, if possible, location (such as city, state, or country). Start here:

EmailChange.com Search for someone's email address by name or their last known email address (http://www.emailchange.com).

MESA Search several search engines simultaneously to look for someone's email address by name (http://mesa.rrzn.uni-hannover.de).

NedSite Search for someone's email address by name, phone or fax number, street address, college attended, ancestors, or military history (http://www.nedsite.nl/search/people.htm#top).

If you don't know the person's location, or if the preceding search engines can't trace an email address, try Google Groups (http://groups.google.com/, shown in Figure 10-3). Maybe your target has contributed messages to a newsgroup recently. If so, searching Google Groups for his or her name will find the message, and the elusive email address.

PROTECTING YOURSELF

Now that you know how to track someone down, you also know how others can track you down, and you can take steps to protect your private information. If you don't want to find your name and home address splashed across the World Wide Web, try one or more of the following techniques:

→ Get an unlisted phone number. This prevents most of the people-tracking websites from finding your name, address, and phone number (it won't be in the telephone directory).

→ Use a fake or misspelled name. The phone company doesn't care what name you use, just as long as you pay your phone bill on time. A fake name

128

Figure 10-3

The Google Groups website can help you track down messages left by a particular email address.

will throw off the majority of these people-tracking websites, even if someone knows your actual phone number.

→ Avoid listing your street address. This way, even if someone finds your phone number in a phone directory, they still won't be able to find out where you live.

→ Contact the people-finding website directly and request that your name be removed from their listing. Unfortunately, with so many people-finders popping up all the time, this might mean having to contact a dozen different websites—and then there's still no guarantee that a new people-finding website won't turn up with your information anyway.

If you don't want to make your email address available to anyone who might be searching for it, try one or more of the following techniques:

→ Use an anonymous remailer before posting any messages to a Usenet newsgroup. This method also helps keep your email address off mailing lists used by spammers.

→ Change email addresses frequently. If receiving email isn't that important to you, use multiple email accounts, and shut them down periodically. If you include a signature file with every email you send out, make sure you don't give out any personal or important information in that signature file, such as a home phone number or a website address that could list even more information about you.

→ If you really need to hide, avoid leaving a paper trail of any sort. Don't sign up for telephone service (or, if you must, use a fake name); avoid using credit cards; pay cash for everything; and avoid magazine subscriptions that use your real name. Eliminating your paper trail can be a lot of work, but it might be worth it if you're hiding from someone dangerous (like the Internal Revenue Service).

Despite your best efforts, you may wind up becoming an online stalker's next victim anyway. The moment someone starts sending you harassing emails or instant messages, send them exactly one message asking them to stop. In many cases, a firm and short message such as, "I'm sorry you feel that way, but I feel that you are crossing some boundaries for me, and I would prefer it if we end our communication here," will be enough to stop most people who may simply be angry at you for whatever opinions you may have expressed. If the person continues harassing you, do not reply. Some stalkers simply enjoy harassing people, so the minute you stop responding in any way, they'll get bored and look for easier prey.

The more frightening stalkers are the ones who specifically target you either because they know you or because they hold a grudge against you simply because of something you might have written in a chat room. If you continue receiving harassing emails, examine the email header to find out the harasser's ISP, and then send an email informing the ISP of the harassment. Often the ISP will send a warning to the harasser, which will end the harassment.

If the harasser's ISP doesn't respond to you and the harassment continues, store copies of every form of harassment for evidence. If the stalker makes a direct threat to you or your family, such as naming what schools your children go to or what color car you drive, contact the police immediately and give them copies of all the evidence (such as harassing email messages) you may have received. Sometimes stalkers delight in terrifying victims from afar and have no intention of harming or getting anywhere near you, but you never know, so it's better to play it safe and protect yourself.

Just as you would never wander around a dangerous neighborhood and not expect trouble, so you shouldn't roam the Internet without taking precautions. For more information about protecting yourself from cyberstalkers, visit the following sites:

Antistalking Web Site	http://www.antistalking.com/
CyberAngels	http://www.cyberangels.org/stalking
Online Harassment	http://www.onlineharassment.com
SafetyEd International	http://www.safetyed.org
Who@	http://www.haltabuse.org

PART 3

BREAKING AND ENTERING COMPUTERS

11

PROBING A TARGET

SOMETIMES HACKERS TARGET SPECIFIC COMPUTERS, BUT MOST OF THE TIME, THEY JUST LOOK FOR THE EASIEST COMPUTER TO BREAK IN TO. Once they break into a computer, they can use that computer to store incriminating files that they don't want found on their own computers. Other times they may use a compromised computer as a launching pad for attacking larger, more sensitive computers, such as those belonging to government agencies. That way when the government tries tracking down the hacker, the trail leads to your computer instead of the hacker's.

Of course, nobody can attack your computer if they can't find it. If you keep your computer disconnected from the phone lines and the Internet, and then lock it up so no one but you can touch it, you can be pretty sure that no one will ever be able to hack into your computer. Unfortunately, most people use their computers to connect to the Internet or a local area network, which means that every computer can be a potential target for a hacker, including every computer that you use.

When an army needs to find a target, they send out scouts who attempt to sneak across a battlefield to report back on what they find. Likewise, when a hacker wants to break into a computer, he needs to scout out possible targets to determine which ones to attack. Three common ways that hackers scan for targets include wardialing, port scanning, and war-driving.

WAR-DIALING

The most common way to access another computer is through the Internet, but just cutting off Internet access won't stop a hacker. After installing firewalls and intrusion detection systems, many companies essentially circumvent their own defenses by installing modems connected to outside telephone lines so that sales people or telecommuting workers can access that computer from any telephone line in the world.

Individuals may also be vulnerable if they run remote access programs such as pcAnywhere on their computers. Whenever you connect a computer to a modem and an outside telephone line, that telephone line suddenly opens a doorway into your computer.

To prevent unauthorized people from accessing these computers, corporations and individuals keep the telephone numbers of their computers secret and unlisted. While this may stop the majority of people, it won't stop a hacker.

To find a telephone number leading to a computer, hackers start out by using educated guessing. If they want to attack a specific target, they first find out the telephone numbers that a company may use. For example, if a hacker wants to find the telephone number to a computer that belongs to the local corporate office, he just looks in the telephone book to find all the phone numbers that lead to that particular building. Generally when the telephone company assigns numbers to a corporate office, all the telephone numbers share the same prefix, such as 234-1090 and 234-3582.

So if there's a vulnerable computer with a modem stored anywhere in this company, chances are nearly 100 percent that the telephone number that reaches this computer also begins with the same 234 prefix. While a hacker could spend all night dialing different telephone-number combinations until he reached a modem on the other end, hackers simply let their computers do this tedious work instead, by running a special program called a *war-dialer* or *demon dialer* (see Figure 11-1).

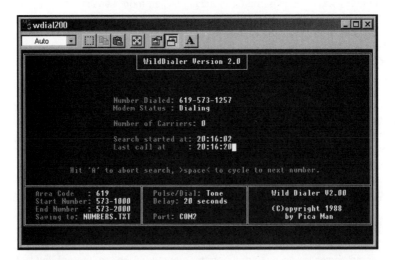

Figure 11-1

A war-dialer dials a range of telephone numbers and keeps track of all numbers that lead to a computer.

If a hacker knew that a certain company's telephone numbers all started with 234, he could program his war-dialer to dial every number from 234-0000 to 234-9999. Each time the war-dialer finds a telephone number that leads to a computer modem (such as 234-3024), the war-dialer saves that number for the hacker to examine later. This means that if there's a telephone number that allows others to access a computer, it's only a matter of *when*, not *if*, a hacker will find that telephone number.

After a war-dialer finds all the telephone numbers that connect to a computer, a hacker can then probe each telephone number individually. Before a computer will allow access through a telephone line, it usually asks for a password. All the hacker needs to do now is guess the correct password, and the computer will open its gates and let the hacker inside.

One of the simplest defenses against war-dialing is a call-back device. The moment someone (a valid user or an intruder) calls the computer, the call-back device hangs up and dials a prearranged telephone number that only a valid user would be at. Of course, a determined hacker would simply find out the phone number that the call-back device will dial and then use call forwarding on that number to reroute the call to the hacker's phone number.

PORT SCANNING

While some computers allow access through a telephone line, more computers allow access over the Internet. Instead of having a unique telephone number that identifies a computer over the phone network, Internet-connected computers have a unique Internet Protocol (IP) address that identifies them over the Internet. Instead of using a war-dialer to find computers on the Internet, hackers use a hacking tool called a *scanner* (also called a port or network scanner). See Figure 11-2.

Some popular scanners include NetScanTools (http://www.nwpsw.com), Nessus (http://www.nessus.org), iNetTools (http://www.wildpackets.com), SAINT (http://www.wwdsi.com/products/saint_engine.html), SARA (http://www-arc.com/sara), SATAN (http://www.fish.com/satan), and Nmap (http://www.insecure.org/nmap).

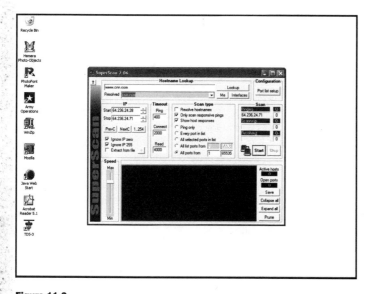

Figure 11-2

A port scanner can search for a range of IP addresses for a computer to attack.

Scanning works much like war-dialing, but instead of dialing multiple phone numbers to find a way into a computer, scanners probe a range of IP addresses. When the scanner finds a computer at a particular IP address, it then examines the ports on that computer to see which ones could be exploited.

A port isn't a physical cable or opening in your computer. Instead, a port represents a specific way for a computer to communicate over the Internet. When a computer connects to the Internet, it needs to know when it's receiving email and when it's accessing a web page. Since information from the Internet flows into the computer through the same physical connection (a telephone line or cable modem), computers create separate channels or ports that only accept certain data. That way, whenever information flows into a computer through a specific port, the computer knows how to handle that data.

To identify different ports, computers give each port a number. So if a computer wants to access a web page stored on another computer, it asks for this information through port 80. Computers that display web pages (also known as *web hosting computers*) simply keep port 80 open and wait for another computer to ask for a web page through port 80.

Every computer connected to the Internet uses ports, which means that ports open up a door that hackers can use to access a computer. Table 11-1 lists the more common ports, but keep in mind that a computer may have several hundred ports that could be open at any given time.

Table 11-1: Ports Commonly Available on Every Computer on the Internet

SERVICE	PORT
File Transfer Protocol (FTP)	21
Telnet	23
Simple Mail Transfer Protocol (SMTP)	25
Gopher	70
Finger	79
Hypertext Transfer Protocol (HTTP)	80
Post Office Protocol, version 3 (POP3)	110

When a computer wants to communicate with another computer through a port, it sends a SYN (synchronize) message to that computer, which essentially tells the other computer, "I'm ready to connect to your port." When the target computer receives this message, it sends back a SYN/ACK (synchronize/acknowledgment) message, which says to the first computer, "Okay, I'm ready." When the first computer receives this SYN/ACK message, it sends back a return ACK (acknowledgment) message to the target computer so the first computer knows the port is open and the other computer is ready to send data through the port.

Port scanners use this basic sequence of events to find open ports and probe them for vulnerabilities.

Ping sweeping

Ping sweeping checks for computers at a specific IP address by sending a message to that computer. If the computer responds by returning the data, this tells the ping sweeper that the target computer is up and running. If the scanner doesn't receive a return ping, it concludes that there is either no computer at that IP address or that the computer normally connected to that IP address is temporarily offline.

An ordinary ping uses a protocol called *Internet Control Message Protocol* (ICMP), which defines the way two computers transfer messages to one another. ICMP pings are harmless and not necessarily considered an attack, although some firewalls may block ICMP pings to certain ports to guard against ping flooding (one of the earliest and most primitive denial of service attacks, also called the "Ping of Death," where the attacking computer simply sends more pings than the receiving computer can handle).

If an ICMP ping can't get through to a computer that a hacker knows should be up and running, they often try using a port scanner, such as Nmap (see Figure 11-3), to send an ACK message (ping) to the target computer. ACK pings sometimes fool firewalls because they trick the target computer into thinking that it's receiving an acknowledgment message from another computer that the target computer already contacted. Because the firewall assumes that the target computer initiated the communication, the firewall lets the ACK ping through, which tells a scanner like Nmap that the target computer is available even though an ordinary ICMP ping couldn't find that same computer.

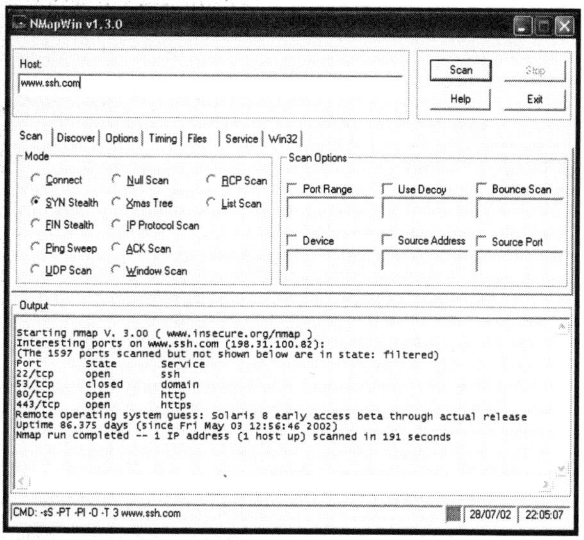

Figure 11-3

Nmap can probe the Internet for vulnerable computers.

Pinging a range of IP addresses can be slow and time-consuming, because your computer needs to send a ping and then wait for a reply. To speed up this process, some scanners send a flood of pings without waiting for replies; each acknowledged ping reveals a computer that is a potential target.

Port scanning

To attack a computer, you need your target's IP address, which you can get either through ping sweeping or by looking up a domain name on the Network Solutions website (at http://www.networksolutions.com/cgi-bin/whois/whois and shown in Figure 11-4). Once you know a computer's IP address, the next step is to find which ports are open so you know which ones you may be able to use to access the target computer.

Figure 11-4

The WhoIs command can help you identify the IP address of any website.

Some common port-scanning techniques include:

TCP connect scanning   Connects to a port by sending a synchronize (SYN) packet, waits for a return acknowledgment packet (SYN/ACK), and then sends another acknowledgment packet (ACK) to connect. This type of scanning is easily recognized and often logged by target computers to alert them of a possible hacker attack.

TCP SYN scanning   Connects to a port by sending a SYN packet and waits for a return acknowledgment packet (SYN/ACK), which indicates that the port is listening. Known as half-scanning, this technique is less likely to be logged and detected by the target than ordinary TCP connect scanning because the scanning computer never sends back an acknowledgment packet (ACK).

TCP FIN scanning   Connects to a port by sending a "No more data from sender" (FIN) packet to a port. A closed port responds with a Reset (RST) message, while an open port simply ignores the FIN packet, thereby revealing its existence.

Fragmentation scanning   Breaks up the initial SYN packet into smaller pieces in order to mask your actions from a packet filter or firewall. This is used in conjunction with other scanning techniques, such as TCP connect, TCP SYN, or TCP FIN scanning.

FTP bounce attack   Requests a file from an FTP server. Because the request contains the IP address and port number of a target computer, an FTP bounce attack masks the source of the attack and can bypass any firewalls or other security measures aimed at keeping outsiders (but not other computers on the same network) from accessing the target computer. A successful file transfer indicates an open port.

UDP (User Datagram Protocol) scanning   Uses UDP instead of TCP. When a port receives a probe, its closed ports send an ICMP_PORT_UNREACH error. Ports that don't send back an ICMP_PORT_UNREACH error are open.

Fingerprinting the operating system

Finding a computer and an open port can get you into a computer, but finding an open port is not enough. Hackers must find out which operating system the computer uses so they can know which commands to use and how to take advantage of any known vulnerabilities in the software that could save them from having to guess the computer's password.

Most webservers use a variation of Unix (such as Linux, Digital UNIX, or Solaris), but many run a version of Microsoft Windows. A handful of webservers may even use OS/2 or the Mac OS.

Operating system probing works by sending data to different ports. Since different operating systems respond differently depending on the data they receive at a specific port, hackers can deduce the type of operating system used on a target computer. These are some common probing techniques:

→ **FIN probing**: Sends a FIN ("No more data from sender") packet to a port and waits for a response. Windows responds to FIN packets with RST (Reset) messages, so if a RST message returns from your FIN probe, you know the computer is running Windows.

→ **FIN/SYN probing**: Sends a FIN/SYN packet to a port and waits for a response. Linux systems respond with a FIN/SYN/ACK packet.

→ **TCP initial window checking**: Checks the window size on packets returned from the target computer. The window size from the AIX operating system is 0x3F25 and the window size from OpenBSD or FreeBSD is 0x402E.

→ **ICMP message quoting**: Sends data to a closed port and waits to receive an error message. All computers should send back the initial IP header of the data with an additional eight bytes tacked on. Solaris and Linux systems, however, return more than eight bytes.

By using a program like Nmap, hackers can also scan a target computer and narrow down (or pinpoint) the operating system name and possibly even the version number as well.

Probing can be difficult to block, since it's difficult to tell the difference between a probing hacker and a legitimate connection with another computer. These hacker probes can often go unnoticed by firewalls or system administrators since their probing actions may appear completely harmless. Once a hacker knows the IP address, the open ports available, and the type of operating system for a target computer, the hacker can plan his strategy for breaking into the computer much like a burglar might study a house before trying to break into it.

WAR-DRIVING

Rather than physically connect computers with cables to form a network, many companies and individuals are turning to a wireless network standard known as *802.11b* or *Wi-Fi* (wireless fidelity) instead. The idea is simple. You just plug in a device known as an *access point* as part of your network, and that access point relays signals from your network to any computer with a wireless *network interface card* (NIC), which can then access that network as if it were physically connected through a cable. If you use an AirPort card with a Macintosh computer, you're using an 802.11b wireless network.

Every computer with a wireless card can access a wireless network. Unfortunately, that means that a wireless card plugged into a hacker's laptop computer across the street can also access that same network. A wireless network is essentially the equivalent of a normal wired network with cables sticking out of every window of the building, and anyone can plug in and access your network at any time without your knowledge.

To prevent unauthorized users from accessing a wireless network, most wireless networks use *encryption* (dubbed *WEP* for wired equivalent privacy) and authentication. WEP encryption hides the data passing through the airwaves and authentication only allows pre-defined computer access to the wireless network. Like most security measures, these two methods can stop some, but not all, hackers from getting on a network. WEP encryption is relatively weak and can be cracked easily. Only allowing pre-defined computers access to a wireless network can stop most hackers, but many people don't bother turning on this feature. Even if this feature is turned on, hackers simply trick a computer that they are actually authorized to use the wireless network.

Hackers can scan for wireless networks by driving around any neighborhood with a laptop computer, a wireless network interface card, an antenna to pick up the signals broadcast by the network, and a scanning program to detect the presence of the wireless network (see Figure 11-5). Sometimes hackers also include a global positioning system (GPS) for mapping out the exact location of a wireless network. This whole process of driving around scanning for wireless networks is called *war-driving*, and with so many corporations and individuals setting up wireless networks, it is fairly easy to find one. (There is also war-strolling, war-flying, and war-boating, but the main idea is the same: Cruise a neighborhood and search for wireless networks.)

For more information about the different techniques, hardware, software, and news about war-driving, visit the WarDriving.com site (http://www.wardriving.com). To read "The Definitive Guide To Wireless WarX'ing," visit http://www.kraix.com/downloads/TDGTW-WarXing.txt. For more information about Wi-Fi networks, pick up a copy of *The Book of Wi-Fi* by John Ross, published by No Starch Press.

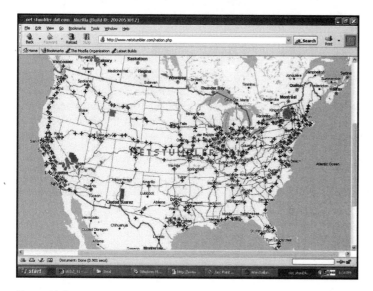

Figure 11-5

A North American map showing the location of all known wireless networks found by the NetStumbler program.

The key to finding a wireless network is a wireless sniffer program as shown in Figure 11-6. Some of the more popular ones include NetStumbler (http://www.stumbler.net) for Windows, MiniStumbler (http://www.netstumbler.com) for Pocket PC, Kismet (http://www.kismetwireless.net) for Linux, and MacStumbler (http://www.macstumbler.com) for the Mac OS.

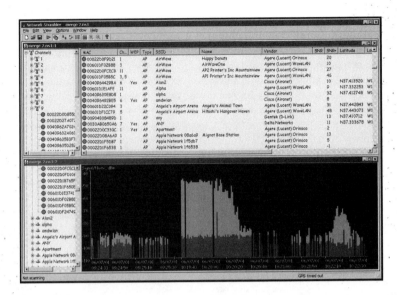

Figure 11-6

A wireless sniffer program can help you find and identify wireless networks nearby.

To make finding a wireless network even easier, hackers have adopted the techniques of the hobos, who used to carve or draw marks on trees or buildings to alert other hobos to unfriendly towns, sympathetic households, or good places to hop on a passing train. Similarly, war-chalking (http://www.warchalking.org) involves drawing marks in a neighborhood to identify the location and features of a particular wireless network, as shown in Figure 11-7.

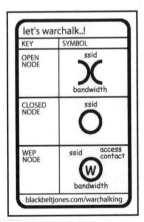

Figure 11-7

War-chalking symbols identify the location and status of a wireless network.

Once that first hacker discovers a wireless network and leaves behind a war-chalking mark, other hackers will likely explore that same wireless network. With so many unwanted intruders poking around a network, it's only a matter of time before one of them accidentally or purposely disrupts, deletes, or alters some important files.

AFTER THEY FIND A WAY INTO A COMPUTER

Through war-dialing, port scanning, or war-driving, hackers can locate nearly any computer that communicates with another computer through a network, a phone line, or the Internet. Unfortunately, once hackers find a computer, they often can't resist the temptation to explore and break into that computer, and once a hacker has broken into a computer, the results could range from simple browsing to trashing the entire system and wrecking everything in sight.

12

SNEAKING INTO A COMPUTER

FINDING A COMPUTER TO ATTACK IS THE FIRST STEP. BREAKING INTO THAT COMPUTER IS THE SECOND STEP. Generally, hackers don't succeed because of some innate brilliance on their part. Most hackers succeed in breaking into a computer by exploiting the carelessness, ignorance, or outright laziness on the part of the people who use or maintain the computer.

Once a computer offers an outside connection to the world through a telephone line, the Internet, or a wireless network, the first line of defense for stopping a hacker is usually a password.

Success seems to be largely a matter of hanging on after others have let go.

—WILLIAM FEATHER

ASK AND YE SHALL RECEIVE: THE ART OF SOCIAL ENGINEERING

The easiest way to get into any computer is to ask someone to give you access. Naturally, computer administrators aren't going to give access to anyone who asks, so hackers just ask the people who have regular access to the computer but little interest in protecting that computer. In other words, hackers target the ordinary user.

Phone anonymity

Most people see computers as a necessary nuisance, so when they receive a call from someone claiming that they're having trouble using the computer, they can sympathize with that caller. When that caller claims to be in a rush to complete a project before a looming deadline, they can once again understand the caller's frustration. And when that caller rattles off company phrases and names of corporate executives or projects with the familiarity of a long-time worker, most people accept the caller as legitimate.

So when that caller finally asks for help, whether it be for a telephone number to the computer or even a password to an account on the computer, most people are only too happy to help out what seems to be a fellow coworker. The trouble is that the caller might actually be a hacker using social engineering tactics to get you to volunteer valuable information that the hacker needs in order to break in and access a computer. The beauty of social engineering is that the hacker can get other people to help him without them ever knowing the hacker's ulterior motive. Even better, the hacker can get information just by picking up a phone. If one person fails to give him the information he needs, the hacker can just dial another number and talk to someone else until he eventually gets the type of information he wants.

Sometimes hackers practice reverse social engineering. Rather than call someone and try to get information out of them, reverse social engineering gets other people to call you and volunteer information on their own initiative.

One type of the reverse social engineering scam works by a hacker disrupting a network in a small but noticeable and obvious annoying manner. After sabotaging the network, the hacker posts his telephone number and name (usually not his real name) for all computer users to find. Inevitably, someone will call this telephone number, thinking that it leads to a computer administrator when it really belongs to the hacker.

At this point, the hacker requests certain information from the user, such as the user's account number or name and the accompanying password. The user who initiated the call isn't likely to suspect that the hacker is anyone but a helpful technician, so that person freely volunteers this information. Once the hacker gets this information, he can fix the problem that he created in the first place. The user is happy and the hacker has the information he needs to break into the computer.

To mask their own identity, some hackers are adept at mimicking different voices such as an older man or a young woman. By drastically altering their voice, hackers can often milk the same person for information without raising any suspicions.

Because they may only get one chance to break into a computer, hackers can afford to be patient. They can take days, weeks, or even months gathering information about a particular target from different sources so that they can talk about a company or computer with the jaded familiarity of someone who has worked there for years.

Social engineering in person

Talking to people over the phone has the advantage of hiding the hacker's appearance from sight. After all, if most people knew that the person who sounds like their boss is actually a twelve-year-old kid, they would definitely not give out any information.

However, social engineering over the phone has its limitations. You may want direct access to a computer, which means that you have to show up in person. Although deceiving someone in person takes a lot of confidence, most people never dream that someone standing right in front of them would deliberately lie about who they are or what they're doing, which means they'll be more likely to cooperate without questioning the hacker's true intentions.

When hackers use social engineering in person, they often masquerade as a consultant or temporary worker, since that explains the hacker's unfamiliarity with the building layout and their presence in the office in the first place. Once on the premises, hackers may simply scout the site to get more information about the company and the way it uses its computers. If the opportunity presents itself, hackers may access the computer directly, claiming to be security consultants or technicians.

Under the guise of repairing or maintaining the computer, the hacker may secretly install a back door to the computer so that they'll be able to access that computer after they leave. While wandering through an office, hackers may look for passwords taped to the sides of monitors or engage in shoulder surfing and peek over the shoulder of someone as they type in their password.

As an alternative to masquerading as someone else, hackers may simply get jobs working as night janitors. This gives them free access to all the office computers without the nuisance of other people getting in the way.

Whether the hackers do their social engineering over the phone or in person, the goal is still the same: Find a way into the computer, whether that way be through a password conveniently given to them by an unsuspecting worker or through direct physical access to the computer where they can shoulder-surf a password, find a password written on a slip of paper stuck to a monitor, or simply type and guess different passwords at the computer terminal itself.

PASSWORD CRACKING

The first line of defense for many computers is a password. Although passwords restrict access to a computer, they're the weakest link in any security system. The most secure passwords are lengthy, consisting of random characters, but most people tend to choose simple, easy-to-remember passwords and use the same password for several different systems (for example, their work computer, their America Online account, and their Windows screensaver). If hackers discover a person's password, they'll often have the key to their other accounts, as well.

When a computer requires a password, but you don't know what that password may be, you have several options:

→ Steal a valid password

→ Guess the password

→ Discover the password with a brute-force attack

Stealing a password

If you can get physical access to a computer, the easiest way to steal a password is by *shoulder surfing*—peeking over someone's shoulder as they type in a password. If that option isn't available, poke around the person's desk. Most people find passwords hard to remember, so they often write them down and store them where they can easily find them, like next to their monitor or inside their desk drawer.

Still can't find that pesky password? Try one of these methods:

→ A keystroke logger

→ A desktop-monitoring program

→ A remote desktop-monitoring program

→ A password-recovery program

NOTE: All of these programs require that you have access to the victim's computer so you can install or run the programs without the user's knowledge.

Using a keystroke recorder or logger

Keystroke recorders or *loggers* record everything a person types, and either sends their typing to a monitoring computer or saves it to a file. The simplest keystroke loggers record anything a user types (see Figure 12-1), which can include incriminating email messages, credit card numbers, and passwords.

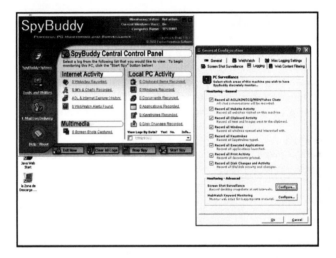

Figure 12-1
You can configure what you want a keystroke logger to capture.

When the user leaves the target computer, you can remove the keystroke logging program from their machine and retrieve the logging file that contains the password and anything else they typed (see Figure 12-2). The more advanced keystroke loggers can email the log file of a user's keystrokes to you so you can monitor their activities from another location.

To avoid detection, keystroke loggers run in *stealth mode*, which means that they hide their presence from the user, although they can still be spotted if you know what and where to look. Unless someone suspects that someone has planted a keystroke logger on their computer, chances are good they will never look for, let alone find, a keystroke logger hidden in stealth mode.

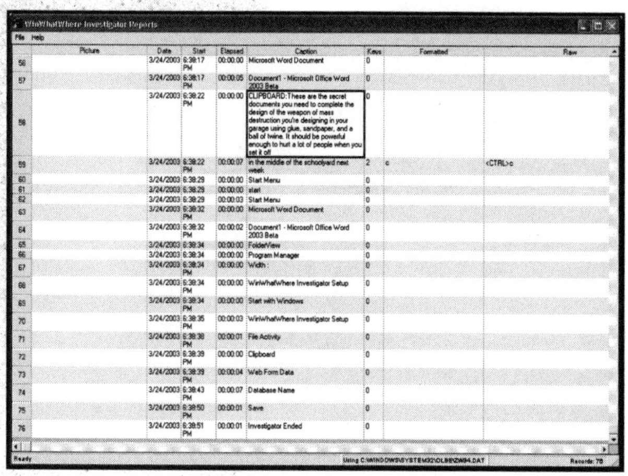

Figure 12-2

A keystroke logger can capture keystrokes so you know what someone typed and what program they used at the time.

To avoid giving away their presence at all, some keystroke loggers are available as hardware devices that plug in between the computer and the keyboard. Such hardware keystroke loggers can be spotted easily just by looking at the back of the computer, but their presence is completely invisible to any software running on that computer. Best of all, unlike their software equivalents that only work under specific operating systems, hardware keystroke loggers work with any operating system running on that computer, such as FreeBSD, Linux, Windows XP, or OS/2.

Some popular hardware keystroke loggers include KeyGhost (http://www.keyghost.com), Hardware KeyLogger (http://www.amecisco.com), and KEYKatcher (http://www.tbotech.com/key-katcher.htm). To find a software keystroke logger, visit Keylogger.org (http://www.keylogger.org), which rates the different keystroke loggers by their features and ease of use.

Spying with a desktop-monitoring program

More powerful than keystroke loggers are *desktop-monitoring programs*. Like a computer surveillance camera, desktop-monitoring programs secretly record the programs a person uses, how long the person uses each program, the websites viewed, and every keystroke the user types. To show you what a user might be doing, some desktop-monitoring programs can periodically capture the contents of the screen or secretly turn on a webcam to record the person sitting in front of the computer.

Many desktop-monitoring programs can store days of recordings, and some can be set to record at specifically designated times, when certain applications are run, or when a user logs on to the Internet (see Figure 12-3).

To find a desktop-monitoring program, visit Computer Monitoring Software http://www.computer-monitoring.com or try these programs:

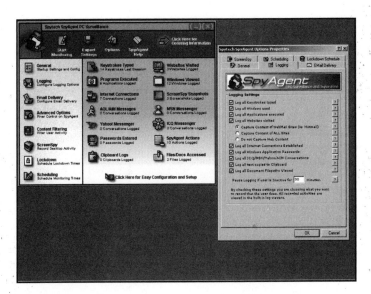

Figure 12-3

A desktop-monitoring program can track every program and keystroke used on a specific computer.

AppsTraka	http://appstraka.hypermart.net
Desktop Surveillance	http://www.omniquad.com
iSpyNOW	http://www.ispynow.com
Net Vizor	http://www.mi-inc.com/netvizor.htm
Spector	http://www.spectorsoft.com
SpyBuddy	http://www.agent-spy.com
WinWhatWhere Investigator	http://www.winwhatwhere.com
WinGuardian	http://www.webroot.com

Remotely viewing another computer's desktop

Desktop-monitoring programs are useful if you have regular access to the computer you want to watch. But if you don't, you can use a remote desktop-monitoring program instead. Just install a program such as Q-Peek (http://www.qpeek.com), Spector (http://www.netbus.org), or PC Spy (http://www.softdd.com) on the computer you want to monitor. Then, anything anyone types, views, or manipulates on that computer will appear live on your computer's screen.

Using a password-recovery program

Because typing a password over and over again to access a program can be a nuisance, many programs let you store passwords directly in the program, hidden behind

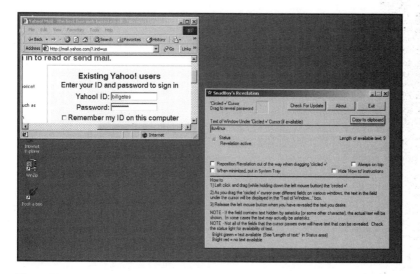

Figure 12-4

The Revelation password-recovery program can reveal the password needed to access a user's Internet account.

a string of asterisks (see Figure 12-4). Because people often forget these passwords and then can't access their programs or files, *password-recovery programs* have been developed to retrieve these lost or forgotten passwords. You can, of course, also use these programs to retrieve other people's passwords.

There are many commercial and free versions of password-recovery programs, such as these:

iOpus Password Recovery XP	http://www.iopus.com
Passware Kit	http://www.lostpassword.com
Peek-a-boo	http://www.corteksoft.com
Revelation	http://www.snadboy.com

Besides blocking access to a program, passwords can also block access to files, like WordPerfect documents or Microsoft Excel spreadsheets. To retrieve or crack password-protected files, get a special password-cracking program from one of these companies (see Figure 12-5):

AccessData	http://www.accessdata.com
Alpine Snow	http://www.alpinesnow.com
Crak Software	http://www.crak.com
ElcomSoft	http://www.elcomsoft.com
Password Crackers	http://www.pwcrack.com
Passware	http://www.lostpassword.com

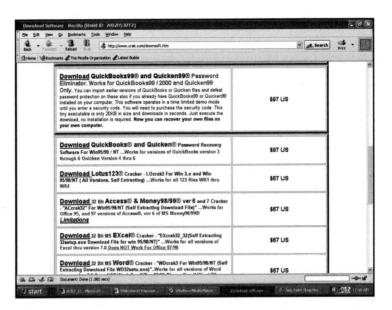

Download QuickBooks99® and Quicken99® Password Eliminator. Works for QuickBooks99 / 2000 and Quicken99 Only. You can import earlier versions of QuickBooks or Quicken files and defeat password protection on these also if you already have QuickBooks99 or Quicken99 installed on your computer. This software operates in a time limited demo mode until you enter a security code. You will need to purchase the security code. This tiny executable is only 20KB in size and downloads in seconds. Just execute the download, no installation is required. **Now you can recover your own files on your own computer.**	$97 US
Download QuickBooks® and Quicken® Password Recovery Software For Win95/98 / NT ...Works for versions of QuickBooks version 3 through 6 Quicken Version 4 thru 6	$97 US
Download Lotus123® Cracker - LOcrak3 For Win 3.x and Win 95/98/NT (All Versions, Self Extracting) ...Works for all 123 files WK1 thru WK4	$67 US
Download 32 Bit **Access® & Money98/99®** ver 6 and 7 Cracker - "ACcrak32" For Win95/98/NT (Self Extracting Download File)" ...Works for Office 95, and 97 versions of Access®, ver 6 of MS Money98/99® _Limitations_	$67 US
Download 32 Bit MS **EXcel®** Cracker - "EXcrak32_32(Self Extracting 32setup.exe Download File for win 95/98/NT)" ...Works for all versions of Excel thru version 7.0 Does NOT Work For Office 97/98	$67 US
Download 32 Bit MS **Word®** Cracker - "WDcrak3 For Win95/98/NT (Self Extracting Download File WD32setu.exe)"..Works for all versions of Word	$67 US

Figure 12-5

A variety of password-cracking programs are readily available for purchase over the Internet.

Guess a password with a dictionary attack

Most people choose easy-to-remember passwords, which means the odds that someone will choose an ordinary word for a password are extremely high. To find passwords that use ordinary words, hackers have created special password-cracking programs that use *dictionary files* (sometimes called *word lists*), which contain actors' names, names of popular cartoon characters, popular rock bands, Star Trek jargon, common male and female names, technology-related words, and other common words found in most dictionaries.

The password-cracking program takes a word from the dictionary file and tries this word as a password to access a computer. If the first word isn't the right password, the password-cracking program tries another word from its dictionary list until it either finds the right password or runs out of words. If the password works, you have access to the program you want. Of course, if it runs out of words in its dictionary file, you can try another dictionary file until you find a valid password or run out of dictionary files. If a password is an ordinary word, it's only a matter of time before a dictionary attack will uncover it.

To increase the odds of uncovering a password, some password-cracking programs will not only try every word in a dictionary file, but also subtle variations of each word, such as spelling the word backwards or adding different numbers on the end. So even though a password like SNOOPY12 won't be found in an ordinary dictionary file, the password-cracking program can still uncover this password by manipulating each word in its dictionary file.

For an example of a dictionary attack tool sold commercially for people to test the security of their networks, visit SolarWinds (http://solarwinds.net). For one of the largest collections of word lists, visit the Wordlist Project (http://wordlists.security-on.net), which offers word lists in various languages, including English, Spanish, Japanese, and Russian.

Brute-force password attacks

Dictionary attacks can find ordinary words or variations of words, but sometimes a password may consist of random characters. In these cases, the only solution is to use a brute-force attack.

As the name implies, a *brute-force attack* is like prying a password out of a computer by smashing it with a sledgehammer. Instead of trying common words that most people use as passwords, the brute-force method simply tries every possible combination of characters in varying lengths. So, if someone's password is as obscure as NI8$FQ2, a brute-force attack will find that password (and every other password on that computer) eventually.

Brute-force attacks are especially popular when cracking Unix systems, because most Unix systems store the list of account names and passwords in the /etc/passwd file. To provide a small degree of security, Unix encrypts each person's password using an *encryption algorithm* (also called a *hash function*), usually using the Data Encryption Standard (DES).

To gain access to Unix computers, hackers simply copy the /etc/passwd file to their own computer so that they can run a dictionary or brute-force attack on that file at their convenience, without risk of being spotted. With a copy of the passwd file on their own computer, hackers can take as much time as they need until either the dictionary or brute-force attack succeeds. Once it finds just one password, the hacker can use that password to gain access to that unlucky person's account.

To find password-cracking programs that use word-list or brute-force attacks, visit these sites:

BlackCode	http://www.blackcode.com
AntiOnline	http://www.antionline.com
New Order	http://neworder.box.sk

SOFTWARE LOOPHOLES AND FLAWS

Rather than trying to get a password, many hackers take the alternative (but not always reliable) route of trying to exploit a flaw in the operating system or application server, thus bypassing the target computer's security altogether. *Exploits* (called *'sploits* among hackers) that use software flaws are especially popular with novice hackers, called *script kiddies*, because they can use them to sneak into a system without knowing much about the system they're breaking into. In fact, script kiddies are often more dangerous than more technically skilled hackers because a script kiddie may damage or delete files through sheer clumsiness, while a more technically sophisticated hacker would know how to avoid causing accidental damage (although he would know how to do even more serious damage if he wanted).

Buffer overflows

Perhaps the most common flaw in many operating systems and in server software is the *buffer overflow*, which occurs when you feed a program too much data, or sometimes a type of data that the program isn't expecting. In many cases, overflowing a computer with data simply crashes it.

While crashing a computer might be fun for some people, buffer overflows have a potentially dangerous flaw. If a hacker floods a target computer with too much data along with a program, the overload of data tricks the computer into running the program, which can tell the computer to open a port, wipe out files, or give the hacker access to parts of the computer that only an administrator should be allowed to modify.

To see how prevalent buffer overflow vulnerabilities are in a variety of programs, including ICQ, Microsoft Internet Information Server (IIS), WS-FTP, Macromedia Flash, HP Tru64 UNIX, and AOL Instant Messenger, visit the CERT Coordination Center (http://www.kb.cert.org/vuls) and search for "buffer overflows" as shown in Figure 12-6.

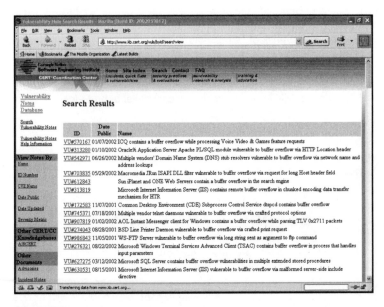

Figure 12-6

An ever-growing list of known buffer overflow vulnerabilities.

Hidden back doors

When creating software, programmers often create *back door* or *default* accounts and passwords to test their software, so they can bypass the login process and quickly access and test other portions of the program. Before the company ships the finished program, the programmers need to remove any back door accounts and passwords, but inevitably they forget a few, which leaves a back door open to any hacker who can find it.

When Red Hat shipped its Linux Virtual Server (LVS) software (nicknamed "Piranha"), the developers inadvertently left in an undocumented backdoor account with the username set to "piranha" and a password set to "q", giving anyone who knew of this exploit access to servers running on Red Hat's LVS.

The piranha problem highlights the double-edged nature of open source software, such as Linux. While revealing the source code can help strengthen its security by allowing others to study the program, it also allows hackers the chance to find flaws they might not otherwise have been able to discover and exploit.

Default settings

Many programs, such as operating systems or webserver software, come packed with plenty of built-in security. The only problem is that when you install the software, it fails to install any of its security features unless you specifically tell it to do so. Since most people rarely customize the installation of their software, it's possible and common for someone to install a perfectly secure program with all the security features turned off.

If you're using Windows XP, you may not realize that it comes with a built-in Internet firewall to protect your computer from unauthorized access over the Internet. Unfortunately, many manufacturers install Windows XP with the firewall turned off, because it can interfere with someone's Internet connection if they don't realize that the firewall is turned on.

To turn on (or off) the Windows XP firewall, follow these steps:

1. Click the Start button and click Control Panel.

2. Click Network and Internet Connections.

3. Click Network Connections.

4. Click the Local Area Connection icon.

5. Click Change Settings of This Connection, which appears in the left side of the Network Connections window. A Local Area Connection dialog box is displayed.

6. Click the Advanced tab.

7. Click in the "Protect my computer and network by limiting or preventing access to this computer from the Internet check box." (If the check box already has a check mark in it, the firewall is already turned on.)

8. Click OK.

9. Click the close box of the Network Connections window.

Finding more software exploits

Every program has flaws, and someone discovers a new one practically every day, so website administrators spend much of their time just keeping up with the latest information and installing the latest patches. Inevitably, some administrators won't hear about a particular patch, which means that a commonly known exploit can often be found in computers years after the vulnerability has been discovered. Sometimes installing a patch to fix one flaw accidentally creates and opens up another flaw, which means installing another patch again in the future.

To exploit these flaws, hackers create tools that allow anyone to probe a computer and test for commonly known flaws, which is how novices (script kiddies) can access a computer without even understanding what they're doing.

To read about the latest security exploits for Windows, visit Microsoft's Security & Privacy site (http://www.microsoft.com/security) and download patches, or read bulletins describing just how insecure your Windows network may really be.

To stay up to date with the latest security breaches in products as diverse as Windows 2000, Linux, ColdFusion, Solaris, FreeBSD, and Unix, visit these sites:

Insecure.org	http://www.insecure.org
Security Administrator	http://www.ntsecurity.net
SecurityFocus	http://www.securityfocus.com
Packet Storm	http://packetstormsecurity.nl
SecuriTeam	http://www.securiteam.com
Linux Security	http://www.linuxsecurity.com
Zone-H	http://www.zone-h.org

BREAKING INTO A WIRELESS NETWORK

Wireless networks deal with the paradox of making access easily available while also making it secure, which means that most wireless networks emphasize convenience over security. While many wireless networks don't take any security measures at all, a few use the built-in wireless encryption standard known as *WEP* (Wired Equivalent Privacy).

Of course, WEP is considered insecure, which means it's like locking your screen door and expecting that to keep intruders out. To defeat any WEP-encrypted wireless networks, war-drivers have created a program called AirSnort (http://airsnort.shmoo.com), which passively gathers encrypted packets off a wireless network. When it has gathered enough of them (approximately 5 to 10 million), it can guess the encryption password, thus granting anyone access to the wireless network.

To ensure that you can crack WEP encryption, try another program called WEPCrack (http://wepcrack.sourceforge.net). Both AirSnort and WEPCrack come with source code so you can study how the programs work and either add new features or create a similar program on your own.

For added security, wireless network manufacturers also include two additional features: *SSID* (Service Set Identification) and *MAC* (Media Access Control) address authentication. SSID identifies every wireless network with a unique identifier, so only computers that know this identifier can access that particular wireless network. Likewise, every wireless access point can include a list of MAC addresses of computers that it will allow into the wireless network. If a computer has a MAC address that doesn't match the list of allowable MAC addresses, the wireless access point won't let the computer use the network.

Both SSID and MAC addresses act like passwords, but many people don't bother turning either of these features on. If they do turn these features on, they don't customize the settings. As a result, most wireless networks use the default passwords that every wireless network manufacturer ships with their products. Hackers also know these default passwords, so they just try these known passwords until they find one that works.

PASSWORDS: THE FIRST LINE OF DEFENSE

Choosing a unique, hard-to-guess password will likely stop all but the most determined hackers. To foil most hackers, just sprinkle some random characters (such as symbols and numbers) in your passwords, or use a special password-generating program such as Quicky Password Generator (http://www.quickysoftware.com), Masking Password Generator (http://www.accusolve.biz), and Randpass (http://www.randpass.com), which can create truly random passwords of varying lengths.

Unfortunately, the more people who use a computer, the more likely one of those users will choose an easy-to-guess password. All it takes is one password to allow a hacker to break into a computer. If you thought keeping hackers out of a computer was tedious and difficult, finding a hacker on your computer and kicking him out is a lot more work.

13

DIGGING IN

BREAKING INTO A COMPUTER ISN'T EASY, SO ONCE A HACKER GETS INTO A COMPUTER, THE FIRST GOAL IS TO MAKE SURE HE CAN GET BACK INTO THAT COMPUTER AT ANY TIME. The best way to do this is to gain a system administrator account on the computer, otherwise known as a *root account* or just plain *root*.

To gain root access, hackers have created special tools called *rootkits*, which are designed to punch holes in a computer's defenses. That way, if a system administrator finds and blocks the first way the hacker broke into the computer, the hacker can still use one of many alternative ways to get back into that same computer.

Some of the more common rootkit tools include sniffers and keystroke loggers (for snaring additional passwords), log-cleaning tools (for hiding the hacker's presence on the system), programs for finding common exploits (for taking advantage of flaws in the operating system or server software), and Trojan horses (for opening up back doors into the computer and masking the intruder's activities). Once a hacker has installed a rootkit on a computer, he can sneak back into that computer at any time without worrying about being detected.

> Opportunities multiply as they are seized.
>
> —SUN TZU

CLEANING OUT THE LOG FILES

Log files track the activity on a computer so administrators can see who has used the computer, what they did, how long they stayed connected, and where they came from. Since a log file can also record the activity of an unauthorized intruder, much like a surveillance camera can record a burglar breaking into a store, hackers look for the log file as soon as they get access into the computer.

Script kiddies often delete the log files to prevent the administrator from seeing exactly what they did on the computer. Unfortunately, deleting the log file reveals the presence of an intruder as blatantly as using a stick of dynamite to get rid of a surveillance camera. The moment an administrator notices that someone has deleted the log file, he or she immediately knows that a hacker must be on the system.

Rather than announce their presence by deleting the log files, the smarter and more technically skilled hackers selectively modify the log files to hide their presence by deleting their own activities from the log files but otherwise leaving the log files intact. At a cursory glance, a system administrator would find the log files seemingly untouched, thereby giving the hacker a chance to infiltrate the computer without alerting the administrators.

The log file typically contains the following information:

→ The IP address of the machine that performed an action or "request" on the target computer.

→ The username, which simply identifies the account being used. A perfectly valid username could mask the presence of a hacker who has secretly hijacked a valid user's account.

→ The date and time that the user did something.

→ The exact command or "request" that the user gave the target computer.

→ The HTTP status code that the target computer returned to the user. That status code shows what action the target computer did as a result of the user's command or "request."

→ The amount of bytes transferred to the user.

In many cases, simply editing the log files can hide a hacker's tracks, but system administrators have their own ways to ensure the integrity of their log files. One of the simplest involves printing out the log files as they're generated. That way, if a hacker does delete or modify the log files, he will never be able to destroy or change the printed copy. If the system administrator suspects something is wrong, he or she can compare the log file on the hard disk with the printed-out log file. While tedious, this virtually guarantees that a hacker cannot hide his presence by modifying the log files alone.

Another way to preserve log files involves creating duplicate copies. The original log file appears where hackers expect to find it, while a duplicate copy of that same log file gets stored on another computer altogether, preferably one that no one else (including anyone with a root or administrator account) can modify or delete. The system administrator can use *log-file analysis programs* that can compare the two log files and notify the system administrators of any discrepancies, which can indicate the presence of a hacker.

To learn about the capabilities of various log-file analysis programs, take a look at one or more of the following programs:

Analog	http://www.analog.cx
WebTrends	http://www.netiq.com
Sawmill	http://www.sawmill.net
NetTracker	http://www.sane.com
Webalizer	http://www.mrunix.net/webalizer

KILLING THE MONITORING SOFTWARE

Modifying the log files can hide what a hacker has done in the past, but hackers still need to hide their presence while they're logged on to a computer. So, after the log files, the second target that hackers go after are the programs that can help system administrators notice any changes on their computers. In the world of Unix and Linux, the most common commands that hackers try to alter include the following:

→ find—Looks for groups of files

→ ls—Lists the contents of the current directory

→ netstat—Shows the network status, including information about ports

→ ps—Displays the current processes that are running

→ who—Displays the names of all the users currently logged on

→ w—Prints system usage, currently logged-on users, and what each user is doing

Planting Trojaned programs

When they introduce malicious programs onto a computer, hackers simply substitute the computer's current programs or binaries with their own hacked or Trojaned versions. If an unsuspecting system administrator uses these hacked versions, the commands may appear to work normally, but they secretly hide the hacker's activities from view. The longer it takes system administrators to find the hacker, the more time the hacker has to cause damage or to open additional back doors to ensure that he can return at a later time.

Of course, when a hacker replaces the original programs or binaries with his own deceptive versions of those same programs, he risks giving away his presence. This danger occurs because every file contains two unique properties: a creation date and time, and a file size. If a system administrator notices that a program's creation date was yesterday, that's a sure sign that the programs have been altered.

To protect their files from alterations, system administrators use *file integrity programs* that calculate a number, called a checksum, based on the file's size. The moment someone changes a file's size, even by a small amount, the checksum changes.

To avoid being detected by a file integrity checker, a skilled hacker may run the file integrity checker program and recalculate new checksums for all the files, including the modified ones. Now, if a system administrator didn't keep track of the old checksum values, the file integrity checker won't notice any differences.

With a little bit of tweaking, hackers can make their altered versions of certain programs the exact same size as the files they're replacing. This means that if they just change the date and time of this altered file to match that of the real file, any checksum comparisons won't notice the substitution.

A system administrator using a file integrity checker must run it right after setting up a computer. The longer the system administrator waits, the more likely a hacker will have time to change files, and then the file integrity checker will think the changed files are actually the valid ones.

Even more importantly, system administrators need to calculate a cryptographic checksum using an algorithm such as MD5. Unlike ordinary checksums, a cryptographic checksum can be nearly impossible to fake, which means that hackers can't fake the checksum values for any files they modify.

To learn more about the various file integrity programs that system administrators use, visit these sites:

Samhain	http://www.la-samhna.de
Tripwire	http://www.tripwiresecurity.com
GFI LANguard	http://www.gfi.com
AIDE (Advanced Intrusion Detection Environment)	http://www.cs.tut.fi/~rammer/aide.html

Loadable Kernel Module (LKM) rootkits

The simplest way a system administrator can defeat any altered or Trojaned programs is by storing unaltered copies of all the common programs that hackers try to modify, and just recopying them back on the computer. By using these clean copies of various monitoring programs, a system administrator can hunt around the computer and likely find new traces of a hacker that the Trojaned versions hid from sight.

To get around this problem, hackers have started exploiting *loadable kernel modules*, commonly found in Unix-like systems such as Linux. In the old days, if you wanted to add a feature to Linux, you had to modify and recompile the entire source code of your operating system. Loadable Kernel Modules (LKMs) eliminate this task by letting you attach new commands to the Linux kernel (the heart of the operating system) through an LKM. This means you don't have to recompile the kernel over and over again, and it also prevents any changes you made from keeping Linux from loading altogether—if you modified the Linux source code incorrectly, it might never work again. If you modify code as an LKM, the Linux kernel can still load, and if the code in your LKM fails, it won't crash the entire operating system.

Hackers can also take advantage of LKMs. Rather than replace any existing programs and risk detection, LKM rootkits simply load their programs into memory. If a system administrator checks the file integrity of the various monitoring tools, they appear untouched (because they are). But if the administrator tries to run these seemingly untouched programs, the hacker's LKM module intercepts the commands and runs its own commands, which mask the hacker's presence. As far as the system administrator can see, the monitoring programs are untouched and working fine.

Some popular LKM rootkits sport odd names like SuckIT, Knark, Rial, Adore, and Tuxkit. To learn more about various tools used to make up a rootkit, visit Rootkit (http://www.rootkit.com), shown in Figure 13-1.

Figure 13-1

Rootkit.com provides source code for various rootkit tools, including Trojan horses and patches to hide a hacker's activity.

OPENING A BACK DOOR

The most common way to open a back door in a computer is by opening a port, usually one of the more obscure ports that won't likely already be in use (unless another hacker has gotten there first). The rootkit often sets up a default password, such as "password" so the next time the hacker connects through this particular port, he or she just needs to type in this default password to get back into the computer.

If the hacker had taken time to insert Trojan versions of monitoring programs beforehand, these Trojaned monitoring programs will ignore both the open port (reporting it as closed when it's really open) and any activity coming from this back door.

If a hacker opens a port as a back door, a system administrator might discover this open port during a routine port scan of the system. To mask their presence even further, hackers may create special "open sesame"-type back doors that remain shut until the hacker transmits a certain command to the computer. When the computer receives this seemingly innocuous command, the back door opens a port and the hacker slides right through.

SNIFFING FOR MORE PASSWORDS

Another component of a rootkit is a sniffer or a keystroke logger, which the hacker can plant on a system to snare passwords, credit card numbers, or other valuable information transmitted across the network. A hacker may install a keystroke logger on one or more computers, though this increases the chance that the keystroke logger program may be detected.

Sniffers are less obvious because a hacker only needs to install it on one computer and then set that computer's *network interface card* (NIC) to promiscuous mode. Normally, each computer on the network only peeks at traffic specifically addressed to that computer, but when set in promiscuous mode, the computer peeks at any data passing through.

Once the sniffer retrieves one or more passwords, the hacker can use those valid passwords to hijack a legitimate user's account. Now the hacker can enter the computer under the disguise of a legitimate user, even in the middle of the night on a weekend when few legitimate users would be on the system. As a seemingly legitimate user, a hacker can leisurely browse a computer to better understand the software being used and the configuration of the network.

If the sniffer happens to snare the password of a system administrator, the hacker can use the system administrator's account to gain root access. With root access, the hacker can create additional accounts, even accounts with system administrator privileges, so the hacker can get back into the computer through a phony "legitimate" account later.

To learn more about the capabilities of sniffers, take a look at these programs:

WinDump	http://windump.polito.it
Ethereal	http://www.ethereal.com
Sniffer	http://www.sniffer.com
EtherPeek	http://www.wildpackets.com
Analyzer	http://analyzer.polito.it
tcpdump	http://www.tcpdump.org
Sniffit	http://reptile.rug.ac.be/~coder/sniffit/sniffit.html

Sniffers actually have legitimate users for analyzing and fixing a network. However, few people want a total stranger running a sniffer on their network. Rather than check to see if a computer's NIC card may be running in promiscuous mode, system administrators can run a variety of anti-sniffer tools (such as AntiSniff, shown in Figure 13-2) to help them find any rogue sniffers running on their network. Here are a few anti-sniffer programs:

AntiSniff	http://packetstorm.decepticons.org/sniffers/antisniff
PromiscDetect	http://ntsecurity.nu
PromiScan	http://www.securityfriday.com
The sentinel project	http://www.packetfactory.net/Projects/sentinel

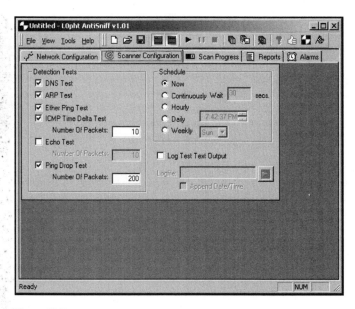

Figure 13-2

The AntiSniff program can check for hidden sniffers on a network.

KILLING ROOTKITS

It may be impossible to keep a computer hacker-free. A system administrator may diligently wipe out all rootkits and shut down all the back doors a hacker may have set, but there's still no guarantee that there still isn't one back door that the system administrator may have missed. If even one back door remains, the hacker can return, install more rootkits, and open up more back doors once again. The only sure way a system administrator can remove hackers from a computer is by erasing everything and reinstalling everything from scratch.

Since erasing everything can be a drastic measure, most system administrators have to balance their time between keeping a computer up and running, and trying to keep hackers out of the system. Despite their best efforts, system administrators can't be perfect, while hackers only need one lucky break to slip into a computer undetected.

To help tilt the balance in favor of the system administrators, many people have developed dedicated rootkit detectors. These rootkit detectors scan a computer for signs that betray the existence of a rootkit, such as files that a specific rootkit is known to plant on a computer. Two popular rootkit detectors are chkrootkit (http://www.chkrootkit.org) and Carbonite (http://www.foundstone.com), which can search a computer for LKM rootkits.

Besides running rootkit detectors periodically, system administrators should also run a port scanner to detect any ports that may be open. An open port may be a signal of sloppy administration or of a back door left behind by a hacker.

When a system administrator first sets up a computer, he or she should create cryptographic checksums of all the important files and store these checksums in a separate location, such as on a CD that can only be written to once. Along with the checksums of important files, system administrators should also save spare copies of crucial program utilities on the CD as well. Now if a hacker breaks into a computer, the system administrator can at least be certain that the files stored on the CD can be trusted.

Finally, system administrators need to keep up with the latest security flaws and vulnerabilities so they can patch them up, or at least watch out for hackers who may exploit the latest known flaws.

Still, no matter what a system administrator does, there will always be a chance that a hacker could be lurking in a computer at any given time. Some system administrators leave hackers alone as long as the hackers leave their important data alone, but most system administrators must constantly try to throw hackers off their system, while the hackers can keep coming back with new techniques, tools, and ideas again and again and again. . . .

PART 4

PROTECTING YOURSELF

14

COMPUTING ON A SHOESTRING

ONE OF THE BIGGEST BARRIERS TO COMPUTERS IS THE PRICE TAG.
Computer manufacturers would love you to think that you need the absolute latest
computer that just coincidentally costs more than you want to spend. The trick to buying a computer is knowing that few people need the most advanced computer
available: New computers plummet in value faster than new cars. To cut costs, do a little research and you could save hundreds of dollars on your next computer—and,
with a little creativity, load it with software for nothing, or next to nothing.

GETTING A COMPUTER ON A BUDGET

If you need another computer, never buy a new one. Instead, save money and buy a
used or refurbished computer. Since computer prices drop every day, even the latest
computer will become obsolete and overpriced within a few weeks. With a little bit of
careful shopping, you may even be able to get the latest computer at a cut-rate price,
but only if you know where to look first.

Refurbished computers

Refurbished computers are products that someone either returned because of a
defect or because they didn't like it for some reason—even though it may be working
perfectly well. Once a manufacturer receives a returned computer, they tear it apart,
test every component, and then put the computer back together again so it's just like
new—but with one problem. Legally, manufacturers can't sell a returned computer as
new, so they have to sell it as a refurbished computer.

Since the manufacturer has already lost money accepting a returned computer,
they offer to sell it at a greatly reduced price just to get rid of it. If the computer were to
fail a second time and force someone to return it, the manufacturer would lose even
more money. So when manufacturers receive a returned computer the first time, they
actually test it more rigorously than a new computer, because they want to make sure
that customers won't have a technical reason to return the computer again.

Refurbished computers come with the same technical support and warranty as
the identical new model, but at a much lower price. Perhaps the one major drawback

with refurbished computers is that you may have to customize them to get all the features you want. When you buy a refurbished computer, you can only buy what the manufacturer happens to have in stock that day. So if you want a computer with a 120Gb hard disk but the manufacturer only has a refurbished computer with an 80Gb hard disk, you'll either have to wait until the manufacturer gets a computer with a 120Gb hard disk or just buy the computer with the 80Gb hard disk and replace the hard disk (or add a second one) later.

Still if you don't mind getting a computer that someone else may have opened and used, buying a refurbished computer can be a great way to get a top-of-the-line machine without paying top-of-the-line prices. You won't find refurbished computers sold at your favorite store, though. Most computer manufacturers only sell refurbished computers through websites.

Amazon.com   Although best known for selling books, Amazon.com also sells new and refurbished computer systems and accessories (http://www.amazon.com; 800-800-8300).

Astak   Sells various name-brand computer systems and parts, many of which are *OEM* (Original Equipment Manufacturer) parts that computer dealers normally buy to build and repair computers, so manuals may be missing or non-existent, and products arrive in plain cardboard boxes (http://www.astak.com; 408-519-0401).

HP Shopping   Hewlett-Packard's online computer store that also offers a special outlet section for selling discontinued and refurbished desktop and laptop computers. In addition to computers, you can also buy refurbished printers, monitors, and handheld computers (http://www.shopping.hp.com; 888-999-4747).

Dell Computer   Dell Computer is another mail-order computer giant that has its share of returned products, which it sells at a discount (http://www.dell.com/factoryoutlet; 877-471-DELL).

Gateway   Gateway sells refurbished desktops, laptops, and servers (http://www.gateway.com; 1-800-846-3614).

Opportunity Distributing   Opportunity Distributing contacts companies that are upgrading their computers and sells their old equipment to the public (http://www.opportunitydistribute.com; 952-936-0221).

Overstock.com   Besides selling refurbished and discontinued products from various manufacturers, including Gateway, Sony, Dell, and Toshiba, Overstock.com also sells consumer-oriented software at cut-rate prices, such as children's games and educational programs (http://www.overstock.com; 800-989-0135).

PC Factory Outlet   Packard Bell, eMachines, and NEC sell their returned or discontinued models here (http://www.pcfactoryoutlet.com; 800-733-5858).

PCnomad Specializes in selling refurbished laptop computers, including those from IBM, Toshiba, Dell, and Compaq (http://www.pcnomad.com; 800-278-4009).

PCRetro Buys computers and office equipment from failed or bankrupt companies, and refurbishes them for sale to the public (http://www.pcretro.com; 877-277-3872).

TigerDirect Sells new and refurbished computers and computer parts, so you can build your own computer if you have the desire (http://www.tigerdirect.com; 800-800-8300).

UsedComputer.com Offers a clearinghouse for a variety of dealers who specialize in selling used and refurbished computer and office equipment at prices way below retail (http://www.usedcomputer.com/classifieds/XcClassPro.asp; 877-277-3872).

Floor models and returns

Every computer store has floor models that customers can bang away at for a test drive while browsing through the store displays. If you must have the latest technology, consider buying a floor model. Most stores will be happy to cut the price a bit to make a sale.

Alternatively, consider buying a returned or "open box" machine. Many of the larger computer stores allow customers to return new computers within a specified period of time. Usually stores will have one or two returned models that are perfectly good but out of their original packaging or in an opened box, so the store will sell them at lower prices.

Online auctions

If your local computer store doesn't sell returned or floor models, try online auctions or resellers. Online auctions are a great place to buy inexpensive computers and computer parts. The computers, computer parts, and even "antique" computers sold on these sites come from individuals off-loading their old hardware or from liquidators and brand-name distributors (such as Dell Computer) that need to dump their surplus or old stock. And, if you hunt around long enough, you just may find that elusive part you need to keep your computer running, and get it at a bargain price to boot.

Since online auctions offer so many different computers and accessories, make sure you know what you're buying before you dive in. With a little research and plenty of patience, you can buy new or used equipment or software at prices far below what you could ever find through mail order or in a retail store. Just be careful that you don't get so fixated on buying a particular item that you wind up bidding more than the retail price.

To find computer equipment through an online auction, visit one of the following websites:

CNET Auctions	http://auctions.cnet.com
eBay	http://www.ebay.com
Dell Auction	http://www.dellauction.com
CompUSA Auctions	http://www.compusaauctions.com
uBid	http://www.ubid.com

Government auctions

Every year, police departments around the country confiscate property from criminals. After taking the good stuff for themselves, the police hold an auction to get rid of what's left and to raise money.

At police auctions (usually held monthly, depending on where you live) you'll see everything from cars and yachts to houses, office furniture, and, of course, computers. (Call your local police department to see when they hold property auctions.)

Before the auction begins, try to inspect the equipment to make sure it's working. (This may not always be possible.) Auctioned computers come with no guarantees, so either assume they won't work and be prepared to strip them for parts, or just hope for the best.

Recycled computers

A few computer companies have popped up that buy old computers from corporations, refurbish them, and then resell them. Although you won't get the latest models when you buy recycled equipment, you can get a fairly decent used machine with a warranty to boot. Just make sure that the cost of the recycled computer really is less than buying a refurbished computer, a floor model, or an auctioned computer.

Here are some good sites for recycled machines:

Comp-Recycle.com	http://www.comp-recycle.com
RE-PC	http://www.repc.com
RecommIT	http://www.recommit.co.uk
Used-PCs.com	http://www.used-pcs.com

Build it yourself

If you're handy, you can build your own computer. Depending on the parts you buy, you could either save a lot of money building a bare-bones model or create a souped-up computer for the same price you might pay for an ordinary name-brand computer. Best of all, you get the experience of building your own machine, so you'll know how to fix and upgrade it later.

Look online or in any issue of *PC Magazine*, *PC World*, or *Computer Shopper* to find tons of dealers who sell computer parts, or find a local computer store (usually one without a fancy franchise name), and buy the parts you need. If you need help, pick up a do-it-yourself computer book that explains how to build your own PC

176

(although the best way to learn is simply to watch someone else build one), or search online where you'll find lots of tutorials and reviews of various hardware (try http://www.pcguide.com, http://www.storagereview.com, http://www.tomshardware. com, or http://www.anandtech.com).

Computers are relatively easy to build because they consist of easily purchased and replaceable components that you simply snap or screw together. If you can build a toy house out of Lego building blocks, you should have little trouble putting together your own computer. It just takes a little more fiddling around to get it to work.

The biggest hassle with building your own computer is getting the right parts, and getting them to work correctly together. Even new computers crash, so don't expect a computer you've built to be any different.

Buy a new computer

Sometimes you absolutely must have the latest computer model available. While you could wait a few months until people start returning these models so you can buy a refurbished computer, you may just want to go ahead and buy the latest computer right now. For people who can't wait, at least make sure you don't spend more than necessary.

To help you find the lowest prices on the Web, visit these sites:

StreetPrices.com	http://www.streetprices.com
PriceWatch	http://www.pricewatch.com/
iBuyernet.com	http://www.ibuyer.net
Shopper.com	http://shopper.cnet.com
BizRate.com	http://www.bizrate.com
PriceSCAN.com	http://www.pricescan.com

By using these websites, you can search for the lowest price offered by various online retailers for the exact same piece of equipment. Once you've found the lowest price, you can buy your new computer knowing you got the best price available at the time.

When you're in the market for a new computer, consider buying machines with processors from a company other than Intel. Because Intel is the leader in the processor market, their prices are usually higher than those of compatible rivals, such as Advanced Micro Devices (AMD). AMD processors are often just as fast (or sometimes even faster) than their Intel rivals, yet AMD processors almost always cost much less.

Soup-up your old computer

Many people want another computer because their current one is too slow. But rather than buy another computer, those on a budget might consider just yanking out their current processor and replacing it with a faster processor. If the computer won't accept a new processor, you can often yank out the entire motherboard and replace it with a new one that accepts a faster processor. The cost of a new processor and a motherboard will almost always be less than buying another computer.

For an even cheaper way to boost the performance of your computer, try over-clocking it. Basically, *overclocking* means tweaking your hardware (typically the main processor but sometimes the video cards too) at a higher clock speed than what the manufacturer designed it to run. Overclocking may void your equipment's warranty and even overheat and damage your equipment if you're not careful, but with a little bit of care, you can boost the performance of an ordinary computer into a super power-house, using the equipment you already own.

For more information about overclocking your equipment, visit ClubOC (http://www.cluboverclocker.com) or Extreme Overclocking.com (http://www.extremeoverclocking.com), or pick up a copy of *The Book of Overclocking* by Scott Wainner and Robert Richmond, published by No Starch Press.

SAVE ON PRINTER SUPPLIES

When you buy a computer, you'll probably need a printer to go along with it. For ordi-nary black and white printing, get a laser printer. Although a laser printer initially costs more, the cost to print pages on a laser printer is much less than printing on an inkjet printer. If you need color though, you'll have no choice but to buy an inexpensive inkjet printer (or a really expensive color laser printer).

Watch out, though. Many printer manufacturers seduce you with low prices on their inkjet printers, but when you buy replacement ink cartridges, you'll find that the cost of two or three ink cartridges alone equals the original price of the inkjet printer. Even worse, inkjet printers tend to suck up ink rapidly, so over the lifetime of your inkjet printer, you may wind up spending several times more for inkjet cartridges than you did for the printer in the first place.

To help reduce your ink usage, try a program dubbed InkSaver (http://www.strydent.com), which claims to reduce the amount of ink your printer uses without any noticeable difference in print quality. InkSaver works with most Epson, Canon, and Hewlett-Packard printers, but you can download a trial version of InkSaver to see if it works with your particular inkjet printer.

No matter how much ink a program like InkSaver can help you save, you'll eventually need to buy replacement inkjet cartridges. Instead of buying inkjet car-tridges from the printer manufacturer, buy refill kits or alternative inkjet cartridges from Amazon Imaging (http://www.amazonimaging.com) or Rhinotek (http://www.buyrhinotek.com). To find more online retailers that sell replacement inkjet cartridges, visit Buy Ink Cartridges (http://www.buyinkcartridges.com).

These third-party ink companies sell refill kits and replacement inkjet cartridges for most inkjet printers, at as low as half the amount that an original manufacturer's inkjet cartridge would cost. Visit their websites and see if they sell replacement car-tridges for your particular inkjet printer.

If you're shopping for an inkjet printer, compare the prices of replacement ink cartridges at Amazon Imaging or Rhinotek first. You may find that the inkjet printer that looks so appealing today might wind up costing you several hundred dollars in the future for replacement inkjet cartridges alone. Look for the cheapest replacement inkjet cartridges, and then look at the printers that work with them.

To foil companies (such as Amazon Imaging and Rhinotek) that make replacement inkjet cartridges, printer manufacturers have come up with several tactics to force consumers to buy only inkjet cartridges from the printer manufacturer.

Both Hewlett-Packard and Epson are planning to put computer chips in the inkjet cartridges to prevent them from being refilled. The moment the cartridge runs out of ink, the computer chip implanted in that cartridge prevents that cartridge from ever being used again, no matter how much you may refill the cartridge with replacement ink. Hewlett-Packard's DeskJet 2000C supposedly uses such a computer chip in its inkjet cartridges. Lexmark and Hewlett-Packard have even patented the print heads on certain inkjet cartridges, thereby preventing anyone from making a compatible replacement inkjet cartridge. So if you can't find a third-party replacement inkjet cartridge for your printer, now you know why.

If you have a laser printer, don't throw away your old toner cartridges. Check your local Yellow Pages under computer supplies, and look for local stores (or contact Amazon Imaging) that refill or sell used toner cartridges for your particular laser printer model.

ALMOST-FREE SOFTWARE

Once you have your computer, you'll need an operating system and software. Many computers come bundled with an operating system (such as Windows XP or Linux), but if you build your own computer or buy a used computer, you may still need an operating system.

Because Microsoft Windows is still so popular, you might be tempted to buy a brand new copy of Windows XP. But if you can find an old copy of Windows 98 or Windows Millennium Edition (Me), you can buy the upgrade version of Windows XP and save money over the full version. Just load Windows 98/Me on your computer, and before you start installing any software, load the upgrade version of Windows XP.

Be careful though. If you can only find an old copy of Windows 2000, you must upgrade to the Windows XP Professional Edition instead of the Home Edition. Naturally, the Professional Edition costs more, so you may find it's easier just to wipe Windows 2000 off your hard disk, install Windows 98/Me, and then upgrade to the Home Edition of Windows XP.

If you plan to use Linux, you can download a copy for free. Some popular Linux distributors that offer free copies include Red Hat (http://www.redhat.com), Mandrake Linux (http://www.linux-mandrake.com), and Debian (http://www.debian.org).

If you don't have the time or patience to download a copy of Linux and you don't want to buy a boxed retail version from a store, you can order Linux CDs from CheapBytes (http://www.cheapbytes.com).

For true computer renegades, skip both Windows XP and Linux and go for a pure Unix environment in the form of FreeBSD (http://www.freebsd.org) or OpenBSD (http://www.openbsd.org).

Shareware and freeware

Shareware programs can be used for free during a trial period (usually 30 days or so) after which they generally ask you to pay a reasonable amount if you continue using them. Shareware programs are often just as good (or even better) than their higher-priced, brand-name counterparts. No matter what type of program you need (virus scanner, word processor, paint program, and so on), you can almost always find a good shareware version that equals the features of a commercial program.

Freeware programs are given away—you can legally use and own them without ever paying for them. Freeware may be software that has been abandoned by a company, or it may be a limited version of a program given away to help market the full-featured commercial version. (The idea is that if you like the freeware version, you might want to upgrade to the commercial version later to get more features.) To find great collections of freeware and shareware, visit the following sites:

Download.com	http://download.cnet.com
Simtel.Net	http://www.simtel.net
Jumbo	http://www.jumbo.com
Tucows	http://www.tucows.com

Buying software at an academic discount

College and university bookstores usually sell academic versions of nearly all major software at a substantial discount—the software companies want to get students hooked on using their program instead of a competitor's. So a program that normally costs $495 might be sold by a university bookstore for $100.

Of course, the catch is that if you want to get this academic discount, you must have a student ID. If you know of someone in college, ask them to buy software for you (and in exchange, you can buy them beer). As another alternative, just sign up for one class, get your student ID, and then drop out (just pretend you're a football player). Now you can use your student ID to buy all the software you want, at academic discounts.

Upgrade offers

In an effort to grab as much market share as possible, nearly every software publisher offers two different prices: an ordinary retail price and a discounted upgrade price for people who own the previous version of the program (or sometimes a similar rival program). Unless you have more money than sense, you never need pay full retail price for any software.

To qualify for the upgrade price, you may need proof that you own either a previous version or a rival program, or have an actual copy of a previous version or rival program on your hard disk. Microsoft typically sells special upgrade versions of their software that peeks at your hard disk for a previous version or rival program. If neither one exists, the upgrade version won't install itself.

Here's where you can get creative. If you're buying software directly from the software publisher, they'll ask that you mail or fax them proof that you own a previous version or a rival program, such as the front page of the manual. So if you want the upgrade version of Microsoft Excel, you'll need to prove that you own a rival spreadsheet, such as Lotus 1-2-3 or Quattro Pro.

The simplest way to handle this is to find a friend who owns the program you need (such as Lotus 1-2-3), and fax a photocopy of the manual's front page.

If you can't find anyone with the program you need, try to find an older version of the program either online or at your local computer store. By buying an older version (which you can always sell on eBay), you'll qualify for the less-expensive upgrade. The cost of the upgrade plus a boxed older version will nearly always be less than the full retail price for any program. Or maybe better yet, just use the older version of the program—who needs the latest version anyway?

Try these sites for older versions of software:

Ellen's Software Collection	http://www.ellens.com
Oldsoftware.com	http://www.oldsoftware.com
Surplus Computers	http://www.softwareandstuff.com
ComputerCost	http://www.computercost.com

Low-cost Microsoft Office alternatives

Most computer stores and mail-order dealers sell the most popular software, but unless you know better, you might think that what you see in the stores or mail-order catalogs is the only software available. Rather than spend hundreds of dollars paying for commercial software, hunt around the Internet and look for alternatives instead.

If you need to share work with others, chances are good you'll be stuck using Microsoft Office. Of course, Microsoft Office costs hundreds of dollars and offers hundreds of features that most people never need or use, so rather than torture yourself using and learning Microsoft Office, try one of the many Microsoft Office alternatives listed below:

EasyOffice	http://www.e-press.com
OpenOffice	http://www.openoffice.org
PC602 Pro PC Suite	http://www.software602.com
SOT Office 2002	http://www.sot.com/en/linux/soto
ThinkFree Office	http://www.thinkfree.com

Pirating software

Sometimes even the best shareware or freeware programs don't come close to offering what a commercial version offers. So rather than buy software, many people just copy it instead, a practice known as *software piracy*.

Legally, you could be practicing piracy every time you install a program on two or more computers, even if all those computers belong to you and you're the only one who uses them. Because software piracy laws can seem ludicrous at times, many people feel no qualms about copying and using software that they never bought.

When "borrowing" a friend's copy of a program, you'll probably find that you need a CD key or registration number to install it. If you're installing from an original CD, the CD key is usually printed on a sticker glued to the back of the CD case. If you don't have the CD key or it's missing, you have two choices:

→ Visit a hacker website that lists valid keys for various programs, and pick the one you need (search for the product you're looking for together with the search term "serial," "crack," or "appz").

→ Use a special CD key generator program (on a friend's computer if yours isn't working yet) to create a key for your particular program, and use the generated key to install your software (see Figure 14-1).

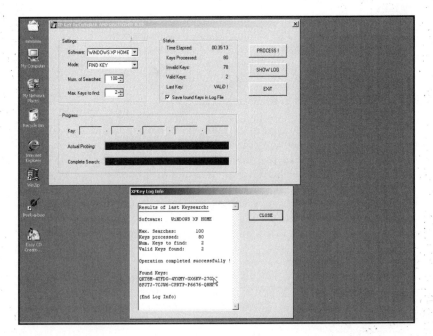

Figure 14-1

The XPKeyGen program claims it can create valid codes necessary to activate illegal copies of Windows XP.

If you can't be bothered with borrowing a CD (or you can't find anyone to lend one to you), there's another simple solution to getting software—find and download your programs online. Many hacker websites post entire pirated programs, called *warez* or *appz*, that have been cracked to remove annoying copy-protection schemes. Just visit one of these websites and download all the software you want.

NOTE: Most pirated programs on websites are games, but if you hunt around, you'll find all kinds of pirated programs.

Needless to say, warez and appz sites with serial numbers, CD key generators, or pirated software move around a lot. To find them, search for "serial numbers" (see Figure 14-2), "pirated software," "warez," "cracks," "serials," or "CD key generator."

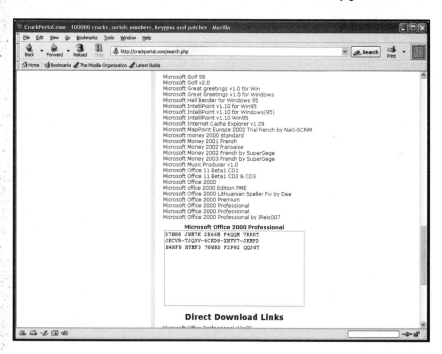

Figure 14-2
Many websites contain lists of valid keys for a variety of programs.

Just don't forget the risk involved in using warez. Sometimes the programs aren't complete, so you could waste time downloading them only to find they don't work. Even worse, many hackers like to infect warez with viruses or Trojan horses to "punish" people for trying to use software they haven't bought.

Cracking software

But don't let someone else do all of the work—why not crack some software yourself? Software cracking involves modifying a program to either turn a trial version into a fully functional one, or to shut off a shareware program's nag screen that keeps reminding you to register. Essentially, cracking allows you to trick a program into thinking it's registered when it's not.

To crack Windows software, you need several tools:

→ A disassembler to reveal the program's assembly language source code, so you can see how it works, such as IDA Pro (http://www.datarescue.com/idabase).

→ A debugger to examine how a program runs, so you can identify the part of the program that you want to change (generally the part requiring a registration number), such as MULTI Source-Level Debugger (http://www.ghs.com/products/MULTI_debugger.html).

→ A hex editor to modify the executable version of a program, such as UltraEdit (http://www.ultraedit.com) or Hex Workshop (http://www.hexworkshop.com).

→ A Windows registry viewer to modify any Windows registry entries necessary to make the cracked program run properly, such as Registry Crawler (http://www.4developers.com/regc) or Registry Toolkit (http://www.funduc.com/registry_toolkit.htm).

Remember, software cracking requires an intimate knowledge of assembly language, so it's not for the beginner. To learn how people crack software or how to become a software cracker yourself, search Astalavista (http://www.astalavista.com) or CyberArmy (http://www.cyberarmy.com) for the programs and tutorials you'll need. To read more about cracking software and how programmers try to defend their programs against crackers, pick up a copy of *Crackproof Your Software* by Pavol Cerven, published by No Starch Press.

FREE MUSIC

Nearly all new computers come with a CD-ROM drive, a sound card, and speakers, which can turn any computer into a simple CD audio player. You can play your own audio CDs on your computer, but you may have more fun scouring the Internet for free music to play from your hard disk or a *CD-R* (CD recordable) drive.

One reason there are so many free music files on the Internet is the restrictive nature of the recording industry. In the old days, recording artists could only get massive public exposure by signing with a major record label. If they couldn't get a contract, they were rarely heard by the general public.

To get around this problem, a few renegade musicians offered samples of their music for free over the Internet. However, in the early days of digital sound (prior to the arrival of MP3), a high-quality sound file of a single song could be as large as 30MB.

Then came *MP3*—Moving Picture Experts Group Audio Layer-3 compression technology. MP3 allows entire songs to be compressed into relatively small files (a few megabytes), while retaining the audio quality of the original recording. Fast Internet access (such as cable or DSL modems) has made downloading and sharing MP3 files fast and convenient. Many enterprising bands and musicians regularly release their songs in MP3 format for people to download, copy, and enjoy for free, hoping that if you like their songs, you'll buy their albums.

Of course, that's the legal, sanctioned use of MP3 technology. Many people use MP3 illegally to record songs from their favorite CDs, store them as MP3 files, and trade them with others over the Internet, violating copyright laws and cheating artists out of their royalties.

Once you have your favorite songs stored in MP3 format, you can use a recordable CD drive to create your own audio CDs. Just as cassette tape decks have allowed people to record, copy, and trade their favorite songs with one another on blank cassette tapes, the MP3 format has done the same thing on a global scale using the power of the Internet.

To take advantage of music stored in MP3 format, you need a player (so you can hear the music stored in MP3 format), a ripper (for saving your MP3 files on a CD), and one or more websites where you can download MP3 files.

MP3 players

Here's where to get some of the more popular MP3 players:

MuzicMan (for Windows)	http://www.muzicman.com
Sonique (for Windows)	http://sonique.lycos.com
Winamp (for Windows)	http://www.winamp.com
RadioDestiny (for Windows and Macintosh)	http://www.radiodestiny.com
Mpg123 (for Unix)	http://www.mpg123.de

MP3 rippers

These programs will let you save your MP3 files to CD so that you can play them back later:

AudioCatalyst (for Windows and Macintosh)	http://www.xingtech.com/mp3/audiocatalyst
Cdparanoia (for Unix)	http://www.xiph.org/paranoia
Play & Record (for Windows)	http://www.hycd.com

MP3 search engines

Start with these sites when searching for MP3 files:

MP3.com	http://www.mp3.com
Lycos Music	http://music.lycos.com/downloads/
Musicseek	http://www.musicseek.net
Yahoo! Digital	http://launch.yahoo.com/downloads

An alternative to using an MP3 search engine is to run an MP3 *peer-to-peer sharing program* that lets you connect with others and swap music files. These are some of the more popular peer-to-peer sharing programs:

Blubster	http://www.blubster.com
Gnutella	http://www.gnutella.com
Grokster	http://www.grokster.com
Kazaa	http://www.kazaa.com
iNoize	http://www.inoize.com
Madster	http://www.madster.com
Morpheus	http://www.morpheus-mp3-music-download-ic.com

While law-abiding citizens may use peer-to-peer sharing programs to exchange their favorite recipes or tips for winning at computer games, others have used peer-to-peer networks to exchange pornography or copyrighted materials, such as MP3s or commercial software.

FREE INTERNET ACCESS

Network television is free because advertisers pay the cost of producing the shows in return for marketing their products to a vast audience. Similarly, many Internet providers now provide free Internet accounts in exchange for displaying advertisements on your computer screen or tracking your online usage for marketing purposes. Many of these free Internet accounts have limitations or restrictions that change over time, so read their descriptions carefully.

To find the latest and greatest free Internet accounts, visit the Internet 4 Free website (http://www.internet4free.net), or try one of the following:

DotNow	http://www.dotnow.com
Juno	http://www.juno.com
NetZero	http://www.netzero.net

Rather than set up your own Internet account, just visit one of the larger public libraries that have computers connected to the Internet. Libraries offer free Internet access, although they may place a time limit and charge a fee if you need to print anything out.

FREE EMAIL

Free email accounts are perfect if you need to send email that can't be easily traced to you, and so that, if your boss scans your work email account, there won't be any embarrassing messages.

Many free email accounts offer special features such as encryption (to protect your email from prying eyes), a self-destruct capability (to wipe out your email after a specified period of time), support for multiple languages, and anonymity (to hide your true identity from the rest of the world).

To sign up for a free email account, visit your favorite search engine and search for the string "free email." For a quick overview of what the different free email services have to offer, visit one of the following websites:

MSN Hotmail	http://www.hotmail.com
Mail.com	http://www.mail.com
HushMail	http://www.hushmail.com
Yahoo! Mail	http://mail.yahoo.com

FREE FAX SERVICES

If you need to send a fax to someone, you don't need a fax machine or even fax software. Various free services let you send a free fax anywhere in the world. Some even capture faxes that others send to you and forward them to your email account as graphic files for later viewing. Try these:

eFax.com	http://www.efax.com
FreeFax	http://www.freefax.com.pk
ZipFax	http://www.zipfax.com

FREE WEBSITE HOSTING

Many online services or Internet providers give you several megabytes of storage space so you can put up your own website. Unfortunately, the amount of space available may be too small, or the Internet provider may censor what type of information you can post. For example, online services like America Online tend to frown on anyone using their service to post anti–America Online comments on a website.

If the rules or storage space of your current Internet provider aren't satisfactory, try one of the many companies that offer free websites. These companies usually don't care what type of information you post—all they really care about is attracting people to their own website so they can sell ads. Search for "free website" or "free web page" to find a company that offers free websites, or try these:

GeoCities	http://geocities.yahoo.com
Netfirms	http://www.netfirms.com
Theglobe	http://www.theglobe.com
Free Website Hosting	http://www.freewebsitehosting.com
Free Web Hosting	http://www.freewebhosting.com
Tripod	http://www.tripod.lycos.com

COMPUTING ON A BUDGET

Although the cost of computers can widen the gap between the haves and the have-nots, this doesn't have to be the case. With a little creativity and a lot of persistence, everyone can access the Internet. Who knows? Using your access to the Internet, you might one day help change political policy, meet new friends, or just broaden your mind by exploring the whole world from the comfort of your home—all without going bankrupt buying lots of expensive computer equipment that you don't really need after all.

15

PROTECTING YOUR DATA AND YOUR PRIVACY

DESPITE THE LIP SERVICE PAID TO NOBLE-SOUNDING PRINCIPLES LIKE HUMAN RIGHTS AND PERSONAL FREEDOM, MOST GOVERNMENTS HAVE NO QUALMS VIOLATING EITHER PRINCIPLE FOR POLITICAL EXPEDIENCY AND SHORT-TERM ECONOMIC PROFIT. Because governments are less interested in protecting the rights of individuals than they are in protecting their own members, the only person who has the most interest in protecting your individual rights is you.

The issue is privacy. Why is the decision by a woman to sleep with a man she has just met in a bar a private one, and the decision to sleep with the same man for $100 subject to criminal penalties?

—ANNA QUINDLEN

PROTECTING YOUR DATA

Whether you store confidential business secrets on your computer, personal notes, incriminating email, financial records, or just plain ordinary information that you don't want other people to see, you have the right to keep your data private. Of course, having the right to privacy is one thing—exercising that right can be a completely different problem.

Besides blocking physical access to your computer (see Chapter 20), you can password-protect your data, encrypt it, or hide it and hope no one knows where to find it. Better yet, combine several of these methods and you can make access to your data as difficult as possible for someone other than yourself.

Password protection

Passwords are only as good as their length and complexity. Still, if you choose a good one, you can block access to most would-be data thieves. Rather than rely on the weak password protection available in screensavers, use a dedicated *password-protection* program instead. Not only can a dedicated password-protection program block access, but it can prevent someone from rebooting your computer to circumvent your password protection.

Windows users can try Posum's Workstation Lock (http://posum.com), which can password protect your computer; Password Protection System (http://www.necro-cosm.com/ppsplus/index.html), which can password protect individual files, such as data files and actual programs; or WinLock (http://www.crystaloffice.com), which restricts access to certain programs to people with the correct password.

Encrypting your data

Password-protection programs can restrict access, but don't rely on them to keep your data safe. For further protection, use *encryption* to scramble your data beyond recognition. Of course, encryption is only as good as your password—if someone steals your password, encryption will be as useless as a bank vault without a lock.

Besides choosing a weak password, another flaw is choosing a weak encryption algorithm. *Encryption algorithms* define how the data is scrambled, and not all encryption algorithms are alike.

Proprietary encryption algorithms are often the worst, since hiding the way an algorithm works (known as "security by obscurity") won't disguise the fact that it scrambles data in a predictable manner that can be used to crack the encryption. Any program that claims their proprietary encryption algorithm is secure most likely doesn't know anything about encryption in the first place.

The better encryption programs use algorithms that have been published worldwide and survived the scrutiny of security experts over the years. That doesn't mean that they don't have any flaws—it's just that no one has found any weakness yet–or the NSA has and isn't telling. (Studying an encryption algorithm can reveal how that algorithm encrypts data, but it won't necessarily show you how to crack it.)

Some of the more popular encryption algorithms include the Data Encryption Standard (DES), International Data Encryption Algorithm (IDEA), Rivest Cipher #6 (RC6) (http://www.rsasecurity.com/rsalabs/rc6/index.html), Blowfish and Twofish (http://www.counterpane.com/labs.html), and Advanced Encryption Standard (AES) (http://csrc.nist.gov/encryption/aes).

Encryption scrambles your data, but passwords protect it. In the world of encryption, two types of password methods have emerged: private-key encryption and public-key encryption.

Private-key encryption uses a single password to encrypt and decrypt data, which means that if you lose or forget your password, you can't get your data, and anyone who discovers your password can decrypt your files. Even more troublesome is that if you want to send someone an encrypted file, you have to figure out a safe way to send them the password first so they can decrypt the file when they receive it.

To overcome the flaws of private-key encryption, computer scientists developed *public-key encryption*, which gives you two passwords: a private and a public key. The private key is (hopefully) known only to you. The public key can be given freely to anyone.

You can use your private key to encrypt a file, and anyone with your public key can decrypt it. If someone wants to send you data, they have to encrypt it using your public key. Then that encrypted file can only be decrypted using your private key.

One of the most popular encryption programs is Pretty Good Privacy (http://www.pgp.com and http://www.pgpi.com), written by Phil Zimmermann, who is generally credited with making public-key encryption widely available by releasing the source code to his Pretty Good Privacy program (PGP) over the Internet. When the source code managed to find its way to other countries, the U.S. government began a fruitless five-year criminal investigation to determine whether Phil had broken any laws that classified encryption technology as a "munition." Eventually the government dropped the charges after realizing they didn't have a case and popular opinion was against them.

Similar to PGP is a free and open source version dubbed GNU Privacy Guard (http://www.gnupg.org). Besides PGP, there is other encryption software:

Kryptel	http://inv.co.nz
PC-Encrypt	http://www.pc-encrypt.com
Absolute Security	http://www.pepsoft.com
CryptoForge	http://www.cryptoforge.com

To read a free monthly newsletter covering encryption, visit the Crypto-Gram Newsletter (http://www.counterpane.com/crypto-gram.html) written by Bruce Schneier, author of *Applied Cryptography*. Or, to discuss encryption, visit one of these newsgroups: alt.security, alt.security.pgp, comp.security.misc, or comp.security. pgp.discuss.

Defeating encryption

The simplest way to defeat encryption is to steal the encryption password. Failing that, you can try a brute-force attack, which essentially involves trying every possible password permutation until you eventually find the correct one. Brute-force can defeat every encryption algorithm, but the stronger encryption algorithms have so many possible combinations that to exhaustively test for each one would take even the fastest computer millions of years, so in practice the encryption is secure.

The faster and more powerful computers get, the easier it will be for brute-force attacks to pry open weaker encryption algorithms. On June 17, 1997, a team of college students used a brute-force attack to crack a DES-encrypted file in a $10,000 contest sponsored by the RSA Security. This "cracking" program, code-named DESCHALL (http://www.interhack.net/projects/deschall), was distributed and downloaded over the Internet so volunteers could link thousands of computers together and attack the problem simultaneously. Now, if a team of college students can crack DES using ordinary computer equipment, think what governments can do with their higher budgets and specialized hardware. The moral of this story is that if the strongest encryption algorithm a program offers is DES, look elsewhere. Triple-DES (a derivative of the DES encryption standard) is stronger than ordinary DES, although many encryption programs prefer the newer AES encryption standard.

Hiding files on your hard disk

One problem with encryption is that it can alert someone that you're hiding something important. Because no form of encryption can be 100 percent secure (someone can always steal the password or crack the encryption method), you might try a trickier method: Hide your sensitive files. After all, you can't steal what you can't find.

To do so, visit PC-Magic Software (http://www.pc-magic.com) and download their Magic Folders or Encrypted Magic Folders program. Both programs let you make entire directories invisible so a thief won't even know they exist. Encrypted Magic Folders hides and encrypts your file, so even if someone finds the directory, they won't be able to peek at its contents or copy any of its files without the proper password.

Similar programs that can hide and encrypt your hidden folders include the following:

bProtected	http://www.clasys.com
Hide Folders	http://www.fspro.net
WinDefender	http://www.rtsecurity.com/products/windefender

Encryption in pictures

Since few people encrypt their email, those who do use encryption immediately draw attention to themselves. If you want to use encryption while looking as if you aren't, use steganography, a term derived from the Greek words *steganos* (covered or secret) and *graphy* (writing or drawing), literally meaning "covered writing." *Steganography* is the science of hiding information in an apparently harmless medium, such as a picture or a sound file.

For example, suppose government agents decide to snare every email message sent to and from a particular website. With unencrypted email, spying computers could easily search for keywords like "nuclear," "missile," "nerve gas," or "bomb" and store copies of these messages for further analysis. If you encrypt your email, they can just as easily grab copies of your encrypted messages and use their supercomputers to crack them open later.

But if you use steganography, you can send seemingly innocent graphic files of famous paintings, antique cars, or bikini-clad models that actually contain hidden messages inside. These ordinary files could easily contain underground newsletters, censored information, or simply ordinary text that you want to keep private. If someone intercepts your email, they'll see only a picture. Unless a snoop is certain that the picture contains hidden messages, he'll most likely ignore it.

Steganography programs break up your data (either text or encrypted text) and bury it within a graphics or sound file, such as a GIF or WAV file. In the process, the steganography program slightly corrupts the graphic or sound file, so the more data you try to hide, the greater the degradation.

You can use two techniques to prevent total degradation (which would flag the fact that a graphic or sound file contains hidden information). First, use black-and-white instead of color graphic files, because slight degradation in a black-and-white graphic isn't as noticeable as it is in color graphics. Second, store small files in multiple graphic or sound files rather than cramming all the information into a single graphic or sound file.

To toy around with steganography programs and learn more about this relatively obscure branch of encryption, visit the StegoArchive website at http://steganography.tripod.com/stego.html and look for popular steganography programs such as S-Tools, Invisible Secrets, or Hide and Seek.

You might also like to visit Stego Online (http://www.stego.com), download the free Java source code, and practice encrypting text files within GIF files on your own hard disk. If you're serious about encrypting your data and disguising that fact, browse through the steganography newsgroup at alt.steganography.

In an effort to help people communicate against their government's wishes, a group of hackers from the Cult of the Dead Cow developed a steganography tool called Camera/Shy (http://hacktivismo.com/projects). Once you hide a message inside a GIF image using Camera/Shy, you can post that GIF image on a web page. Anyone with a copy of Camera/Shy and the right password can browse your web page and display the hidden messages in each GIF image (see Figure 15-1).

Figure 15-1

The Camera/Shy program can hide messages in GIF images on a web page so other people can read them.

Although steganography might seem like the perfect way to communicate in secret, it can be detected. Two programs, Stegdetect (http://www.outguess.org) and Stego Watch (http://www.wetstonetech.com) can scan graphic, sound, and video files to look for hidden messages. While they may not necessarily be able to read any hidden messages buried inside a graphic image, both programs can alert someone that a hidden message exists. Depending on what part of the world you live in, that could cause the authorities to watch you more closely or give them a "reason" to make you disappear in the middle of the night.

To learn more about encryption, visit Cryptography A-Z (http://www.ssh.fi/tech/crypto) to find links to free encryption software, companies selling encryption packages, and universities offering encryption course materials, and as much about encryption as you care to learn, provided (of course) that the government hasn't already confiscated your computer.

SPYING ON YOUR OWN COMPUTER

Sometimes the biggest threat doesn't come from an unknown stranger but from someone you already know, whether it's a coworker, a relative, or even your own spouse. When you're away from your computer, how can you be sure that nobody is using it in your absence? If you know that someone is using your computer, maybe you're suspicious of what they're really doing with your computer.

In cases like these, you may want to spy on your own computer. That way you can see who is using your computer, what programs they are running, and even what they are typing at any given time. Perhaps your employees are giving trade secrets away, your children are looking at pornography, and your spouse is setting up extra-marital liaisons with people through chat rooms.

Spying with a webcam

With the right software, you can turn any webcam into a surveillance camera. The moment someone steps within view of the webcam, the webcam software detects the motion and starts recording video or still images so you can see exactly who used your computer at a specific time and date. For greater security, the webcam program can even email the images to you or post them on a website. That way, if the intruder erases your hard disk, you'll still have copies of the images that can identify who the perpetrator may be.

Sometimes you may want to monitor an area where people come and go all the time, such as inside a store. Just tell your webcam program what time to start and stop capturing images, and how long you want your computer to store those images before deleting them (see Figure 15-2). Now if something unusual happens, such as someone robbing the cashier, your webcam will capture it all on your computer.

Figure 15-2
You can program your webcam to capture images in secret and email them to you.

To turn your webcam into a surveillance camera, download Microsoft's free Webcam Timershot (http://www.microsoft.com) or try these programs:

i-Catcher	http://www.icode.co.uk/icatcher
Video Security	http://www.honestech.com
MelCam	http://www.melioris.com

Spying with software

A webcam may show you who used your computer, but it won't necessarily show you what they did while they were using your computer. To find out this type of information, you need to use a desktop-monitoring program that can show you which programs someone used, what they typed to someone else in a chat room or instant messenger program, and even what images they saw on the screen (see Figure 15-3).

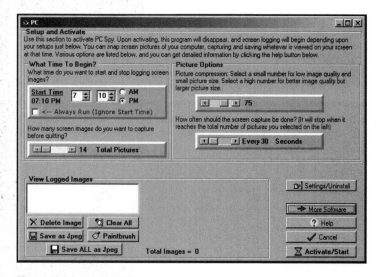

Figure 15-3

A desktop-monitoring program can capture screen images so you can see exactly what the other person did on your computer.

By using a desktop-monitoring program, you can capture proof of someone's illegal activities that you can use to confront them with later, or just keep it a secret so you can gather even more incriminating evidence later. (See Chapter 12 for more information about desktop-monitoring programs.)

COVERING YOUR TRACKS

If you use the Internet, you may not want others to know which websites you've been visiting. Unfortunately, anyone with access to your computer can find this type of information just by looking at the Internet cookies and browser cache stored on your computer, so if you want to cover your tracks, you have to erase every file that traces your activity.

Stopping cookies

When you visit some websites, they may store information on your computer in a *cookie* file, which contains the address of the website along with any additional information you may have typed, such as your name or email address.

When you return to that site, the cookie sends the information stored on your machine to the website computer. Cookies allow the website to customize or personalize its web pages, such as displaying the message, "Welcome back, John Doe!" at the top of the page.

While cookies themselves are harmless (they cannot spread a virus or delete any of your files), they can reveal your favorite websites to anyone who looks around in your web browser settings. Neither teenagers nor employees will want their parents or boss to know they've been visiting the Penthouse website during working hours, but no matter how discreet you are, the tell-tale cookie will give the game away.

If you don't like the idea of websites hiding cookies on your computer, you can change your browser's preferences to refuse them. To do this in Internet Explorer 6.0 for Windows, follow these steps (see Figure 15-4):

Figure 15-4
Changing the way the Windows version of Internet Explorer handles cookies.

1. Choose Tools → Internet Options. An Internet Options dialog box appears.

2. Click the Privacy tab.

3. Click the Advanced button. An Advanced Privacy Settings dialog box appears.

4. Click the "Override automatic cookie handling" check box so a check mark appears.

5. Click the Accept, Block, or Prompt radio button to choose how you want Internet Explorer to handle cookies.

6. Click OK in this settings dialog box, and then click OK in the main Options dialog box.

To delete existing cookies and filter incoming ones, use a cookie utility program like these:

Cookie Crusher	http://www.thelimitsoft.com
Cookie Pal	http://www.kburra.com
MagicCookie Monster	http://download.at/drjsoftware

Cookie programs can filter cookies as you browse, allowing some to pass (like cookies from shopping sites that store your shopping preferences) while blocking others (like cookies from companies that want to track how long you've spent browsing their site). Best of all, these cookie crushers can find and delete existing cookies on your hard disk automatically (see Figure 15-5).

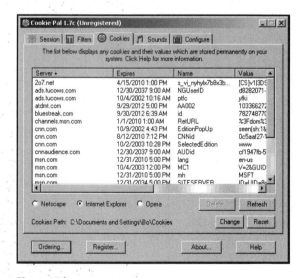

Figure 15-5

A program like Cookie Pal can show you all the cookies already stored on your hard disk.

Cleaning out your web browser cache

Besides storing information about your web browsing habits in cookie files, your browser may also store pictures, web pages, and the addresses of the last few websites you visited (your "history") in a temporary folder (buried inside the Windows folder), as shown in Figure 15-6.

Figure 15-6
You can find the addresses of the last few websites someone visited in the Address Bar list box.

To clean out this information in Internet Explorer, follow these steps:

1. Choose Tools → Internet Options. An Internet Options dialog box appears.

2. Click the General tab. The History group shows how many website addresses the browser stores (such as 20).

3. Click the Clear History button. A dialog box appears, asking if you want to delete all items in your history folder.

4. Click Yes.

5. Then click the Delete Files button in the Temporary Internet files group.

6. Click OK.

To avoid having to always manually clean up these files, try running one of these programs:

CyberClean	http://www.thelimitsoft.com
MacWasher or Window Washer	http://www.webroot.com
SurfSecret Privacy Protector	http://www.surfsecret.com

These programs can automatically clean out your Temporary Internet Files and History folders along with deleting cookies, old email messages, and any downloaded program files at the same time. By running a clean-up program regularly, you can make sure no one can trace your web browsing usage and violate your privacy (see Figure 15-7).

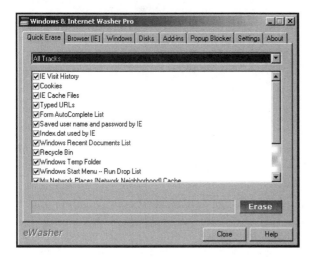

Figure 15-7
Window & Internet Washer Pro can delete all traces of your browsing history.

SHIELDING YOUR PRIVACY

Besides protecting your privacy from snoops who can access your computer, you may want to shield your privacy from websites, government agencies, and corporations that may be curious about your Internet browsing habits. While it's unlikely that the National Security Agency or Central Intelligence Agency is spying on your computer, the thought of leaving your personal life exposed to others can be as disturbing as trying to disrobe in private while living in a glass house. To protect your privacy, consider browsing the Internet anonymously and encrypting every email you send. Here's how.

Anonymous browsing

Because purging your Internet usage history from your hard disk can be troublesome, most people won't bother doing it. But what if you could prevent your Internet usage information from being stored on your computer in the first place? Or, if you could browse in secret?

Anonymous browsing services, like IDzap.com (http://www.idzap.com), Anonymizer.com (http://www.anonymizer.com), and Rewebber (http://www.rewebber.com), block access to your computer so websites can't plant a cookie on your computer, detect which type of browser you're using, or identify your IP address. When you visit them, you simply type in the URL you want to visit, and the anonymous browsing service takes you there—in secret. Best of all, they provide their basic services for free. To find other anonymous web browsing services, visit the Anonymous Browsing Quick-Start Page (http://anonbrowse.cjb.net).

One caveat though—anonymous browsing services aren't always reliable. You'll probably run into difficulty with many shopping sites (which rely on cookies), and other sites that want to detect your browser and such. Still, they're a free and simple way to browse discreetly.

Browsing as someone else—sort of

Bell Labs and AT&T Labs have a really interesting twist on anonymous browsing in their Crowds service (http://www.research.att.com/projects/crowds). The idea is similar to blending in with a crowd in a public place.

When you use Crowds, you're randomly thrown into a crowd of other randomly chosen users. Rather than accessing a web page yourself, the computer randomly selects another user in the crowd to access the web page and pass it along to you (which could have the unwanted side-effect of revealing what one individual in the crowd may be doing). By masking any individual's actions within the larger actions of a group, Crowds shields the privacy of everyone because no one can tell which actions any specific individual has taken at any given time.

Freedom WebSecure software from Zero-Knowledge Systems (http://www.zeroknowledge.com) allows you to connect to the Zero-Knowledge Systems' server, which then redirects you to any website you want to see. If a website tries to track you, they can only trace you as far as the Zero-Knowledge Systems server.

While many people worry about giving away their web surfing information, you may just want to sell this information to others instead. Visit Lumeria's SuperProfile (http://www.superprofile.com) and you can do just that. Not only can you control who gets your personal information, but you can also (theoretically) make some money in the process.

Sending anonymous email

If you want to express your opinion, leak information in secret, or even simply participate in medical or other support groups in confidence, send your email anonymously and securely. One way to do so is to keep opening and closing free email accounts, but anonymous email services, like Sendfakemail.com (http://www.sendfakemail.com) can protect your privacy for a fee. Then again, another way to keep your identity private is to use any free email service and simply fake your personal information. For more information about sending email anonymously, visit eMailman (http://www.emailman.com/anonymous).

If these anonymous email services aren't enough, try a secure, encrypted, anonymous email service, like these:

Hushmail	http://www.hushmail.com
CryptoMail.org	http://www.cryptomail.org
PrivacyX	http://www.privacyx.com
CertifiedMail.com	http://www.certifiedmail.com
ZipLip	http://www.ziplip.com

Like other anonymous email services, encrypted anonymous email services don't require a name, address, phone number, or other method of tracing you, so your email can remain truly anonymous. ZipLip will even shred your email after it's been read.

Using a remailer

Still another way to mask your identity through email is to use an *anonymous remailer*, such as Anonymous.To (http://anonymous.to). An anonymous remailer sends your email from your computer to a remailer, which is another computer connected to the Internet. The remailer masks your identity by stripping away your real name and address and replacing it with a phony one before sending your email to its final destination.

You can even use multiple remailers to cover your tracks even further. Send your email to the first remailer (which strips out your address), then tell it to send your email to another remailer. Continue this process for two or more anonymous hops, and it will be nearly impossible for anyone to trace or monitor where your email came from.

Although each remailer may work differently, a typical one works as follows. The message you write starts out looking like this:

```
From: Name@YourAddress.com
To: remailer@RemailerAddress
Subject: Anything
::

Anon-To: destination@address
This is my message.
```

Your real address appears only when you're sending email to the remailer. Once the remailer gets your message, it ships it off to the address defined by the Anon-To field. (The two colons let the remailer know a destination address will follow. That way, the remailer doesn't think the Anon-To field is part of your real message.)

To filter your email through multiple remailers, your message might look like this:

```
From: Name@YourAddress.com
To: remailer@RemailerAddress
Subject: Anything
::
Anon-To: second@RemailerAddress
::
Anon-To: destination@address
This is my message.
```

In this example, you're sending your email to the first remailer located at the remailer@RemailerAddress. This first remailer then sends your message to a second remailer located at second@RemailerAddress. The second remailer then sends your email to its final destination at destination@address. For the truly paranoid, you can keep adding remailer addresses indefinitely.

To further protect your privacy, ask an anonymous remailer to hold your email for a random period before forwarding it to its final destination. This delay can prevent snoops from tracing the origin of your email by noting that it arrives at the remailer at 4:00 and then leaves exactly one minute later.

But don't think that anonymous remailers allow you to conduct criminal activities. If you harass others through email, send out death threats, or plot bomb attacks, remailer administrators will likely help the police find and prosecute you. Don't abuse the privilege.

The biggest problem with remailers is that they appear and disappear as quickly as democracies in Third World countries. Running an anonymous remailer costs time and money, and most remailers don't charge for their services because asking someone to pay by check or credit card destroys their anonymity. And some anonymous remailers aren't really anonymous. Some require that you open an account with them, which means that whoever runs the remailer has a record of your real email address.

Although anonymous remailers and encryption can help protect your privacy, nothing can guarantee absolute privacy. Anonymous remailers are only as secure as the people running them. Anyone can set up a phony anonymous remailer and read every message that passes through it. Although encryption can protect your email to some extent, the real danger lies in exposing your real email address. For this reason you should use a remailer in another country.

For example, someone living in communist China should view a Chinese remailer with suspicion. But that same person would probably be safer using an anonymous remailer located in Finland, Canada, or Mexico, because its administrators probably won't care about Chinese citizens, and the Chinese authorities are less likely to be able to access the remailer's records.

To learn from people who are using anonymous remailers, browse the Usenet group alt.privacy.anon-server to read the latest developments.

Your own Private Idaho

If the idea of trying to combine anonymous email with encryption seems cumbersome, you might want to try a program designed to simplify this process. Private Idaho (http://www.eskimo.com/~joelm/pi.html) works with the Pretty Good Privacy (PGP) program to encrypt your email. PGP is a highly regarded encryption program that is considered to offer encryption tough enough to resist cracking even by well-funded intelligence organizations, such as the CIA and NSA.

Best of all, Private Idaho is free and comes with complete Visual Basic source code so you can modify it or just study the source code to make sure it doesn't contain any back doors that government authorities can use to spy on your email. For a 32-bit version of Private Idaho, visit the Private Idaho email website (http://www.itech.net.au/pi).

Chatting anonymously

Besides sending emails anonymously, you may also want to chat with people in IRC (Internet Relay Chat) rooms anonymously. Normally when you visit an IRC chat room, someone can use the whois command to identify your IP address. If you download the Invisible IRC Project software (http://www.invisiblenet.net/iip), though, you can mask your true IP address from strangers.

PROTECTING YOUR IDENTITY

In the 1990 movie "Darkman," a scientist develops a synthetic skin, but before he can announce his discovery to the world, mobsters blow up his laboratory with him in it. Although he survives, he's badly burned and hides his disfigured face from society. Using his synthetic skin and his knack for mimicking the voices of other people, he assumes the identity of various people to get back at the criminals who tried to destroy him.

Of course, the idea of imitating another person so perfectly is so far-fetched that nobody believes it could ever happen to them. Unfortunately, in today's world, no one has to mimic the way you look, speak, and act because everyone's identity is wrapped up in a string of numbers and words that define that person in a computer database. Just steal certain information that only your victim is supposed to know, such as that person's Social Security number, and as far as the computer is concerned, you are that other person.

Once someone has stolen your identity, they can do anything they want while you get blamed for their actions. Identity thieves have opened credit card accounts under other people's names and racked up thousands of dollars worth of debts before disappearing, essentially wrecking the victim's credit rating. Other identity thieves have purchased new cars, opened cell phone accounts, and taken out loans.

By the time an identity thief has wrecked your credit rating and saddled you with legal and financial bills, he (or she) can simply repeat the whole process all over again with another innocent victim. A smart identity thief can work for years off other people's credit and never get caught or punished, which means that you could be the next target and not even know it.

Guard your personal information

To steal your identity, a thief just needs to copy any numbers or passwords that uniquely identify you, such as your Social Security number, driver's license, checking account, and credit card numbers; passport information; or personal information, such as a home address, mother's maiden name, and birth date.

The first step to protecting yourself against identity theft is to strip your wallet or purse as clean of any of this information as possible. After all, how many times during the day do you really need your Social Security card, birth certificate, or passport? And if you can't remember your mother's maiden name or PIN number, then you probably have bigger problems than worrying about identity theft anyway.

Stripping your wallet of as much unnecessary identification as possible can protect you against pickpockets or just plain forgetfulness, in case you leave your wallet or purse behind somewhere.

After purging your wallet or purse, the next step requires a more conscious effort. Be careful about giving out your personal information to others. Don't print your Social Security number or driver's license number on your check, and be sure to shred any pre-approved credit card applications you get in the mail.

Dumpster diving, a popular hacker technique for finding useful information among the trash, can also be used by identity thieves who can fill out any credit card applications you've tossed in the trash, write in a new address, and have a new credit card (in your name, of course) sent to the identity thief's home (or phony) address instead. Armed with a credit card that you've never seen before, an identity thief can go on a shopping spree, leaving you stuck with the bill months later.

Rather than steal your personal information without your knowledge, identity thieves may take the less obvious, but more effective, route of just asking you for your personal information directly.

Obviously if a total stranger asked for your Social Security number, you would be suspicious, but imagine if you've recently lost your wallet and a concerned bank employee calls to verify your ATM personal identification and account number. Without thinking, most people would automatically give out this information over the telephone, not realizing that the phony bank employee is actually an identity thief.

One particularly devious scam targets elderly African-Americans. Flyers often appear around churches, nursing homes, or through email with headlines boasting:

Apply for Newly Approved Slave Reparations!
Claim $5,000 in Social Security Reimbursements!

The flyers claim that elderly African Americans are eligible for slave reparations under a fictional "Slave Reparation Act" or for Social Security funds due to a "fix" in the Social Security system.

To be eligible for this money, people must contact someone who then asks for their name, address, phone number, birth date, and Social Security number to process their request for this nonexistent money. Once the identity thieves have the information they need, they can open up credit card accounts under the victims' names.

Although identity theft has been around since long before computers, the Internet has brought renewed attention to identity theft. Hackers can break into a corporate website and steal credit card information. Less likely, but still a real possibility, is that someone could plant a remote access Trojan horse (such as Back Orifice or NetBus), which can capture keystrokes as you type your credit card information over the Internet.

While you may be defenseless against hackers who infiltrate corporate databases containing your credit card information, you can guard your personal computer against Trojan horses by installing a firewall (which can block suspicious activity on the Internet) and antivirus or anti–Trojan horse programs that can detect the presence of a Trojan horse and wipe it off your hard disk.

If it happens to you

Despite any precautions you may take, there's always the chance that you'll be the next identity theft victim. Once you find out that someone has stolen your identity, you need to take action immediately by canceling every credit card you have, including bank cards, department store cards, gasoline cards, and even video store cards.

After shutting down your existing charge accounts to minimize any damage from the identity thief, contact the following three credit agencies and explain that you've been a victim of fraud. These credit agencies will place your accounts on a fraud alert list that can further protect you from any charges run up by the identity thief.

EQUIFAX
PO Box 105069
Atlanta, GA 30348
(800) 525-6285

TRANS UNION
PO Box 6790
Fullerton, CA 92634
(800) 680-7289

EXPERIAN
PO Box 1017
Allen, TX 92634
(888) 397-3742

Since trying to repair your credit rating can be time-consuming and frustrating, consider subscribing to a fraud protection service that your credit card company might offer. Such a service limits your liability from identity theft and can help repair your credit rating quickly.

Of course, fraud protection services only protect you for a single charge account, so you might want to consider the services of a company such as PromiseMark (http://www.promisemark.com), that can protect your entire identity. PromiseMark offers an Identity Theft Protection Plan that can help you through the process of repairing your credit and establishing new accounts. That way you can minimize the financial damage and get your life back in order as quickly as possible, without going through the frustration and hassle of repairing your credit rating all by yourself.

For more information about identity theft and ways to prevent, protect against, or recover from identity theft, visit Victims Assistance of America (http://victimsassistanceofamerica.org), the United States Department of Justice (http://www.usdoj.gov/criminal/fraud/idtheft.html), or the United States government's dedicated website about identity theft (http://www.consumer.gov/idtheft/index.html).

So what are the chances that you may lose your identity? Probably not that great, but ask Oprah Winfrey, Steven Spielberg, Warren Buffett, or Martha Stewart what they might have thought about becoming an identity theft victim. Or visit the Privacy Rights Clearinghouse (http://www.privacyrights.org/identity.htm) to read the long list of ordinary citizens who lost their identities and spent months (or even years) trying to repair the damage.

To help you recover from identity theft, buy a copy of the Identity-Theft Survival Kit, available from IdentityTheft.org (http://www.identitytheft.org). This kit includes a book to help you understand what you can do after being victimized by identity theft, attorney-written form letters to protect your legal rights and help you reestablish credit, and six audio cassettes that explain how to recover from identity theft.

The odds of getting in a car crash aren't that great, but most of us probably have car insurance anyway. So if the thought of losing your identity frightens you, perhaps a little bit of protection might not be such a bad thing after all. Just make sure that any organization you trust with your identity isn't really an identity thief in disguise.

206

16

WAGING WAR ON SPAM

NO MATTER HOW INFREQUENTLY YOU USE THE INTERNET, YOU'RE GOING TO GET SPAMMED. Instead of finding important messages from business associates, friends, or your favorite newsgroup, you find a long list of junk email from companies advertising totally useless products, like bogus vitamins, "free" vacation giveaways, or money-making schemes. Unlike newspaper or magazine advertisements that you can ignore without losing a moment's thought, spam just doesn't seem to leave you alone.

Spamming means sending unsolicited messages to multiple email accounts or Usenet newsgroups. Victims of spamming must then take time to delete the unwanted messages so they can make room in their mailboxes for useful email. Some of the more common spams are chain letters or other suspicious "business opportunities" like this:

> *$$$$$$$$ FAST CASH!!!! $$$$$$$$*
>
> *Hello there, Read this it works! Fellow Debtor: This is going to sound like a con, but in fact IT WORKS! The person who is now #4 on the list was #5 when I got it, which was only a few days ago. Five dollars is a small investment in your future. Forget the lottery for a week, and give this a try. It can work for ALL of us. You can edit this list with a word processor or text editor and then convert it to a text file. Good Luck!!*
>
> *Dear Friend,*
>
> *My name is Dave Rhodes. In September 1988 my car was repossessed and the bill collectors were hounding me like you wouldn't believe. I was laid off and my unemployment checks had run out. The only escape I had from the pressure of failure was my computer and my modem. I longed to turn my avocation into my vocation.*
>
> *This January 1989 my family and I went on a ten day cruise to the tropics. I bought a Lincoln Town Car for CASH in February 1989. I am currently building a home on the West Coast of Florida, with a private pool, boat slip, and a beautiful view of the bay from my breakfast room table and patio.*

A speech is like a love affair. Any fool can start one, but to end it requires considerable skill.

—LORD MANCROFT

I will never have to work again. Today I am rich! I have earned over $400,000.00 (Four Hundred Thousand Dollars) to date and will become a millionaire within 4 or 5 months. Anyone can do the same. This money making program works perfectly every time, 100 percent of the time. I have NEVER failed to earn $50,000.00 or more whenever I wanted. Best of all you never have to leave home except to go to your mailbox or post office.

I realized that with the power of the computer I could expand and enhance this money making formula into the most unbelievable cash flow generator that has ever been created. I substituted the computer bulletin boards in place of the post office and electronically did by computer what others were doing 100 percent by mail. Now only a few letters are mailed manually. Most of the hard work is speedily downloaded to other bulletin boards throughout the world.

If you believe that someday you deserve that lucky break that you have waited for all your life, simply follow the easy instructions below. Your dreams will come true.

And so on.

WHY COMPANIES SPAM THE INTERNET AND HOW THEY DO IT

Nobody likes to receive spam because it wastes time and clogs email accounts, yet many companies continue to send it anyway because, unlike direct mail advertising, spamming is essentially free. For the cost of a single Internet account, anyone can reach a potential worldwide audience numbering in the millions. In the eyes of spammers, even if they upset 99 percent of the people on the Internet, having 1 percent buy their product can make spamming worth it.

When sending spam, you don't need to type multiple email messages either. Just as bulk mailers never lick their stamps, many companies use bulk emailing software that automates the addressing process. Click a button and you, too, can scatter unwanted email messages across the Internet.

Many ISPs respond to users' outrage at spam by blocking mail from the accounts of known spammers, though some groups question the legality of doing so, because it amounts to a form of censorship.

Spammers are often stereotyped as scammers and con artists, but that's not necessarily the case. Many are like you or me, just trying to make a buck—but just going about it the wrong way. To learn more about how spammers think and the techniques and software they use, visit the Bulk Email Store (http://www.easybiz.com) and read some testimonials from spammers satisfied with their spamming software.

Retrieving email addresses

Before spammers can start flooding the Internet with their messages, they need a list of email addresses. Although lists of email addresses can be bought, they are not always accurate or up-to-date. Rather than rely on purchased lists that may contain too many obsolete addresses, spammers use programs that extract email addresses to build their own lists. These programs harvest email addresses from three sources: newsgroups, websites, and database directories.

Newsgroup extractors

When you post a message to a CompuServe forum or Usenet newsgroup, your message appears with your email address. Newsgroup extractors download the messages from online services (like America Online) and Usenet newsgroups, strip away the text, and store the return email addresses in a list to produce a free, up-to-date email list.

Even better (from the bulk emailer's point of view), online service forums and Usenet newsgroups focus on specific topics, such as health and fitness, computer programming, or sports. So if, for example, they're selling vitamins, they can simply visit any America Online forum or Usenet newsgroup related to health and fitness, and bingo! They've got a valid list of prospective customers' email addresses.

Website extractors

Website extractors work like newsgroup extractors except that they pull their email addresses from websites. That's because spammers know that if someone puts up a personal or business websites (as shown in Figure 16-1), they're likely to post a contact email address on the web page.

Website extracting programs browse the Internet to find websites based on similar topics, such as camping or stock markets. Then they scan these websites until they find one or more email addresses.

Database directory extractors

Database directory extractors pull email addresses from people-finding directory services like Bigfoot. While the list they produce won't be as tightly targeted as those found on websites or in newsgroups, they can produce useful lists targeted toward specific geographical groups or people with particular surnames.

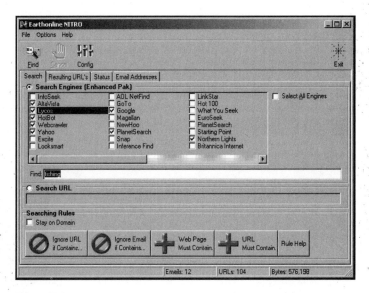

Figure 16-1

Bulk email programs can use popular search engines to find websites that list valid email addresses.

Masking your identity

Spammers often incur the wrath of several hundred (or several million) irate victims. Some respond with angry messages; others launch their own email bombing attacks, sending multiple messages to the spammer's email address, clogging it and rendering it useless.

Unfortunately, crashing or clogging the spammer's ISP can also punish innocent customers who happen to use the spammer's ISP, as well. To avoid such counterattacks, many spammers create temporary Internet accounts (on services such as Hotmail or Juno), send their spam, and then cancel the account before anyone can attack them. Of course, this means constantly creating and canceling multiple Internet accounts, but getting kicked off an ISP and opening new accounts is just part of the game that bulk emailers play. When an interested customer responds, the spammer sends out an actual email address, phone number, or postal address so the prospective customer can learn more.

Of course, for those spammers who can't be bothered opening and closing email accounts, there's an easier way. Many bulk emailing programs, like Email Magnet, simply omit or forge the sender's email address to avoid counterattacks.

Finding a bulk emailing program

You probably won't find a bulk emailing program sold at your local computer store, but you'll find lots of them on the Web. Two sites that sell a variety of bulk emailing programs include Bulk Email Software Superstore (http://www.americaint.com) and Send-Bulk-Email.co.uk (http://www.send-bulk-email.co.uk). (See Figure 16-2.)

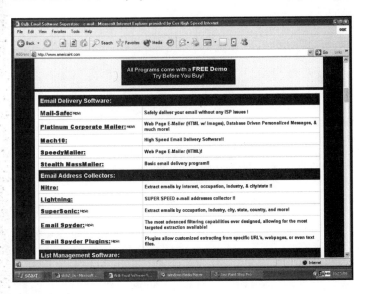

Figure 16-2
Anyone can buy a bulk emailing (spamming) program from websites all over the Internet.

Since publishers of bulk emailing programs make tempting targets for spam avengers, they protect their identity by selling their programs through individual distributors who create their own websites and then, in typical pyramid-scheme fashion, sign up others to sell those same programs through their websites too. By using this multilevel marketing approach to sell their software, bulk emailing publishers can remain relatively anonymous while ensuring that their software will be available from multiple locations, no matter how many times anti-spam activists try to attack and shut down a website that offers spamming software.

PROTECTING YOURSELF FROM SPAMMERS

Now that you know spammers retrieve email addresses, how can you fight back? Depending on your mood and temperament, your response may range from politeness to hostility. While you may ignore and simply delete most spam, some may enrage you.

Complain to the spammer

When you receive spam, the message may include an email address that you can write to in order to remove your address from the spammer's email list. Sometimes this works, but more often this email address itself is phony, or replying simply alerts the spammers that your email address is valid, which can encourage them to sell your email address to others and keep sending spam to you.

Complain to the spammer's ISP

To protect themselves against retaliation, most spammers either strip out or fake their return email addresses. But even if you can't find a valid return address in the email to respond to, you may still be able to uncover one. To do so, search the spam's header for the ISP's address, such as earthlink.net, buried in the From or Message-ID header. Once you identify the ISP, you can complain directly to them.

In the following example, a quick search of the email header reveals that the spammer's ISP is example.com (which could be forged to hide the spammer's true ISP).

```
Subject: Absolutely NOT Risky ! Nothing to lose !!!
From: Hidden <noname@example.com>
Date: Fri, 01 Aug 1997 00:02:54 +0800
Message-ID: <33E0B72E.3796@example.com>
```

Because spam is so annoying, most ISPs prohibit their subscribers from sending bulk email. If they receive complaints, the ISP will often cancel the spammer's account.

To notify an ISP of a spammer, email your complaint to postmaster@spammer.site, root@spammer.site, admin@spammer.site, or abuse@spammer.site, where "spammer.site" is the site the spammer used to send the junk email. ISPs can't monitor all of their users, but if they receive a flood of complaints about one of their customers, they can take action against the spammer and stop future abuses (maybe).

Unfortunately, whenever there's money involved, there's always someone willing to take it regardless of the consequences. While many ISPs explicitly forbid spamming, other ISPs specialize in it, such as EmailSending.com (http://www.emailsending.com), which sells their services solely to bulk emailing customers. Another such ISP even advertises:

> Does your website get shut down as a result of your email marketing campaigns? If so, then Bulk Email Superstore's Bulk Friendly Web Hosting is a must! Our high speed servers are linked to bulk friendly backbones specifically designed to absorb excessive traffic and heat linked to your email marketing campaigns.

So if you complain to a bulk email ISP about one of their customers, chances are you'll just add your valid email address to their "customer lists" that they'll just sell to someone else.

Complain to the Internal Revenue Service

Since many spammers promote get-rich-quick schemes, there's a good chance they may not keep proper tax records of their earnings, so one way to take revenge on these spammers is to contact the Internal Revenue Service (or your own government's tax agency) so they can investigate whether the spammer is properly reporting all income. American citizens can forward spam to either net-abuse@nocs.insp.irs.gov to report fraudulent make-money-fast (MMF) schemes or hotline@nocs.insp.irs.gov to report tax evaders. Reports of tax fraud should be sent directly to your regional IRS Service Center; there is currently no Internet email address for reporting those suspected offenses.

Use an email filter

Email programs like Microsoft Outlook, Eudora Pro, and the web-based email sites like Hotmail and Yahoo! let you filter incoming email based on From addresses, subjects, and keywords. You can set the filtering rules to search for particular spammer email addresses or keywords in messages or subjects (like "MAKE MONEY FAST") and have the filter automatically delete the message or route it to a special folder. Some of the more common keywords found in spam include: "to be removed," "not mlm," "serious inquiries only," "earn $2000-$5000 weekly," "sent in compliance," "at no cost to you," "spam," "work from home," "dear friend," "not multi-level marketing," "xxx," and "call now," so try using these.

Or you can subscribe to an email filtering service like SpamCop (http://spamcop.net), which can screen your email for spam and route suspicious messages to a designated location, so you can review it just in case a legitimate message got routed there by mistake. Anti-spam programs like Spam Buster (http://www.contactplus.com) automatically filter suspicious email, analyze email headers, and track down spammers' ISPs by checking received email against a database of known spammer addresses or by searching for keywords (see Figure 16-3). When the program finds a likely match, it moves the suspect email to a special folder where you can review or delete it later.

Locating the spammer's postal address

Perhaps the most satisfying way to deal with spam is to find the spammer's actual email address, phone number, or postal address—and use it. If a spammer registered a particular address for a website, visit the Network Solutions registry at http://www.networksolutions.com/cgi-bin/whois/whois, type in the domain you want to search, and the Network Solutions database cheerfully provides you with the postal

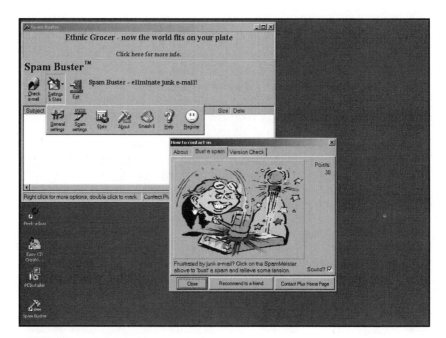

Figure 16-3

Spam Buster can help you track down and locate spammers.

address of the person who registered the domain name, along with the server currently hosting the web pages.

If the spammer doesn't list a web address but gives you his or her real email address, strip away the spammer's ID to find the domain. For example, if the address is spammer@isp.com, remove "spammer" and you're left with the domain name of the spammer's ISP, which in this case is isp.com. By typing this domain into the Network Solutions registry, you can find out how to reach the ISP by mail or phone, or you can add "www" to the front of the domain, which in this example would give you http://www.isp.com, and visit its website, which should list an email address that you can complain to.

Unfortunately, spammers know that their websites will become targets, so they often disguise their real website address through a third-party server, such as a specialized bulk email ISP. When you receive spam, the spammer lists an address that leads directly to the bulk emailing ISP, which then redirects a potential customer's browser to the actual spammer's website. By masking and redirecting the actual website address, spammers can advertise their website without worrying that a hacker will attack it or complain to their ISP.

One bulk emailing ISP even advertises the following:

> IP Tunneling is a method where the recipient of your email message
> accesses your web site through a (non traceable) binary encrypted link
> similar in appearance to the following:

```
(.....unique.site.net.co.fr|https.am2002.opt.com:8096)
```

> Once the recipient clicks the email message, their browser references
> our servers through the binary encoding within the link. Our servers
> (behind the scenes) then call upon your web site's IP which resides
> either on your server or a 3rd party's server. This technology provides its
> users with COMPLETE protection and anonymity.

As a result, it's possible to browse a spammer's website without ever knowing the
exact domain address, which means you can't look up and find the spammer's actual
address and telephone number.

Dealing with forged email addresses

If a spammer opens a temporary email account just to spam the Internet, there's not
much you can do about it—the spammer can keep opening up new email accounts
and shutting them down afterwards. However, if the spammer forges a return email
address, there's still hope.

Forged email addresses may hide the spammer's email address, but the email
itself can reveal the spammer's ISP if you know how to decipher its cryptic-looking
headers, which contain information on the route the email traveled.

Most email programs hide email headers to avoid burying you in irrelevant
technical email–routing details. However, by revealing these headers, you can trace
the route a spam email has taken and possibly identify the spammer. For more information about displaying email headers from a variety of email programs, including
Outlook, AOL, Eudora, Pegasus, Netscape, and WebTV, visit the SpamCop site
(http://spamcop.net).

Let's take a look at some headers sent from a valid email account to see what
they mean.

```
Received: from db3y-int.prodigy.net [127.0.0.1] by
wflda-db3y-int.prodigy.net; Sat, 9 Dec 2000 10:38:19 -
0500
Received: from yorktown.stratfor.com (yorktown.
stratfor.com
[207.8.81.2]) by db3y-int.prodigy.net (8.8.5/8.8.5)
with ESMTP id KAA45964 for <BO@prodigy.
net>; Sat,
9 Dec 2000 10:36:04 -0500
Received: from verdun.stratfor.com (verdun.
stratfor.com
```

```
[207.8.81.26]) by yorktown.stratfor.com (8.8.7/8.8.5)
with SMTP id JAA07105 for <BO@prodigy.
net>; Sat,
9 Dec 2000 09:38:25 -0600 (CST)
Received: by verdun.stratfor.com with Microsoft Mail id
<01BD0485.F3790CC0@verdun.stratfor.com>; Sat, 9 Dec
2000 09:36:39 -0600
```

In the preceding message, the Received headers describe where the email came from, along with the time and date it was sent. Starting with the bottom Received header, you can see that this email came from a domain named stratfor.com, sent on Saturday, December 9, 2000, at 9:36 a.m.

The next Received header (starting from the bottom and working your way up) shows that the email was transferred within the stratfor.com domain (from verdun. stratfor.com to yorktown.stratfor.com) on Saturday, December 9, 2000, at 9:38 a.m. Notice that the stratfor.com domain is also identified by its numeric (IP) address in square brackets, [207.8.81.26].

The next Received header shows that the stratfor.com domain sent the email to the prodigy.net domain on Saturday, December 9, 2000, at 10:36 a.m.

The top Received header shows that the email was transferred within the prodigy.net domain to the receiving email inbox on Saturday, December 9, 2000, at 10:38 a.m. Notice that the prodigy.net domain is also identified by its numeric address in square brackets, [127.0.0.1].

This example shows how each Received header records the transfer of the email from one domain to another. Forged email often omits all the Received headers that show the route of the email, or displays too many Received headers in an attempt to confuse you.

The following example of spam is obviously a forgery, because the Received headers do not show how the email got from the Sender domain (infosonic.com) to the receiving email account, a CompuServe account.

```
Sender: info@infosonic.com
Received: from Blaze.cscent.net ([206.98.109.9]) by
arl-img-10.compuserve.com (8.8.6/8.8.6/2.9) with ESMTP
id TAA09818; Sun, 3 Dec 2000 19:52:30 -0500 (EST)
Date: Sun, 3 Dec 2000 19:52:30 -0500 (EST)
From: info@infosonic.com
Message-Id: <199712040052.TAA09818@arl-img-10.
compuserve.com>
To: info@infosonic.com
Subject: "Earn Insane Profits At Home!"
```

Besides not showing enough Received headers to trace the email's route, another big clue that the email address has been forged is the use of a single capital letter ("B") in the Received header, listing Blaze.cscent.net. (Most Received headers use either all lowercase or all uppercase, but rarely a mix of both.)

NOTE: From first appearance alone, you might conclude that the spammer is using either infosonic.com or cscent.net to send the spam, but in both cases these domain addresses could be forged. Unless you know for sure, you shouldn't complain to either domain, because they might be completely innocent.

Here's another example of a forged email address:

```
Return-Path: <More.Info.1oooooo0@bigger.net>
Received: from relay27.mail.aol.com (relay27.mail.aol.com
[172.31.109.27]) by air27.mail.aol.com (v36.0) with
SMTP; Wed, 13 Dec 2000 14:09:15 -0500
Received: from ul1.satlink.com (ul1.satlink.com [200.0.224.2]) by
relay27.mail.aol.com (8.8.5/8.8.5/AOL-4.0.0) with ESMTP
id MAA21540; Tue, 12 Dec 2000 12:23:29 -0500 (EST)
From: More.Info.1oooooo0@bigger.net
Received: from 34lHT27yw (sdn-ts-003nynyorP15.
dialsprint.net
[206.133.34.66]) by ul1.satlink.com (8.8.8/8.8.8) with
SMTP id OAA13401; Tue, 12 Dec 2000 14:23:04 -0300
(GMT-3)
Received: From j1dqu3p1J (sdn-ts-003nyorP04.
dialsys33.net
[306.203.08.10]) by cor.ibuyitnow22.net (8.8.5/8.7.3)
with SMTP id JJA109; Tue, 12 Dec 2000 12:20:35 -400
(EDT)
```

You can tell this email has been forged because the bottom Received header sports three glaring flaws. First, you can't trace the email from the recipient's email address to the sender's email address (in this case, it's an America Online email account). The top three Received headers show that America Online received the email from ul1.satlink.com, which in turn received it from sdn-ts-003nynyorP15.dialsprint.net. The bottom Received header is garbage designed to confuse you, because it doesn't trace any email being sent to the sdn-ts-003nynyorP15.dialsprint.net domain.

The second flaw in the bottom Received header is the sdn-ts-003nynyorP15.dialsprint.net domain, which claims to have an IP numeric address of [306.203.08.10]. The numbers used in an IP numeric address can only range from 0 to 255, so any number greater than 255 (306 in this example) immediately reveals that this particular Received header is forged.

The third flaw is that the word "From" begins with a capital letter; the other Received headers use "from" instead.

Because the bottom Received header is obviously forged, you can ignore it completely. Studying the remaining Received headers, you can conclude that the email originated from the sdn-ts-003nynyorP15.dialsprint.net domain. To verify that this is an actual domain and not a forged one, look at its numeric address in square brackets. In this case, the numeric address is [206.133.34.66].

DNS lookup programs

Once you have identified a spammer's name and numeric Internet address, you can verify the domain's existence by using a handy online tool called Whois. To run it, visit the Network Solutions registry (http://www.networksolutions.com/cgi-bin/whois/whois). Or run the Whois command using a DNS lookup program like one of these:

DNS Workshop	http://www.evolve.co.uk/dns
NetScanTools	http://www.nwpsw.com
Sam Spade	http://www.samspade.org

For additional help in tracking down spammers, visit the UXN Spam Combat website (http://combat.uxn.com) where you will find more tools for doing DNS lookups, traceroute, DNS probes, and so on (see Figure 16-4).

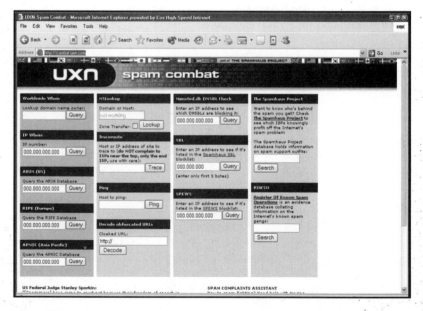

Figure 16-4

The UXN Spam Combat website provides plenty of tools for helping you track down an elusive spammer.

Whichever version of Whois you use, it will tell you whether the dialsprint.net domain really exists. In this example, Whois reports the following:

```
Sprint Business Operations (DIALSPRINT-DOM)
12490 Sunrise Valley Dr.
Reston, VA 22090
US
Domain Name: DIALSPRINT.NET
Administrative Contact, Technical Contact, Zone Contact:
Sprint DNS Administrator  (SDA4-ORG)  dns-admin@
SPRINT.NET
(800)232-6895
Fax- (703)478-5471
Billing Contact:
Sprint Internic Billing
(SIB2-ORG)  nicbills@SPRINT.NET
(800)232-6895
Fax- (703)478-5471
Record last updated on 23-Jan-00.
Record created on 12-Feb-96.
Database last updated on 22-Dec-99 05:27:44 EDT.
Domain servers in listed order:
NS1.DIALSPRINT.NET
206.134.151.45
NS2.DIALSPRINT.NET
206.134.79.44
NS3.DIALSPRINT.NET            205.149.192.145
```

This tells us that dialsprint.net is a valid domain and gives us the administrator's email address.

To further verify that the Received header information is correct, try one of the DNS lookup programs like Sam Spade or NetScanTools to see whether the IP address belongs to a specific domain name. In this example, the last valid Received header is:

```
from 34lHT27yw (sdn-ts-003nynyorP15.dialsprint.
net [206.133.34.66])
```

This shows that the domain name has been masked by the garbled string of characters "34lHT27yw." Examining the other Received headers shows that this string should list the same domain name as that which appears in parentheses (sdn-ts-003nynyorP15.dialsprint.net). Because the spammer deliberately scrambled this information, you can be pretty sure that this information reveals the address of the ISP they used to send the email.

Examining the [206.133.34.66] numeric address with the Name Server Lookup (NSLookup) command confirms that it belongs to the sdn-ts-003nynyorP15.dialsprint.net domain. Thus, we can be pretty sure that the spammer sent email from the dialsprint.net domain. Of course, the spammer might have opened an account with dialsprint.net just to send spam and then canceled it, but at least you can complain to the ISP.

Disguise your email address on a website

To retrieve valid email addresses, many spammers run website extractor programs that grab the HTML code that makes up a web page and searches for an email address. So one way to fool website extractor programs is to disguise your email address with ASCII code equivalents within your HTML code.Normally, an email address appears as raw HTML code in plain English. For example, if you wanted to list your email address as myname@isp.com on a web page, it would look like this in the equivalent HTML code:

```
<p>Email address: <a
href="mailto:myname@isp.com">myname@isp.com</a></p>
```

With the email address clearly visible in the HTML code, website extractor programs have little trouble retrieving any email addresses. But if you substitute each letter of your email address with the ASCII character equivalent, such as typing &#109 for the letter "m", &#121 for the letter "y" and so on, your HTML code now looks like this:

```
<p>Email address: <a
href="mailto:&#109;&#121;&#110;&#97;&#109;&#101;&#64;&#105;&#115;&#112;&#46;&#99;&#111;&#109">&#109;&#121;&#110;&#97;&#109;&#101;&#64;&#105;&#115;&#112;&#46;&#99;&#111;&#109</p>
```

Both versions of the HTML code displays the email address myname@isp.com on a web page, but the ASCII version prevents spammers from retrieving your email address since the spammer programs won't recognize the ASCII code as a valid email address.

To find the ASCII code for each character in an email address, visit ASCII table (http://www.asciitable.com).

Final tactics for avoiding spam

One of the earliest methods for fighting spam was to maintain a database of known spammer email addresses and ISPs. Unfortunately, spammers can change ISPs rapidly, making most anti-spammer databases obsolete. To avoid this problem, the Kill The Spams program (http://www.zipstore.com) uses a list of rules to screen the headers of incoming emails for signs of spam. If a header looks suspicious, the program can flag the email as possible spam or just delete the message automatically.

Programs like Spam Buster (http://www.contactplus.com), SpamButcher (http://www.spambutcher.com), and SpamKiller (http://www.mcafee.com) combine both filtering and a database of known spammers to help keep spam out of your inbox. For more accuracy, Spam Buster can do a DNS lookup on email to verify that the header lists a real address. To avoid having the anti-spam program mistake valid email for spam, many anti-spam programs offer a special Friends list, which tells the anti-spam program which email addresses you will always accept messages from.

To reduce the chances of receiving spam in the first place, give out your email address sparingly. Create a separate email account with a free service such as Hotmail, and use it for posting messages in Usenet newsgroups or when buying online (many companies sell your email address when you register with them). By creating a decoy email account, you can redirect spam to accounts that you rarely use, and keep your everyday email account free from most annoying spam.

ANTI-SPAM RESOURCES

Despite laws, threats, and physical action taken against spammers, spamming is so cost-effective that it's probably here to stay. If spam really irritates you, consider joining and helping CAUCE (Coalition Against Unsolicited Commercial Email) at http://www.cauce.org, an organization consisting of Internet users who have banded together to lobby for new laws to regulate unsolicited email.

To show you how influential one person can be in the fight against spam, visit Netizens Against Gratuitous Spamming (http://www.nags.org). This website offers tips for identifying and dealing with spam and offers an example of "chaff," which is garbage data designed to fool spammers who retrieve email addresses off websites.

To keep up with the latest news regarding spam, and to learn more about how to defeat spam, visit Death to Spam (http://www.mindworkshop.com/alchemy/nospam.html), SpamNews (http://petemoss.com/spam), an e-newsletter provided to ISP administrators so they can learn different ways to fight spam on their own systems, or Junkbusters (http://www.junkbusters.com). Or try Fight Spam, an international anti-spam group (http://spam.abuse.net/spam).

For the latest news about different spammers, or to warn people about new ones, visit the following newsgroups: alt.current-events.net-abuse, alt.current-events.net-abuse.spam, alt.spam, alt.privacy, news.admin.net-abuse.misc, news.admin.net-abuse.announce, and news.admin.net-abuse.email.

17

WEB BUGS, ADWARE, POP-UPS, AND SPYWARE

IN THE WORLD OF ADVERTISING, NOTHING IS REALLY FREE. When you listen to a radio or watch a television show, advertisers pay the costs and earn the right to broadcast their messages any time they want. Most people tolerate radio and television advertising since they've grown accustomed to its constant interruptions.

However, in the world of the Internet, people have a much lower tolerance level for advertisements. While advertisements pay for many free web hosting services and free or low-cost Internet services, there's a fine line between product promotion and invasion of privacy. When you hear or see a commercial on radio or television, you can freely ignore it. Unfortunately, advertisements on the Internet aren't always like that.

Ideally, an Internet advertisement would pop up once and give you the option of making it go away. Instead, Internet advertisements not only pop-up (and keep popping up over and over again), but they may also track which web pages you visit, to determine your preferences, which would be like having a radio or TV that could peek into your living room to see which brand of potato chips you might be eating at the moment. To intrude upon your privacy, Internet advertisers use a variety of tools including web bugs, adware, and a never-ending cascade of pop-up windows.

> Technological progress has merely provided us with more efficient means for going backwards.
>
> —ALDOUS HUXLEY

WATCHING OUT FOR WEB BUGS

Advertisers always need to know how effective their current marketing campaign may be. Since the Internet spans the world, it's nearly impossible to tell how many people looked at a particular ad and who they might be. To solve these two problems, advertisers created *web bugs.*

Tracking the websites you visit

When you visit a website, your browser asks the website server to send your computer all the text and graphic images that make up the web page. Thus, every webserver needs to know the IP address of your computer so it knows where to send the text and graphics.

When your browser receives information about a web page, that information appears in the form of *HTML* (Hypertext Markup Language) code, which tells your browser exactly how to display and position text and graphics. The specific HTML code that your browser receives from a web page defines the name of the graphic file, its size, and the name of the server it came from. In the following HTML example, the graphic file is called dotclear.gif, its width and height are both one pixel, and the server it came from is http://ad.doubleclick.net:

```
<IMG SRC=http://ad.doubleclick.net/dotclear.gif width=1 height=1>
```

Web bugs hide on ordinary web pages as invisible, one pixel by one pixel size images so you won't notice when you're being tracked. When the server sends the web bug to your browser, the server can immediately identify the following:

→ The IP address of the computer that fetched the web bug

→ The specific web page that contains the web bug (useful for seeing which web pages someone might have visited)

→ The time and date the web bug was retrieved

→ The type of browser that fetched the web bug

At the simplest level, web bugs help advertisers determine how many people have visited a particular website and viewed a particular web page. On a more insidious level, web bugs can work with cookies to track which websites each person visits so they can display advertisements specific to that individual.

Using web bugs in spam

Web bugs can sometimes appear in spam too (see Chapter 16), buried inside email so an advertiser can see how many times people read (or at least open) a particular message. If someone doesn't bother to view a web bug in an email, this tells the advertiser that the email address may not be valid or that this particular person didn't bother to read it. In either case, the advertiser will likely remove that person's email address to avoid wasting time sending advertisements that no one will read.

Some companies accused of planting web bugs in email marketing messages include Experian (http://www.experian.com), Digital Impact (http://www.digitalimpact.com), and Responsys (http://www.responsys.com). By browsing their websites, you can get a better idea of how email marketing firms work, and how they might target you sometime in the future.

Bugging newsgroups

Besides slipping web bugs in target email messages, it's possible to embed a web bug into a newsgroup message, too. Not only could this tell an advertiser how many times someone looked at the ad, but it can also track down the specific IP address of each person who downloaded the web bug.

The extremely paranoid believe that web bugs can identify people who subscribe to politically incorrect newsgroups, while less-conspiracy-minded people believe that governments might use web bugs to track down anyone trading child pornography or illegal MP3 files. Since web bugs are invisible, and you aren't likely to even notice their presence, it's possible that a web bug has already given away your IP address and browsing habits to a faceless corporation without you even knowing it.

Protecting yourself against web bugs

Since web bugs often work with cookies to track your browsing habits, your first line of defense is to make sure your browser refuses all cookies. Since this won't always be practical, especially when you visit online shopping sites, visit Bugnosis.org (http://www.bugnosis.org) and download their free Bugnosis tool (see Figure 17-1).

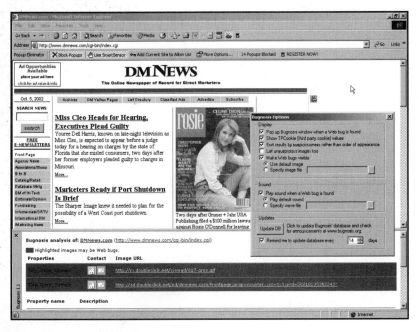

Figure 17-1

The free Bugnosis tool can identify websites that use web bugs.

As you browse through different websites, Bugnosis scans each web page, gives an audible warning, and highlights suspicious web bugs on a web page. By using Bugnosis with Internet Explorer, you can see how prevalent web bugs may actually be, especially if Bugnosis finds suspicious GIF images on your favorite websites, such as the DM News site (http://www.dmnews.com), the *Detroit News* (http://www.detnews.com), or the *New York Times* (http://www.nytimes.com).

ADWARE—SOFTWARE WITH BUILT-IN ADVERTISING

For the longest time, there were four categories of software: commercial programs that you purchased before you could try them, shareware that you could try and purchase if you found it useful, freeware that you could use without ever paying for it (although the programmer retained the copyright), and public domain software that nobody owned so you could freely use it and modify it if you wanted.

When programmers wanted to make money selling a program, they often released their creations as shareware, so people all over the world could try it for free. If the program proved popular, they usually turned it into a commercial product.

Although a handful of shareware programs turned their creators into millionaires, many more simply earned a small amount of change for the programmers and that's it. To increase their odds of success, many shareware programmers decided to turn their creations into a new category of software dubbed *adware*.

As the name implies, adware displays advertisements as the program runs (see Figure 17-2). If you're connected to the Internet, the adware program may access a server and display an ever-changing array of advertisements every time you use the adware program.

Figure 17-2
Adware programs display advertisements every time you run the program.

By incorporating advertisements in their programs, programmers can ensure that they earn a certain amount of money whether people ultimately register and pay for the program or not. Advertisers love adware because it provides access to more potential customers. Unfortunately, the only people who don't seem to care for adware are the people using it.

By itself, adware can be annoying but harmless. However, instead of being content to just display advertisements, some adware programs secretly retrieve information from the user's computer and transmit this information back to the advertiser, which is a characteristic of programs known as *spyware*. This information could be as simple as the type and version of the operating system on your computer, or your IP address along with a list of all the cookies stored on your computer, which an advertiser can examine to determine your browsing habits. When you run an adware program, it's possible that the adware program could be transmitting your browsing and online shopping habits to the advertiser without your consent, which can be as disconcerting as finding a stranger in your kitchen making a note of all the name-brand food products you bought in the past three days.

For more information about adware, visit the Adware.info site (http://www.adware.info). In case you're curious about the types of companies that help programmers develop adware, visit the Software Marketing Resource page (http://www.softwaremarketingresource.com/adware.html).

Defending against adware

Because so many people find the idea of their programs bombarding them with advertisements less than appealing, most adware programs disguise their built-in advertising. To help you find adware programs that may be lurking on your computer, download a free copy of Ad-aware, as shown in Figure 17-3 (http://www.lavasoft-usa.com).

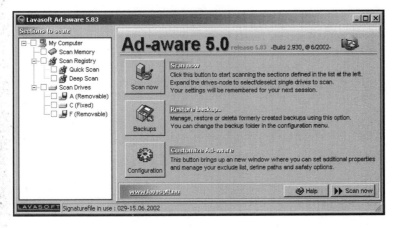

Figure 17-3

Ad-aware can detect and remove adware programs that may be hidden on your computer.

Like an antivirus program, Ad-aware scans your memory, hard disk, and registry file to look for files that may be unique to known adware programs, such as CuteFTP, NetSonic, or Go!Zilla. Once it finds a known adware program, Ad-aware gives you the option of removing it completely from your system.

For another adware removal tool, visit Bulletproof Software (http://www.bulletproofsoft.com) and try their BPS Spyware/Adware Remover. Unlike Ad-aware, BPS Spyware/Adware Remover isn't free, but it does include features to scan and remove any spyware it finds on your computer. (For more information about spyware, see the "Detecting Spyware" section later in this chapter.)

Better yet, visit the Spychecker site (http://www.spychecker.com) before you download that shareware or freeware program. Spychecker has a database of all known adware programs, so you can find out if a program will spy on you before you decide to download and install it.

Adware vs. Ad-aware

Not surprisingly, Ad-aware's efforts have upset a great many advertisers and adware programmers, who see Ad-aware as a threat to their sources of income. One adware program in particular, RadLight version 3.03 release 5.0 (http://www.radlight.net), would scan your hard disk for Ad-aware. If it found Ad-aware lurking on your computer, RadLight would secretly uninstall it without your knowledge. That way it could continue flooding your computer with advertisements and transmitting your data back to the advertiser without Ad-aware's interference.

At the time Igor Janos, author of the RadLight software claimed, "As Ad-aware's behavior was hostile to our bundle, I had to defend."

This immediately set up a backlash against RadLight, so the later version of RadLight 3.03 release 5.2 gives you the option of uninstalling Ad-aware or not. To further distance itself from the negative label of "adware," RadLight now promotes its ad-supported version as "helpware," as if advertisements somehow "help" the user in any way. While this compromise isn't perfect, at least it gives you, the user, a choice in the matter. Naturally, a far more effective choice is to simply avoid using any adware programs at all, while using the Ad-aware program regularly to keep your computer free of such annoyances.

Killing ads in AOL Instant Messenger

With ads popping up in shareware programs, email, and web pages, it was inevitable that ads would start appearing in instant messenger programs. Ads have started appearing in AOL Instant Messenger (AIM), one of the more popular instant messenger services around. As you chat, ads pop up in your AOL Instant Messenger window.

In case you find these ads annoying, you can try to manually kill them by editing the "aim.odl" file with any text editor, such as Notepad. Look for the following code:

```
on_group(5)
{
load_ocm          advert          required
```

```
}
on_group(11)
{
load_ocm          advert        required
}
```

Just put semicolons in front of the load_ocm lines, like this:

```
on_group(5)
{
;    load_ocm          advert          required
}
on_group(11)
{
;    load_ocm          advert          required
}
```

Save the file as "aim.odl" in its original location, and AOL Instant Messenger should no longer annoy you with advertisements. If you don't want to mess around with editing strange files on your hard disk, grab a copy of the DeadAIM program (http://www.jdennis.net/index2.htm), which can remove those annoying advertisements from AOL Instant Messenger automatically.

STOPPING POP-UP/POP-UNDER ADVERTISEMENTS

In the beginning, advertisers relied on banner ads strategically placed around a web page. However, they found that people routinely ignored them, so to force people to at least acknowledge the advertisement's existence, they created pop-up and pop-under ads.

Pop-up ads blanket your screen with windows, advertising anything from lower mortgage rates to vacation trip giveaways (see Figure 17-4). Since these windows cover any web page you're currently browsing, you can't see anything until you close the pop-up ad window. Pornography advertisers have created particularly annoying pop-up ads that spawn three or four more pop-up windows every time you close one.

Pop-under ads are a bit more subtle. They also appear in little windows all over your screen, but they hide under your currently displayed web page, so you won't even see them. The moment you close your browser, though, those pop-under ads seem to magically appear, cluttering up your screen. Since pop-under ads don't intrude upon your browsing activities, advertisers hope that more people will be more receptive to them.

One of the largest email and Internet marketing companies is DoubleClick (http://www.doubleclick.com). It offers the public a way to store a special cookie from DoubleClick that prevents your computer from receiving any more advertisements

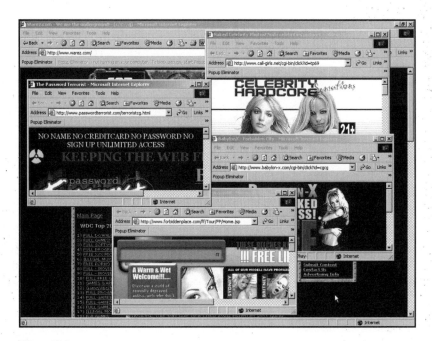

Figure 17-4

Pop-up ads can keep appearing on your screen faster than you can get rid of them.

from DoubleClick. Just visit the DoubleClick site, click to view their Privacy Policy, and follow the directions to opt out from DoubleClick's advertising. Now you just have to worry about online advertising from other companies.

Even if you decide to opt-out from DoubleClick's ads, you may still find yourself bombarded by pop-up and pop-under advertisements. To learn how to stop pop-up and pop-under ads from wrecking your Internet experience, visit the Web Ad Blocking site (http://www.ecst.csuchico.edu/~atman/spam/adblock.shtml).

If you want to automatically block pop-up and pop-under ads from appearing, you'll need to get a pop-up blocker program. Go to WebAttack.com (http://www.webat-tack.com) or Tucows (http://www.tucows.com) and search for "pop-up blocker." Both sites offer plenty of free and shareware pop-up ad blockers, such as the one shown in Figure 17-5, and you can try to find the one you like best.

For a free way to block pop-up ads, stop using Internet Explorer or Netscape and grab a copy of Mozilla (http://www.mozilla.org) or Safari (http://www.apple.com). Both browsers offer commands that let you block pop-up ads from appearing and disturbing your web surfing experience.

DETECTING SPYWARE

The thought of unseen advertisers peeking at your browsing habits may unnerve you, but what may be more disconcerting is finding that someone you know,

Figure 17-5

A pop-up blocker like Stopzilla keeps track of all the pop-up ads it stops.

such as your boss, your spouse, or your parents, are secretly monitoring what you do on your computer through a desktop-monitoring program, otherwise known as *spyware*.

Spyware can capture screenshots of your activity, record every keystroke you type, track every program you use, and log how much time you spend using each program on the computer. Bosses use spyware to catch employees using their computers for personal activities, parents use spyware to make sure their kids don't visit forbidden sites, hackers use spyware to snare credit card numbers and passwords from unsuspecting victims, and spouses use spyware to gather proof that their husband or wife may be cheating on them. To see what type of spyware someone could plant on your computer, visit the Top Secret Software site (http://www.topsecret-software.com) and read about the different capabilities of various spyware programs.

Unlike ordinary programs that appear in a list of running programs tracked by the operating system, such as Windows XP, spyware programs bury themselves out of sight, so unsuspecting victims don't accidentally stumble across the program while it's running. Unless you suspect someone has planted spyware on your computer and you know where to look, chances are good that you'll never detect any spyware on your computer.

Several companies sell anti-spyware programs, such as Nitrous Anti-Spy (http://www.nitrousonline.com), PestPatrol (http://www.pestpatrol.com), SpyGuard (http://www.spyguard.com), and SpyCop (http://www.spycops.com). These programs, like the one shown in Figure 17-6, can search your hard disk for any traces of known spyware programs and keystroke loggers that someone may have slipped onto your computer.

WARNING: Anti-spyware programs will not be able to detect hardware-based keystroke loggers that connect between a computer and the keyboard.

Besides rooting through your hard disk for known spyware files, anti-spyware programs can also monitor the ports on your computer to detect any unauthorized communications being sent from your computer. Such clandestine communication is

Figure 17-6
Anti-spyware programs can keep someone from secretly monitoring your activity on the computer.

almost always the result of either adware, a remote access Trojan horse (see Chapter 8), or spyware, which may be trying to send a record of your activity to the email account of the person spying on you. An anti-spyware program can block such stealth communication from taking place, effectively shielding your privacy.

THE ONLY SURE WAY TO PROTECT YOUR PRIVACY

If you never connect to the Internet, you can protect yourself against the large majority of web bugs, adware, pop-up ads, and spyware. Since that isn't an option for many people, your next best solution is to understand how various threats to your privacy work, and then use protective programs to defend against each threat, such as Bugnosis, Ad-aware, and anti-spyware programs.

Maybe your computer isn't bugged, and maybe nobody is spying on you. But is it worth the risk of losing your privacy not to find out?

PART 5

PROTECTING YOUR COMPUTER

18

FIREWALLS, INTRUSION-DETECTION SYSTEMS, AND HONEYPOTS

IF YOU HAVE A COMPUTER CONNECTED TO THE INTERNET, EXPECT THAT IT WILL BECOME A TARGET FOR A HACKER. While it's unlikely that hackers will specifically target your computer, that doesn't mean they won't leave your computer alone if they happen to find it while prowling around the Internet.

Hackers like easy targets, so even though they may not care about reading your letters to your grandmother or your 2002 tax returns, hackers may break into your computer just for fun to practice attacking a relatively safe computer, to use your hard disk as storage for illegally copied files (music, programs, or videos), or to plant a "zombie" program on your hard disk that can command your computer to flood a specific website with useless data in a denial-of-service attack. Your data may be unimportant to a hacker, but your computer itself can still be a valuable resource.

If you don't like the idea of someone taking control of your computer and having the power to wipe out your data at any moment, you need to protect your computer with a firewall.

Information is the oxygen of the modern age. It seeps through the walls topped by barbed wire, it wafts across the electrified borders.

—RONALD REAGAN

FIREWALLS: THE FIRST LINE OF DEFENSE

At the very least, every computer should have a *firewall*, which acts like a locked door to keep intruders from the Internet out of your computer. A firewall can't provide 100 percent protection against hackers, but it can protect you against a large majority of hackers who simply prowl a range of IP addresses, searching for a vulnerable computer. The moment a hacker finds a computer without a firewall, it's relatively trivial for that hacker to break in. Although computers connected to the Internet through a DSL or cable modem are particularly susceptible to hacker attacks, computers that rely on dial-up access can still be vulnerable.

If you get a firewall, you can choose between hardware or software firewalls. It's possible to use both hardware and software firewalls together, although this will not necessarily give you twice the protection, since the two firewalls may guard (and ignore) the same types of intrusions. Firewalls, like other types of computer equipment and programs, also have their share of bugs, so it's entirely possible to install a firewall only to find that a hacker has found some flaw and managed to bypass it anyway.

How firewalls work

Firewalls work by blocking communication to and from your computer. Many hackers use port scanners to locate potential targets (see Chapter 11), so a firewall can block port scanners to keep the hacker from reaching your computer. At the simplest level, the firewall blocks a port scan, which tells the hacker that a firewall exists. On a more complicated level, the firewall may mask your computer's existence, essentially making it invisible to hackers using port scanners. In this case, the hacker won't know if he found a computer protected by a firewall or just an invalid IP address. In either case, the hacker will likely leave your computer alone and look for an easier target to attack.

Firewalls also serve a second purpose in controlling what your computer can do over the Internet. Many firewalls examine the programs on your computer that connect to the Internet, and allow you to choose the programs that have your permission to connect, such as your browser, your email program, and an instant messenger program. If the firewall detects a program that you haven't specifically approved, the firewall blocks it and notifies you. By blocking unauthorized programs from accessing the Internet, firewalls can stop remote access Trojans (RATs) from secretly connecting to a hacker and giving the hacker control over your computer. Since many spyware programs (see Chapter 17) can transmit records of keystrokes and screenshots of the programs you use to someone who may be spying on you, firewalls can help you detect and block spyware programs, too.

To allow legitimate traffic to pass through a firewall, you may need to tell the firewall what is and is not permissible on your computer. Four criteria that firewalls may use to block illegal traffic are IP addresses, protocols, ports, and specific programs.

IP addresses identify specific computers, so a firewall can either block traffic from certain IP addresses (such as the IP address of *Playboy*'s website) or conversely, only accept connections from specific IP addresses (such as a trusted corporate computer).

Firewalls may also allow or block certain protocols, which are specific ways that computers send and receive data (see Figure 18-1). For example, a firewall may only allow HTTP (Hypertext Transfer Protocol) through, which sends web pages over the Internet (this is the "http" that appears at the beginning of website addresses). Likewise, a firewall may block FTP (File Transfer Protocol), which can send and receive files. Some other types of protocols that a firewall may block include the following:

UDP (User Datagram Protocol)   Used for transmitting information that does not require a response, such as streaming audio or video.

ICMP (Internet Control Message Protocol)   Used to report errors to other computers.

SMTP (Simple Mail Transfer Protocol)   Used for sending and receiving email.

Telnet   Used to access and control a remote computer.

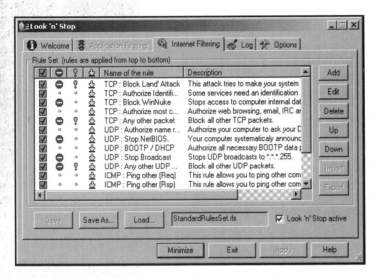

Figure 18-1

You can define the types of protocols that the firewall allows.

By blocking certain protocols, firewalls can prevent certain types of attacks on a protected computer. For example, blocking the Telnet protocol can keep a hacker from controlling and manipulating your computer over the Internet (although it's possible for the hacker to use a different protocol to achieve the same purpose).

Besides blocking certain protocols, firewalls may block certain ports. Ports allow certain types of communication into a computer, so firewalls typically block every port except for the essential ones, such as port 80 (used for browsing web pages) and port 25 (used for sending and receiving email). By shutting down certain ports, a firewall can prevent a hacker from sneaking in through a forgotten open port or from opening an obscure port to transmit information from your computer back to the hacker. Of course, shutting down ports only forces hackers to direct their attacks through the open ports, but it does limit the types of attacks a hacker can use against your computer.

Firewalls may also allow access to the Internet only from certain trusted programs, like a web browser or email program. If any other type of program tries to access the Internet, the firewall blocks its attempt, assuming that the program could be a Trojan horse or hacker trying to send data out from your computer.

Through the combination of filtering IP addresses, protocols, ports, and even specific words or phrases, firewalls can block most unwanted attempts to break into your computer. To find a hardware-based firewall, visit one of the following sites:

Netgear	http://www.netgear.com
TRENDware	http://www.trendware.com
D-Link	http://www.dlink.com

To find a software-based firewall, Windows users can look at these options:

Tiny Personal Firewall	http://www.tinysoftware.com
ZoneAlarm	http://www.zonelabs.com
Look 'n' Stop	http://www.looknstop.com
Norton Internet Security	http://www.symantec.com
Outpost Firewall	http://www.agnitum.com
Sygate Personal Firewall	http://soho.sygate.com
Personal Firewall	http://www.mcafee.com

Many versions of Linux come with a firewall, and if you happen to be using Windows XP, you have a built-in firewall that you can turn on by following these steps:

1. Click the Start button.

2. Click Control Panel.

3. Click Network and Internet Connections.

4. Click Network Connections. A Network Connections window will open.

5. Right-click on the Local Area Connection icon, and when a pop-up menu appears, click Properties. A Local Area Connection Properties dialog box appears.

6. Click the Advanced tab.

7. Click the "Protect my computer and network by limiting or preventing access to this computer from the Internet" check box so a check mark appears.

8. Click OK.

Macintosh users can take a look at these two firewalls: Firewalk (http://www.pliris-soft.com) and NetBarrier (http://www.intego.com). And if you want to contribute your programming skills to developing a firewall for Linux, visit the Falcon Firewall Project (http://falcon.naw.de). By studying the source code to this firewall, you can get a better understanding of how firewalls work and possibly modify the firewall to protect everyone against the latest threats on the Internet.

One of the biggest problems with firewalls is that most novices have no idea how to evaluate them. Besides looking at a pretty user interface, novices aren't likely to understand the capabilities of what each firewall may offer. To learn more about the details of firewalls and how to choose the best one for you, visit the following sites, which offer technical comparisons of the most popular firewalls:

Home PC Firewall Guide	http://www.firewallguide.com
Firewall.com	http://firewall.com
Firewall.net	http://www.firewall-net.com
Free-Firewall.org	http://www.free-firewall.org

How firewalls can be defeated

Perhaps the biggest problem with firewalls is that they take time to configure, which means that most novices will likely configure the firewall incorrectly, which either gives a false sense of security while leaving gaping holes open in the firewall's defenses, or causes increased frustration when the firewall winds up stopping legitimate programs from working, such as an email or instant messenger program. If a firewall gets too aggressive in stopping programs from connecting to the Internet, users may be tempted to just shut off or uninstall the firewall altogether.

Another problem with a firewall is that it can only protect inbound and outbound Internet connections; it can't do a thing to stop someone from accessing a computer through a telephone line, through a wireless access point located behind a firewall (see Chapter 11), or through the keyboard if someone is physically sitting in front of the computer, such as a coworker or the janitor.

Even worse, firewalls can be fooled. If a firewall only allows certain programs to access the Internet, a hacker could simply rename a remote access Trojan horse so that it has the same name as your web browser. Then when this remote access Trojan horse tries to access the Internet, the firewall checks the program's name, finds it matches the list of programs allowed to access the Internet, and falsely allows this program to get through the firewall, which is like a thief fooling a police officer by using a fake picture ID.

Perhaps the most curious way to circumvent firewalls is through a technique known as *firewall tunneling*. Since firewalls may only allow a computer to use certain protocols and ports, firewall tunneling simply uses whatever ports and protocols the firewall allows to sneak data through. This can be as effective as a hijacker sneaking past airport security dressed up as a pilot.

Two products that allow firewall tunneling include RemFTP (http://www.remftp.com) and HTTP-Tunnel (http://www.http-tunnel.com). RemFTP boasts that it is "a program that connects your home and work computers for file transfer, without having to think about firewalls." HTTP-Tunnel advertises that it "allows people behind restrictive firewalls to use previously blocked applications through their firewall." By using either of these commercially available programs, or the firewall tunneling techniques that they're based on, hackers can circumvent practically any firewall with impunity.

Even worse is that you could configure your firewall correctly, and it could still leave gaping holes in your computer's defenses simply because the firewall happens to lack certain vital features that another firewall may offer. Until you buy and try several different firewalls, you may never know how defenseless a particular firewall may actually be. To test the capabilities of your firewall, download some of the following firewall testing programs to determine if your firewall would stop a typical hacker attack:

LeakTest	http://grc.com/lt/leaktest.htm
FireHole	http://keir.net/firehole.html
OutBound	http://www.hackbusters.net/ob.html
PC Flank	http://www.pcflank.com

Port Detective	http://www.portdetective.com
YALTA	http://www.soft4ever.com/security_test/En/index.htm
TooLeaky	http://tooleaky.zensoft.com

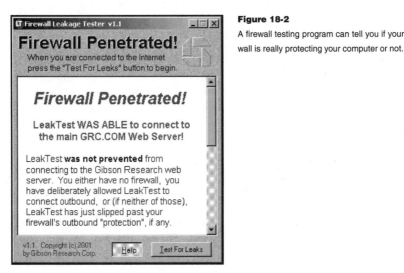

Figure 18-2

A firewall testing program can tell you if your firewall is really protecting your computer or not.

Hardening your operating system

Besides installing a firewall, make sure you update your operating system with the latest bug fixes or security patches. Hackers quickly learn all the flaws in a particular operating system, and if they find that flaw on your computer, they may be able to exploit the flaw to get into your computer, regardless of any firewall you may have installed.

The most secure operating system is OpenBSD (http://www.openbsd.org), but if you're using Red Hat Linux, the friendly folks at the National Security Agency have developed a special version dubbed Security-Enhanced Linux (http://www.nsa.gov/selinux), which can harden your version of Red Hat Linux from attack.

For another way to battle-harden Red Hat Linux, visit Bastille Linux (http://www.bastille-linux.org). Like Security-Enhanced Linux, Bastille Linux adds extra security to your Linux operating system to make sure that all possible flaws in your operating system have been shut down.

INTRUSION-DETECTION SYSTEMS

Firewalls can only deter, not prevent, break-ins. Once a hacker breaks into your computer, a firewall won't provide any protection whatsoever. At this point, you need an *intrusion-detection system* (IDS). Where firewalls act like locked doors and windows leading to your computer, intrusion-detection systems act more like burglar alarms to alert you when an intruder has already broken in. Few personal computers use an IDS, although most corporate computers, such as webservers, use one.

How intrusion-detection systems work

To protect against known hacker attacks, an IDS may do something called *signature analysis*, which means that the IDS recognizes the unique characteristics or "signatures" of common hacker attacks, such as those often created by script kiddies. When an IDS detects the signature of a hacker attack, the IDS will know exactly how to stop that particular attack.

Because hackers keep coming up with new strategies for breaking into a computer, an IDS can't rely on signature analysis alone. To complement signature analysis, an IDS may monitor a network or computer and look for suspicious activity, such as increased traffic coming from an obscure port or repeated attempts to log on to the computer. When the IDS detects suspicious behavior, it contacts the system administrator. By using an IDS, system administrators don't have to search for a hacker by manually scanning the log files or tediously monitoring Internet connections on their own.

Since many hackers often replace some of the computer's existing programs with Trojan horse versions that will let the hacker hide, many intrusion-detection systems include a file integrity checker. This simply calculates a mathematical result (or checksum) for each file based on that file's size. Now if a hacker replaces a file, that file will likely change in size, so when the IDS does a routine check of the computer's files, it will notice the file-size change and alert the system administrator.

To learn more about intrusion-detection systems and to download various IDS programs for Windows and Linux, visit these sites:

Internet Security Systems	http://www.iss.net
Snort	http://www.snort.org
Okena	http://www.okena.com
Talisker	http://www.networkintrusion.co.uk

How intrusion-detection systems fail

An IDS works as an aid to a system administrator, but it isn't meant to replace a real person. By itself, an IDS won't stop a hacker, but it can alert you when a hacker may already be in your computer. Unlike a firewall or an antivirus program, you must respond to every alarm from the IDS. If the IDS generates too many false alarms, the system administrator is likely to get bored and ignore most of the warnings altogether.

To make an IDS fail, hackers often attack a computer, such as with a denial-of-service attack, thereby setting off the IDS alarm. While the IDS and system administrator's attention is focused on the denial of service attack, the hacker can try to slip into the computer undetected.

Since intrusion-detection systems look for signatures of known attacks or evidence of suspicious activity, hackers can alter their attack methods to avoid alerting the IDS. Also, an IDS is nothing more than a computer program with its own share of bugs and flaws, so if hackers can identify the specific IDS program on a computer, they may be able to use known flaws to disable or bypass the IDS completely.

HONEYPOTS

Rather than try to block a hacker (with a firewall) or find a hacker (with an intrusion-detection system), some people prefer the more labor-intensive method of using a *honeypot* instead. A honeypot can serve two purposes. First, it can lure a hacker away from the important data on your computer and isolate the hacker from causing any damage. Second, a honeypot can allow you to study a hacker's methods and techniques so that you can better learn how certain attacks work and how you might be able to defend yourself against them in the future.

Honeypots typically run on a single computer that mimics the activity and breadth of an entire network, even down to emulating the details of a specific operating system, such as Linux, Windows, Mac OS, Solaris, or HP-UX. Although a honeypot looks and behaves just like a real network, it often offers several easily exploitable flaws to encourage the hackers to waste their time exploiting this fictional network.

To learn more about honeypots, visit the Honeynet Project (http://project.honeynet.org), which has been running honeypots and studying hacker techniques for years. The Distributed Honeypot Project (http://www.lucidic.net) plans to create a network of honeypots around the Internet so that system administrators can share the latest hacking techniques. For a list of different honeypots available, visit Talisker (http://www.networkintrusion.co.uk).

The friendly folks at Science Applications International Corporation (SAIC) (http://www.saic.com) have even set up a wireless honeypot near Washington, D.C., to learn the latest war-driving hacking techniques (see Chapter 11).

To learn about the various honeypots currently used by businesses, visit these sites:

Tiny Honeypot	http://www.alpinista.org/thp
NetFacade	http://www22.verizon.com/fns/netsec/ fns_netsecurity_netfacade.html
Symantec ManTrap	http://www.symantec.com
The Deception Toolkit	http://www.all.net/dtk/download.html

Many honeypots are freeware and include source code so you can study how they work and even contribute some ideas of your own.

Because honeypots take time to set up and maintain, most individuals aren't likely to run a honeypot on their personal computer. If you have the time, though, you may want to try running a Trojan horse honeypot—the next time someone tries to access your computer using a remote access Trojan horse, your honeypot can trick the hacker into thinking he has secret access to your computer when he's really isolated from your data and you're watching his activities every step of the way (see Figure 18-3).

Here are some of the many Trojan horse honeypot programs available:

NetBuster   http://surf.to/netbuster
FakeBO   http://cvs.linux.hr/fakebo
Tambu Dummy Server http://www.xploiter.com
The Saint   http://www.megasecurity.org

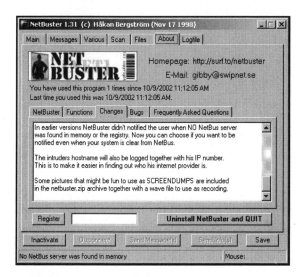

Figure 18-3

NetBuster can create a honeypot to trap hackers trying to access your computer with the NetBus
remote access Trojan.

TRACING A HACKER

Hackers can attack any computer in the world that's connected to the Internet, which
means that someone could be probing your computer right now and checking it for
weaknesses. Even worse is that you may catch a hacker in your computer, but the
second he disconnects, he's gone.

Since hackers can appear and disappear at any time, there's nothing to stop
them from attacking any computer they want, since it's highly unlikely that they'll ever
get caught. To eliminate the hacker's refuge in anonymity, Sharp Technology has
developed Hack Tracer (http://www.sharptechnology.com/bh-cons.htm), which can
trace a hacker back to his Internet service provider (ISP) and possibly even find the
hacker's IP address as well.

Knowing an IP address may identify the hacker's location, but the cryptic series
of numbers that make up an IP address might not give you a clue where the hacker is
located. The next time your firewall or IDS identifies a hacker's IP address, run it

through McAfee Visual Trace, which is part of the McAfee Personal Firewall program (http://www.mcafee.com) or VisualRoute (http://www.visualware.com) to see the hacker's approximate location on a world map (see Figure 18-4). After tracing enough hackers' IP addresses, you may be surprised to find that your personal computer in Nebraska has been targeted by hackers in Korea, Canada, Israel, or Germany.

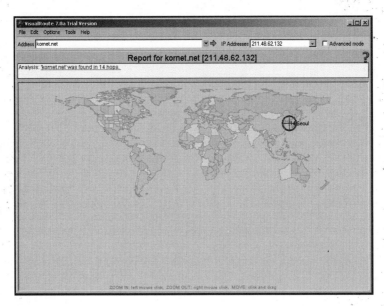

Figure 18-4

With a program like VisualRoute, you can identify the geographical location of a particularly persistent hacker.

To further track down hacker activity, visit myNetWatchman (http://www.mynet-watchman.com) and share hacker attempts on your computer with people all over the world. The more people who pool information about hackers, the more likely myNetWatchman can identify specific types of attacks and pinpoint the IP addresses of the more active hackers in the world (see Figure 18-5).

File Edit View Go Bookmarks Tools Window Help

Back Forward Reload Stop   http://www.mynetwatchman.com/LIS.asp?Queue=HBR1   Search   Print

Home   Bookmarks   The Mozilla Organization   Latest Builds

Incident Summary

Incident Id	Source IP	Source ISP	Incident Score	Agent Count	Status	Response
7484587	211.168.106.155	bora.net	170450	390	Escalated	No Response
9384029	148.223.128.116	uninet.net.mx	79450	3	Escalated	No Response
3361395	211.137.136.118	chinamobile.com	73850	173	Escalation Pending Queue	No Response
7889527	198.092.208.077	internetsite.com	53550	18	Escalated	No Response
8067575	203.093.239.146	cngb.com	50050	74	Escalated	No Response
9512339	063.123.081.241	uu.net	46200	117	Escalated	Provider Acknowledged
9438234	196.025.081.002	saix.net	41300	76	Escalated	Provider Acknowledged
8625146	211.092.141.222	cnuninet.com	36000	264	Escalated	No Response
7974401	066.137.207.210	swbell.net	30100	18	Escalated	No Response
8976039	061.139.048.041	chinanet-sc.cn	29050	67	Escalated	No Response
4747450	066.122.195.132	pbi.net	28350	55	Escalated	No Response
4054674	203.236.003.225	sktelecom.com	28247	51	Escalated	No Response
9425888	066.139.073.010	tier-2.com	26600	70	Escalated	No Response
8115751	216.099.036.080	inaxx.net	26250	70	Escalated	No Response
9393713	216.061.253.253	swbell.net	25550	5	Escalated	No Response
9459360	213.244.090.026	paltel.net	24850	11	Escalated	No Response
8396625	024.098.248.126	attbi.com	24500	62	Escalated	No Response
9689419	194.009.186.118	afripa.com	22400	9	Escalated	No Response
8633608	210.083.203.082	china-netcom.com	22400	36	Escalated	No Response
9329952	211.181.208.116	bora.net	22050	35	Escalated	No Response

Document: Done (0.871 secs)

Figure 18-5

MyNetWatchman can identify the top ISPs used by hackers around the world.

While hackers can always choose when to attack a computer, that doesn't mean that your computer needs to be defenseless. With a good firewall, an intrusion-detection system, a securely patched operating system, and even a honeypot, you can protect your computer and possibly turn the tables on the hacker by tracing him and revealing his location for everyone to see. If enough people contact the ISP used by a particularly annoying hacker, the ISP may disconnect the hacker and force him to look for alternative ISPs. If this happens often enough, this may not discourage the hacker, but at least it can cause him enough trouble that he might restrict his activities and spare many potential victims from future attacks.

19

COMPUTER FORENSICS: RECOVERING AND DELETING DATA

LIKE MOST CRIMINALS, HACKERS OFTEN BRING ABOUT THEIR OWN DOWN-FALL BY FAILING TO REMOVE ALL TRACES OF THEIR CRIME. Not only do many hackers leave incriminating notes and printouts of their latest exploits scattered around their computers, but they also can't resist bragging to others about their exploits in public chat rooms. Yet even this blatant disregard for secrecy and indiscretion wouldn't be so damaging if these same hackers didn't unwittingly leave incriminating evidence stored all over their computers, as well.

DELETING DATA

The biggest problem with data is that once you store it on any form of magnetic media, it stays there forever. When you delete a file, your computer takes a shortcut. Instead of physically destroying the file, the computer simply pretends that the file no longer exists by replacing the first letter of the file name with a special character (hex byte code E5h), which leaves the contents of the file intact.

This process is like taking your name off an apartment building directory to make it look like you no longer live there, but staying in the apartment until someone else moves in. Only when the computer needs the space taken up by the deleted file will it actually overwrite the old file with new data. If your disk has plenty of extra space available, you could go weeks, months, or even years without ever overwriting previously deleted files. (Although, when you defragment your hard disk, your computer will likely overwrite many of these "deleted" files.)

If you delete a file, you can usually undelete it if you run an undelete utility program right away. Undelete utilities simply give a previously deleted file a new name so the computer will recognize it again. However, the longer you wait, the more time your computer will have to overwrite some or possibly all of the deleted file with new data, making it difficult, if not impossible, to recover the original deleted file.

Some utility programs, such as Norton Utilities, come with a file-deletion protection feature that saves any deleted files in a special folder so you can quickly and accurately undelete a file any time in the future. Obviously this feature can save you if you accidentally delete something, but it can also work against you by preserving those sensitive files that you thought you deleted months ago.

This invention involves a device, referred to herein as a "cabinet," which provides physical and biochemical support for an animal's head which has been "discorporated" (i.e., severed from its body).

—UNITED STATES PATENT NUMBER 4666425: A DEVICE FOR KEEPING A SEVERED HEAD ALIVE

To find an undelete program, try one of the following:

Norton Utilities	http://www.symantec.com
Active@UNDELETE	http://www.active-undelete.com
Restorer2000	http://www.bitmart.net
Undelete	http://www.execsoft.com

Executive Software, the makers of Undelete, also offers a free Deleted File Analysis Utility, so that you can analyze your own hard disk and see how many files may still be recoverable, as shown in Figure 19-1. The results may surprise you.

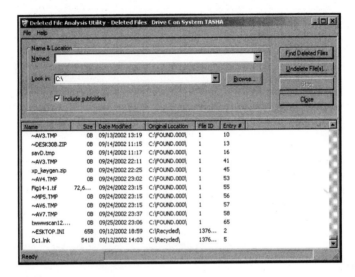

Figure 19-1

The Deleted File Analysis Utility from Executive Software can reveal all the files you deleted in the past that someone may still be able to undelete and read.

File shredders

If you deliberately erase a file and then overwrite it, most undelete programs will not be able to recover it. But if you want to make sure you've deleted a file as much as possible, use a *file shredder* to be sure.

File shredders overwrite deleted files one or more times using random characters, such as zeroes and ones. As a result, when an undelete program tries to recover the deleted file, the file shows only random data.

Levels of file-shredding security

Not all file shredders are equal. A good one offers several ways to shred your files, balancing speed and security (see Figure 19-2). To defeat ordinary undelete programs and wipe files quickly, a file shredder may make one pass at overwriting your deleted file with random data. While this quick wipeout defeats most undelete programs, it will not defeat specialized computer forensics tools.

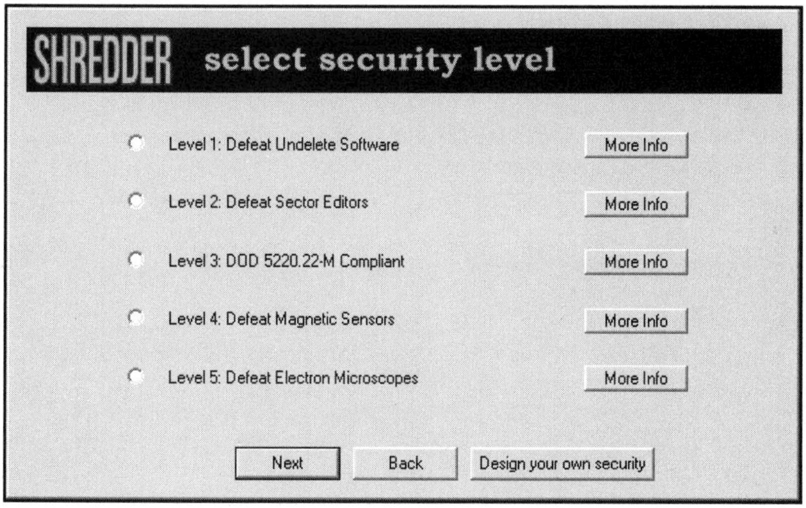

Figure 19-2
A file shredder can offer you different ways to shred your files, giving you a choice between speed and security.

For additional security, file shredders make multiple passes over a deleted file; the more passes, the longer the deletion takes, but the more likely you'll delete all data beyond hope of recovery. The Department of Defense (DoD) even has its own shredding standard, dubbed DoD 5220.22-M (http://www.dss.mil/isec/nispom.htm), which defines the government standards for deleting computer files.

The DoD file-shredding technique wipes a file seven times, each pass replacing the deleted data with a different set of random data. Since each additional pass adds another layer of random data to obscure the original, seven passes can virtually destroy all traces of the original file, although it will always be possible to recover data later using a magnetic sensor or electron microscope (discussed below).

Shredding temporary, web cache, email, and slack-space files

If you shred your sensitive files, don't forget to delete all your temporary and web cache files too. Many file shredders, such as 12Ghosts Wash (http://www.12ghosts.com) or the Macintosh-based ShredIt (http://www.mireth.com/pub/sime.html), can automatically find and destroy these types of files. BCWipe (http://www.jetico.com) can even wipe the slack space of specified files and simultaneously delete temporary and web cache files.

For further security, you can even configure some file shredders, such as the Macintosh-based NetShred (http://www.mireth.com) and the Windows-based Evidence Eliminator (http://www.evidence-eliminator.com), to delete your old email messages.

If you're really paranoid, shred your files and then defragment your hard drive. Then shred the free space remaining on your hard drive to get rid of any traces of files you don't want others to find.

Integrating a shredder into your operating system

Loading the file shredder every time you want to delete a file can be a nuisance, and you may not use it as often as you need to. Fortunately, file shredders such as Shredder95/98/NT (http://www.gale-force.com), CyberScrub (http://www.cyber-scrub.com), and Shred-X (http://www.bsoft.ic24.net) can integrate themselves into your operating system so that when you delete a file, the file shredder automatically shreds the file without any additional effort on your part.

Shredding swap files

One particularly vulnerable area of your computer is the *swap file*. A swap file allocates part of your hard disk for storing data so the computer can free up room in random access memory (RAM) for other programs that may be running.

Any time you run a program such as a word processor, your operating system may temporarily store your data in the swap file. When you save or delete the document, much of your information still remains in the swap file for anyone to look at. For complete protection, make sure you shred your swap file regularly (ideally, every time you turn off your computer) with a file shredder such as AbsoluteShield File Shredder (http://www.sys-shield.com).

Panic-mode shredding

Your file shredder may work perfectly if you methodically delete incriminating files. But what happens if you're sitting at your computer and the police suddenly barge into your house? Some file shredders offer a *panic mode* for just such emergencies. To use it, you define ahead of time which files and directories you want to delete in an emergency; then, you assign a unique keystroke combination to activate the panic mode (see Figure 19-3).

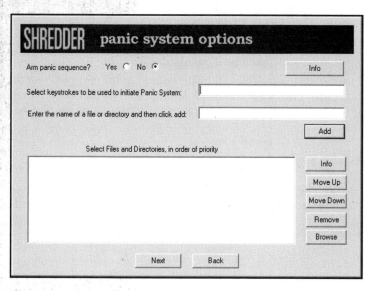

Figure 19-3
Many file shredders offer a panic mode to wipe out your files quickly in an emergency.

When the police (or other unwanted authorities) break in, press your magic panic-mode keystroke and the file shredder starts deleting all your predefined important files. If you're serious about protecting your privacy, a panic-mode feature is essential.

Password protecting your shredder

Since file shredders make undeleting files nearly impossible, they can be powerful weapons in the hands of a particularly malicious person. Just run a file shredder on your enemy's computer and you can irreparably shred the contents of an entire hard disk in minutes. Even worse than having someone deliberately shred your files is if you accidentally shred files you really wanted to keep.

To protect against an enemy or your own clumsiness, some file shredders offer a password protection feature. Before you can shred any files, you have to type in your password. Not only does this keep you from shredding your own files by mistake, but it also keeps your enemies from turning your file shredder against you.

CAUTION: Password protection can stop you from accidentally deleting any files, but you wouldn't want this feature turned on if you might need to use panic-mode shredding to delete a bunch of files instantly.

Writing your own file shredder

If you want to see exactly how a file shredder works, download the source code to the file shredder called Eraser (http://www.tolvanen.com/eraser), written by Sami Tolvanen. Not only is this file shredder absolutely free for anyone to use, but it also includes Microsoft Visual C++ source code, so you can examine how it works and even customize the program for your own particular needs.

Linux users can download a file-deleting program called Wipe (http://gsu.linux.org.tr/wipe). Like Eraser, Wipe is free to use and includes C source code so you can see how the program works and modify the program to add new features if you want.

Self-destructing email

Email can form a long incriminating trail of evidence, so you should also delete your email regularly and shred your email message directories. Since this can be a nuisance, several companies have come up with self-destructing email. The idea is that after a certain amount of time, the email message either shreds itself (using a secure file-shredding method that can defeat ordinary undelete programs) or encrypts itself so it can't be read after a certain date.

Omniva (http://www.disappearing.com) offers a unique self-destructing version of email. When you send a message to someone and run the Omniva Policy Manager program, you receive a unique encryption key from the Omniva Access server. Using this key, you can encrypt your message and send it out on the Internet. When someone wants to read your email, the email has to get the encryption key from the Omniva Access server, which opens the message.

However, once the expiration date of the message has passed, the Omniva Access server destroys the encryption key needed to open the message, effectively locking out anyone who tries to read the message ever again. In this case, the email isn't physically destroyed, but is rendered useless.

Another company that offers self-destructing email is Infraworks (http://www.infraworks.com), which offers a program called InTether. The InTether program consists of a Receiver and a Packager. To send a file (text, video, audio, etc.), you encrypt it using the Packager program. To read, view, or hear the file, another person needs the Receiver program. After a specified date, or after someone opens the file a certain number of times, the Receiver package can delete and shred the file.

While self-destructing email can protect your information in transit and at its final destination, it still won't protect prying eyes from finding traces of your data on the computer where you created the email in slack space, temporary files, and swap files. Self-destructing email can be one step to protecting your privacy, but don't count on it to protect your privacy all by itself.

FINDING ~~DELETED~~ DATA

No matter how many times you've deleted a file, or what methods you may have used, there will always be a way to retrieve it again. While you could extract an overwritten file's data by analyzing its magnetic traces on your hard disk (discussed below), it's far easier to look for electronic traces of it.

The keyboard buffer

Most operating systems store everything you type in a portion of memory called the *keyboard buffer*, so when you create a text document (containing all the subversive actions you plan to take against your government, for example), the keyboard buffer temporarily stores this information in your computer's memory. When you close the file, your computer clears the keyboard buffer by dumping its contents into a temporary copy of that particular file, which you can then view with a computer forensics tool (discussed below).

So if you're trying to get rid of evidence, simply encrypting or deleting a file won't be enough. Encryption or file deletion protects your final file, but it does nothing to hide or erase information dumped in any temporary files created along the way. To ensure you are not incriminated by the keyboard buffer, use your favorite file shredder to delete any temporary files stored on your hard disk.

Cleaning your web browser cache

When you search the Internet, your web browser stores (caches) the web pages you visit in a directory on your hard disk called the *cache directory*. Since the cache directory records all the websites you've visited in the last two weeks, it can leave behind an incriminating trail if you've been visiting sites you're not supposed to visit.

In case you're curious what kind of information someone might find in your web browser cache, run a program such as Cache Auditor (http://www.webknacks.com) for Internet Explorer or Cache, Cookie & Windows Cleaner (http://www.molecule-soft.com) for either Internet Explorer or Netscape. Cache, Cookie & Windows Cleaner shows the contents of your cache files, so anyone can see which web pages you've looked at in the past few days.

Other cache-purging programs include Cache and Cookie Washer (http://www.webroot.com), and IEClean or NSClean (http://www.nsclean.com), which can clean up the cache in Internet Explorer and Netscape. Macintosh users can try MacWasher (http://www.webroot.com) If you're a Windows user running AOL, Internet Explorer, Netscape, or even Opera, try the Complete Cleanup (http://members.aol.com/softdd) program for purging your cache files.

Just remember that purging the cache simply deletes the files and won't physically remove them—anyone can undelete your erased cache directory file later. (For more security, use a file shredder instead, as discussed earlier in the chapter.)

If you think purging your cache, deleting old email messages, wiping out temporary files, and shredding all your files is too much trouble, guess what? That's exactly what computer forensics experts are counting on when they examine a suspect's computer.

COMPUTER FORENSICS TOOLS

Depending on the seriousness of the crime and the skill of the criminal, computer forensics experts generally rely on four basic tools when searching for incriminating data: file undeleting programs, hex editors, magnetic sensors, and electron microscopes.

File undeleting programs

File undeleting programs, readily available in utility programs like Norton Utilities, are often sufficient to catch novices or people unfamiliar with the way computers work. As described previously, they work by renaming undeleted files (if they have not yet been overwritten by your system) so that your system will recognize them again. These programs only work if the files have not been overwritten on your hard disk, so undeleting programs are a relatively weak forensics tool.

Hex editors

If the suspect has deleted files and has overwritten them on his or her hard disk, you can always use a *hex editor* to view any data stored in (or deleted from) both files and disk sectors. A hex editor allows you to peek at the physical contents stored on a disk, regardless of the boundaries of files, directories, or partitions. Hex editors are often used to crack copy-protected software, study how computer viruses work, or in the case of forensics, identify and retrieve information that can't normally be accessed by the operating system.

To understand how hex editors can work, you need to know that all information saved on a hard disk gets recorded in *tracks*, which are concentric rings on the surface of each hard disk platter, like the rings in a tree trunk. Each track is subdivided into sectors, which typically holds 512 bytes of data. These disk sectors are particularly important because they store the keyboard buffer. Figure 19-4 shows a hex editor at work. Hex editors read this physical medium directly and don't rely on operating system services to read "files."

NOTE: For some great online information about how computers work, visit Charles Kozierok's "The PC Guide" at http://www.pcguide.com.

Forensics experts generally use a hex editor to search for evidence in specific parts of a disk—trying to use a hex editor to examine an entire hard disk would be like scouring the inside of a skyscraper for fingerprints. Still, hex editors can often recover

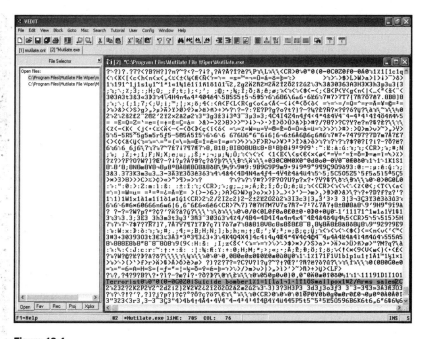

Figure 19-4

A hex editor like VEDIT can display the hidden contents of any disk sector or file.

some or all of the data in a deleted file that you might not otherwise be able to access. To see what a hex editor can find on your hard disk, download and try one of the following:

Hex Workshop	http://www.bpsoft.com
UltraEdit	http://www.idmcomp.com
VEDIT	http://www.vedit.com

Magnetic sensors and electron microscopes

Every file you save leaves magnetic traces on the disk it was saved on. By measuring the changes in magnetic fields on a disk, forensics experts using *magnetic sensors* can reconstruct part or even all of a deleted file—or they can use an electron microscope (expensive, but available to many governments).

Electron microscopes can measure tiny changes in magnetic fields that not even overwriting a file can completely obliterate. Because each time the computer overwrites a file the disk heads may not be aligned directly over the file, fragments of the deleted and overwritten file may remain, which an electron microscope can detect.

Disk splicing

No matter how many times you overwrite a file, or format and partition a hard disk, traces of your original data may still remain. File shredders simply make it progressively more expensive and difficult to retrieve data, but not impossible.

Under the illusion that they'll have complete protection, many people burn floppy or hard disks, crush and mangle them, cut them into pieces, pour acid on them, and otherwise physically manhandle them so that there's no possible way they could ever be used by another computer again. Unfortunately, physical destruction of floppy and hard disks still can't guarantee that your data will be safe, since government agencies such as the FBI and CIA practice a specialized technique known as *disk splicing*.

With disk splicing, someone physically rearranges the pieces of a floppy or hard disk so that it is as close as possible to its original condition. Then they use magnetic sensors or electron microscopes to scan for traces of information still stored on the disk surface.

Obviously, disk splicing is a time-consuming and expensive procedure, so don't expect that your local police force will have the knowledge, skill, or equipment to do it. But if you've destroyed evidence that involves national government agencies such as the NSA, CIA, or FBI, don't expect a mangled disk to hide your secrets from the prying electronic eyes of rich and powerful government agencies either. In fact, the American government even has a special laboratory called Computer Forensics Laboratory (http://www.dcfl.gov), located in Linthicum, Maryland, that specializes in retrieving information from computers, no matter what condition the hardware or disks may be in.

The ultimate lesson is that if you don't want to risk having certain information retrieved from your hard or floppy disk no matter what precautions you may have taken, don't store that information on a computer.

EXPERIMENTING WITH FORENSICS TOOLS

With so many different ways to leave behind a trail of incriminating evidence, you may want to examine your own hard disk for ways that someone could use your data against you.

Free forensics tools

To experiment with a variety of free forensics tools, visit AntiOnline (http://www.antionline.com) or the New Technologies site (http://www.forensics-intl.com/download.html). For example, the dirsnp program can recover previously deleted files, the dd program can read individual sectors off a disk and display their contents, and the readit program can search a file for a particular word or phrase, such as "nuclear missile," "nerve gas," or the name of your boss's mistress.

Since recovered files often contain non-alphanumeric characters (such as smiley faces, triangles, or odd mathematical symbols), the filter program can screen out such useless characters, allowing you to see more clearly the actual data buried inside. To preserve the contents of a suspect's computer, the disable program can turn off the keyboard.

Commercial forensics tools

To learn about some of the tools law enforcement agencies might use against you, visit the Digital Intelligence Inc. website (http://www.digitalintel.com), which sells a unique forensics tool called Drivespy. Drivespy accesses physical drives using pure BIOS (Int13 or Int13x) calls. Not only does this allow Drivespy to access both DOS and non-DOS partitions, but it also ensures that you won't risk having the operating system modify or erase data (such as modifying the swap file) during normal use.

Drivespy lets you do the following:

→ Examine hard disk partitions using a built-in Sector (and Cluster) hex viewer

→ Copy files to a designated work area without altering file access or modification dates

→ Unerase files to a designated work area without altering file access or modification dates

→ Search drives, partitions, and files for text strings or data sequences

→ Store all the slack space of an entire partition to a file for examination

→ Save and restore one or more contiguous sectors to or from a file

For those who need more power than Drivespy offers, Digital Intelligence also sells dedicated computer forensics workstations (whimsically dubbed FRED, for Forensic Recovery of Evidence Device) and a portable version called FREDDIE (for Forensic Recovery of Evidence Device Diminutive Interrogation Equipment). If you ever see the police hauling a FRED or FREDDIE into your computer room, you'll know that they'll be able to copy data from any hard disk or any other removable storage device, such as Zip disks; create images of your entire hard disk; connect directly to your computer and monitor any communications that your friends may be trying to send to you; examine any visible and hidden partitions for data; and capture video images from a camera to record the appearance and location of equipment at the scene of the crime.

You can also visit Guidance Software (http://www.guidancesoftware.com) to learn about its EnCase program. Not only can EnCase examine MS-DOS/Windows computers, but it can also examine Macintosh and Linux computers. EnCase can hook up to a target computer and scan the target computer's hard disk for graphic files (useful for hunting down child pornographers). Once it has retrieved all these graphic files and copied them to another computer, it can display or print the contents of these graphic files.

While searching graphic files may help find child pornography images, searching text and other files can help find evidence against ordinary criminals or terrorists.

Since their information is likely to be stored in word processor documents or email messages, EnCase can search a hard disk for all files that contain certain words or phrases. Once EnCase finds a file containing a specific word or phrase, it can list or copy those files for further examination.

To learn how the American and British governments may be using computer forensics tools to catch criminals, visit the websites of the Electronic Crimes Task Force (http://www.ectaskforce.org) and U.K.'s National Hi-Tech Crime Unit (http://www.nhtcu.org/nhtcu.htm).

PROTECTING YOURSELF

Even if you use a file-shredding program consistently, law enforcement officials can always use a variety of computer forensics tools to pry out any secrets your deleted files may be hiding. So how can you protect your computer from their prying eyes? Basically, you can't. While you can make recovering data harder by periodically purging your cache directory and only storing files on removable disks (such as floppy or ZIP disks) and physically destroying them afterwards, just remember that everything you do on your computer can be recovered and examined later.

Even if you use encryption, guess what? Any information that you encrypt could still be stored in slack space or temporary files, which means a forensics expert can avoid your encryption and uncover your information by finding the unencrypted version of your data elsewhere on your disks.

If you don't want your computer to incriminate you, learn what computer forensics experts are capable of recovering. Experiment with some of the free or commercial forensics tools to recover data on your computer, or see what you can find on other people's computers. Try secretly examining a coworker's computer. You might learn how to better protect your own data.

20

PROTECTING YOUR COMPUTER

YOUR DATA MAY BE THE MOST IMPORTANT PART OF YOUR COMPUTER, BUT THAT DOESN'T MEAN YOU CAN AFFORD TO LOSE YOUR COMPUTER EITHER. No matter how inexpensive computers may get, nobody wants to buy a second computer if they can keep their first one. To keep your computer from disappearing, spend a little extra time and money so that your computer doesn't wind up slipping out of your hands and into the hands of a thief.

    Besides using a little common sense, such as never leaving your laptop computer unattended, you can take some extra precautions, such as locks or alarms. If someone does happen to get your computer, you may be able to find it again with a tracking device. To make a thief's life even more miserable, you may also want to invest in a biometric device that only allows you, or a select group of people you choose, to use your computer.

I thought that a Jewish state would be free of the evils afflicting other societies: theft, murder, prostitution . . . But now we have them all. And that's a thing that cuts to the heart. . . .

—GOLDA MEIR

LOCKING UP YOUR COMPUTER

The simplest way to keep your computer from disappearing is to lock it down with a cable. Most laptop computers have a security slot that can hold a cable, while desktop computers often require a special plate that attaches to the side of the computer, monitor, or desk (see Figure 20-1) with glue.

    Security cables, like bicycle locks, can deter novices and probably slow down opportunistic thieves, but they can't stop determined ones. Given enough time, ordinary nail polish remover can dissolve the adhesives used to glue the cable attachments to the computer, and laptop security locks can be broken with a few well-placed blows from a hammer. As a faster alternative, thieves may just snip the restraining cable in half with a pair of wire cutters.

    Besides locking down your computer, make sure you lock any doors and windows that can allow access to your computer in the first place. The more barriers (motion detection alarms, guard dogs, strong door and window locks, etc.) you put in the way of a thief, the less likely a thief will want to overcome all of them.

    For further protection against theft, make sure you record your computer's model number, make, and serial number in a safe place. Then if someone does steal your computer, you can enter the stolen computer's information into the Stolen

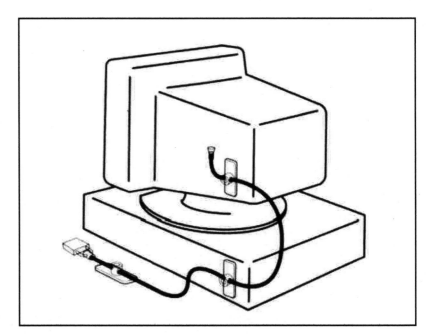

Figure 20-1

A restraining cable can lock your computer to an immovable object, such as a desk.

Computer Registry (http://www.stolencomputers.org), a free service that maintains a database of stolen computers. If someone finds your stolen computer, the Stolen Computer Registry can help get it back to you.

For additional protection, use an etching pen to scratch your driver's license number or other identification on the inside of the computer case (where thieves won't likely find it) or on the outside of the computer case (to reduce the value of the equipment, since the thieves must remove that identification before they can resell it).

PROTECTING YOUR COMPUTER PARTS

Sometimes stealing an entire computer may be too obvious or difficult, but stealing the components inside may be a lot easier. After all, anyone can tell when a computer suddenly disappears from a desk, but who will notice when a computer suddenly loses a hard drive, a video card, an external Zip drive, a trackball, or a memory chip?

To stop someone from walking off with an external device, such as an external hard drive or computer speakers, you can glue a metal plate to each item, thread a computer security cable through these plates, and anchor everything to your computer.

Anti-theft cases

Of course, computer cables may stop someone from stealing the computer, but they may not stop them from opening up the computer case and stealing everything inside. To prevent someone from opening up your computer, you can buy a protective computer cover, which looks like a metal case that fits and locks over your computer. Such protective metal cases deter theft of both the computer itself and any internal components.

To some people, a metal protective case can look ugly and take up space. So rather than cover your computer in a metallic shell, you may just want to get a lock that attaches to the back of your computer, which prevents anyone from opening up the case (but it won't stop anyone from stealing the entire computer).

For another alternative to a protective metal case, you can get a security pad that attaches to a fixed object, such as a desk, and then uses glue to hold the computer (or any other item of value, such as a copying machine or a laser printer) on top of the security pad.

While many people worry about outside hackers breaking into their computers and wiping out their data, the truth is that many hacker attacks come from people who already have legitimate access to the computer, such as coworkers, consultants, or technicians. To prevent insiders from accessing your computer to steal data or to slip a virus or Trojan horse onto your computer, you can also buy protective disk drive locks. These disk drive locks simply cover the front of the disk drive and stop anyone from using that floppy, Zip, or CD drive.

To learn more about physical security devices, such as cables, locks, and protective covers, visit the websites of the following companies:

Compucage	http://www.compucage.com
Compu-Gard	http://www.compu-gard.com
Computer Security Products	http://www.computersecurity.com
FMJ/PAD.LOCK	http://www.fmjpadlock.com
Kensington	http://www.kensington.com
PC Guardian	http://www.pcguardian.com
Secure-It	http://www.secure-it.com
Security Solutions	http://www.securitysolutions.ca

Alarms

An alarm can act as a deterrent to any type of theft, because the last thing a thief wants is noise that draws attention. Many companies make motion-detection alarms that plug into an ordinary expansion slot in the computer and run off their own power, so they can work whether the computer is on or off. When the alarm detects abnormal motion that's likely due to someone moving the computer, the alarm shrieks out a high-pitched wail, scaring off the would-be thief.

For those serious about protecting their computer, consider a unique product by Barracuda Security Devices (http://www.barracudasecurity.com) that works like the exploding dye capsules used by banks to foil heists. (These capsules give a warning, and then they explode, spraying ink over the money and the bank robber so the police can later identify the thief and trace any attempt to put the money into circulation.) The Barracuda Anti Theft Device fits into an internal expansion slot in a desktop computer and detects changes in internal ambient light, signaling that the case has been opened. If the cover is removed without disarming the device with a PIN, an alarm sounds and the device sprays indelible ink across all of the internal components, making them easy to identify as stolen and impossible to resell.

PROTECTING YOUR LAPTOP

In 2001, Safeware (http://www.safeware.com/losscharts.htm) estimated that thieves stole over 500,000 laptops for that year but only 15,000 desktop computers. Laptops make the most obvious and enticing targets because of their small size, light weight, and high resale value, so if you're traveling with a laptop in public, do your best to hide it.

Walk through any airport and you'll see many people carrying their laptops in distinctive black carrying cases, easily recognizable to a thief and nearly impossible to identify by sight if stolen. Instead of carrying your laptop in a case that screams out "Laptop! Steal me!" put it in an ordinary briefcase or backpack, or even in a paper shopping bag to disguise it as a souvenir from an overpriced airport gift shop.

If you're going to lose your laptop in an airport, the most likely place will be at the metal detectors. One person will step in front of you, loaded down with pockets full of metal objects (keys or coins), and wait until you pass your laptop on the conveyor belt for the X-ray machine. Then, while he beeps the metal detector and delays the passengers behind him (including you), an accomplice on the other side of the detector picks up your laptop at the end of the conveyer belt. By the time you get through the metal detector, your laptop is gone—in its unidentifiable black case.

To get through the airport security checkpoints, go in pairs. Have a friend get through it first who can grab your laptop when it gets through the X-ray machine. That way a thief won't be able to grab it first and run off with it.

Laptop alarms

But what if, despite your best efforts, your laptop gets stolen anyway? One option is to try an alarm, like the one sold by TrackIT (http://www.trackitcorp.com) or Caveo (http://www.caveo.com). Unlike desktop computer alarms, laptop alarms consist of two parts: a sensor attached to your laptop and another sensor carried by you (attached to your keychain or kept in your pocket). The moment your laptop gets separated from you by a fixed distance (such as 15 feet), an alarm in the laptop screams out. If this doesn't cause the thief to drop the laptop right away, it calls your attention to your laptop and allows you to follow its piercing whine to retrieve it.

If the thief does get away with the laptop, the motion detection alarm can password-protect and encrypt your hard disk. Now if a thief tries to use the laptop, the password prevents access and the encrypted hard disk prevents anyone from copying any data.

Remote tracking services

Another protective mechanism is a tracing or monitoring program that buries itself on your laptop computer's hard drive. Every time you connect to the Internet, the tracking program contacts a special server and sends the IP address of the current laptop computer's location. The moment you report your laptop stolen, the server waits for your laptop to contact it again. Once the server receives the IP address of the laptop computer's current location, the company contacts the authorities to help track down the missing laptop computer.

Some remote tracking programs even go one step further. Once they receive an IP address from the stolen laptop, the servers can send a command to the remote tracking program to shut off the speakers and search for a telephone line connection. Then the laptop silently dials a phone number that allows the server to trace the phone number to further pinpoint the laptop computer's location.

For added security, the server can also command the remote tracking software to encrypt your hard disk to prevent the thief from accessing any of your data. That way, even if you don't get your laptop back, at least you can rest assured that no one will be able to steal any data on your laptop either.

For more information about various remote tracking programs available for laptop computers, visit the following sites:

Absolute Protect	http://www.absolute-protect.com
Absolute Software	http://www.computrace.com
CyberAngel Security Solutions	http://www.sentryinc.com
zTrace Technologies	http://www.ztrace.com

BLOCKING ACCESS WITH BIOMETRICS

Locks can be broken and alarms can be disabled, so one way to block access to a computer is through *biometrics*, which uniquely identifies authorized users through their fingerprints, retina scans, or voices. The main advantage of biometrics is that they cannot be easily guessed, as poor passwords can. While any hacker can try obvious passwords like SEX or PASSWORD, it's much more difficult to duplicate someone else's fingerprint, retina, or voice. Biometrics works on the principle that every person has unique characteristics that are impossible to duplicate; even identical twins have different sets of fingerprints.

Typically a biometric device works like this. First, you have to store every authorized user's biometric data in the device, such as their fingerprints or retina scans. This creates a database that the biometric device can use to decide who to accept and who to reject.

Once you've given the biometric device a few samples of each person's data, you need to test the device to ensure that the biometric device can accurately identify each person. The biggest problem facing biometric devices is finding the proper balance between false acceptance and false rejection.

As the name implies, *false acceptance* means that the biometric device's criteria accepts too many variations as valid, so anyone whose fingerprint may be slightly similar to an authorized user may still be granted access. *False rejection* means that the biometric device's criteria are too narrow, which means that even authorized users may have trouble getting the biometric device to recognize them as valid users.

Biometric devices

Since most people pick simple passwords or forget their passwords altogether, some people have chosen to get rid of passwords altogether and rely on tokens or smart cards instead. A token or smart card contains information magnetically coded on a plastic card. When you insert the card into a reader device, the computer can tell whether you're authorized to use the computer. Of course, if someone happens to steal your smart card, they can get access and keep you locked out.

Since passwords can be guessed and both passwords and smart cards can be stolen, many people are pinning their hopes on biometric devices to restrict access to their computers. The most common biometric devices and the simplest to implement are fingerprint scanners. These scanners can come as separate units that connect to the computer through a cable or as PCMCIA cards that plug into a laptop computer.

To learn more about fingerprint biometric devices, visit these sites:

DigitalPersona	http://www.digitalpersona.com
KeyTronicEMS	http://www.keytronic.com
Precise Biometrics	http://www.precisebiometrics.com
Siemens	http://www.siemensidmouse.com
Utimaco Safeware	http://www.utimaco.com

Besides fingerprints, no two person's signatures are alike, so several companies market signature-recognition devices. For more information about signature-recognition devices, visit Communication Intelligence Corporation (http://www.cic.com) or Cyber-SIGN (http://www.cybersign.com).

Hook up a camera to your computer, and with the right software you can verify authorized users through face recognition. Users just have to stare into a camera, and once the computer recognizes them as an authorized user, they can get access to the computer. One company that sells face-recognition software is Identix (http://www.identix.com). To learn more about face recognition, visit the face-detection algorithm demonstration by the Robotics Institute (http://vasc.ri.cmu.edu/cgi-bin/demos/findface.cgi). Just upload photographs of different people so you can see how accurately the face-recognition algorithm correctly identifies the same face in different poses and backgrounds.

Offering a unique twist to biometrics, Real User (http://www.realuser.com) offers a program called PassFaces. Instead of forcing people to remember obscure passwords and spell them correctly, PassFaces lets users pick a unique face as their password. When they want access to the computer, the computer flashes several different faces on the screen and the user must choose the right face.

Iridian Technologies (http://www.iridiantech.com) offers an even more exotic biometric device that scans the retina of users' eyes to identify authorized users. Rather than rely on a single biometric measurement, SAFlink (http://www.saflink.com) uses voice, face, and fingerprint recognition to identify authorized users through an ordinary digital camera, microphone, and fingerprint reader. Another company, BioID (http://www.bioid.com), uses face, voice, and lip-movement recognition to identify authorized users. If someone fools one biometric device, they probably won't be able to fool the second or third one at the same time.

For more information about security in general, from protecting your possessions to guarding yourself on the streets, visit Ardent Security Solutions (http://www.security-solutions.com) or the National Security Institute (http://nsi.org). For specific information about protecting the security of your computer and data, visit the Computer Security Institute (http://www.gocsi.com).

Defeating biometrics

The theory is that no one can duplicate a fingerprint, signature, or face scan of another person, so biometrics should be the answer to securing access to a computer, right? Wrong.

Biometrics can be fooled. Besides the cruder methods that involve holding a gun to an authorized user's head and making him scan his retina into the computer, or simply cutting off a person's finger and using the decapitated fingertip to get past a fingerprint scanner, there are subtler, less violent ways to trick biometric devices.

When authorized users put their fingertip on a fingerprint scanner, the computer verifies their access and they walk away. Of course, their valid fingerprint still remains on the fingerprint reader device. Many fingerprint scanners can be fooled just by cupping your hands and breathing over the device to fog it up, which causes the residue of the authorized user's fingerprint to appear on the fingerprint scanner. The scanner sees this valid fingerprint once again and thereby gives you access.

To capture a valid fingerprint for future use, sprinkle graphite powder on the fingerprint scanner and then stick a piece of ordinary cellophane tape over the surface to capture the fingerprint on the sticky side of the tape. Now you can stick this piece of tape over the fingerprint scanner, which will recognize it as the fingerprint of a valid user.

Face-recognition devices are even simpler to fool. Just take a picture of an authorized user, hold that picture up to the camera that scans the face, and chances are good that the biometric facial recognition device will think you're a valid user when you're not. Fooling voice-recognition devices can be just as easy. Hide a tape recorder and stand near an authorized user speaking into the microphone. Then, play back this recording and you've got yourself a valid voiceprint that the biometric device will recognize.

Retina scanners can be fooled the same way, just as long as you can get a picture of an authorized user's retina. Hold the picture of the authorized user's retina in front of the camera, and chances are good that you'll fool the biometric retina scanner.

Perhaps the best way to fool any biometric device is to intercept the data going from the biometric reader to the computer. If you can sneak a hardware device such as USB Agent (http://www.hitex.demon.co.uk) in between the biometric device and the computer, you can intercept data from valid users. Then you can ignore the biometric device altogether and just use the USB Agent to feed the computer the data it expects from a valid user (see Figure 20-2).

Figure 20-2
The USB Agent can intercept and analyze data sent across a USB cable.

Another tool for intercepting data sent across a USB cable is USB Sniffer for Windows (http://usbsnoop.sourceforge.net) or USB Snoopy (http://home.jps.net/~koma). Both programs can snare data so you can analyze what a valid user's biometric data looks like to the computer.

No matter how advanced biometric devices may get, there will always be a way to fool them. Biometric tools can supplement security, but they can't substitute for it. To keep someone from fooling a biometric device, you need a guard to watch over the biometric device. Of course, if you can afford to station a guard by your computer, then you don't really need the biometric device.

All the protective locks, alarms, and biometric devices in the world can only deter a casual thief and slow down a determined one—you can never protect your computer with absolute security. As long as you remember that all protective devices are deterrents, you'll be able to balance security with your budget. But the moment you believe that security can be bought through the latest technology, that's when you're certain to be disappointed—and you'll probably be missing a laptop computer as well.

APPENDICES

A

SOFTWARE

TO HELP PROTECT YOUR COMPUTER AGAINST THE MANY HOSTILE THREATS ON THE INTERNET, HERE'S A LIST OF PROGRAMS THAT YOU MAY FIND HELPFUL IN DEFENDING YOURSELF. These programs include freeware, shareware, free trials, and demos of defensive programs. Whenever possible, we've listed the program's main site which you can visit for the latest version of the software.

PROGRAM TYPES

→ Freeware programs are free for you to use, copy, and distribute without license restrictions. (In some cases, they even include source code that you can study and modify.)

→ Shareware programs are "try before you buy." You get the full program but if you continue to use it you must pay for it.

→ Demoware and trialware are time limited or "crippled" versions of a piece of software. If you like the program you must buy the full version to continue to use it.

To save money, try the many freeware programs first. Many freeware programs offer equal (or better) protection than shareware or commercial software. For example, while BlackICE is a well-regarded (and excellent) firewall program, ZoneAlarm offers similar protection for free.

INSTALLATION SUPPORT

Since installing many of these programs may be tricky, we've made no attempt here to tell you how to install or troubleshoot them. Before you install a program, you should visit the program's website (listed with each program) and follow the software publisher's installation instructions.

Uncompressing, Unzipping, Unstuffing, and So On

Many of the programs you'll find on the Internet are compressed; you'll recognize the compressed files by their extensions.

→ .zip files are Windows files which may be "unzipped" with StuffIt Expander or WinZip.

→ .exe files are program files; double-click them from within Windows to extract them and run the application.

→ .sit and .sea files are Macintosh StuffIt files which may be "unstuffed" with StuffIt Expander.

→ .gz and .tar are gzipped or tarred Linux files which may be uncompressed with LinZip or tar.

You must expand or uncompress these programs before you can run them. Here's a list of useful tools for that purpose.

Utilities

Programs to expand compressed files.

Windows

Aladdin Expander Decompress, decode, convert, and access the most popular compression archive formats, including StuffIt (.sit), ZIP (.zip), UUencode (.uu), MacBinary (.bin), BinHex (.hqx), and more. Freeware. (http://www.aladdinsys.com)

WinZip A straightforward zipping and unzipping utility. Shareware. (http://www.winzip.com)

Macintosh

Aladdin Expander Decompress, decode, convert, and access the most popular compression archive formats, including StuffIt (.sit), ZIP (.zip), UUencode (.uu), MacBinary (.bin), BinHex (.hqx), and more. Freeware. (http://www.aladdinsys.com)

Aladdin DropStuff Compress, encrypt, and make self-extracting archives. Shareware. (http://www.aladdinsys.com)

Linux

LinZip   A full-featured compression utility. Shareware. (http://www.linzip.com)

tar   Compress and manipulate tar archives. Freeware.

ANONYMITY

Hide your identity with these programs.

Windows

No Referrer   Helps you surf anonymously by stripping out identifying information normally sent out by your computer. Freeware. (No installation support.)

Privacy Companion   Protects your privacy by alerting you when a website is trying to give your computer a cookie, which could be used to gather information about your computer. Works with Internet Explorer only. Freeware. (http://www.idcide.com/)

Private Idaho   Email utility program to help you encrypt your email using PGP and anonymous remailers. Freeware. (http://www.eskimo.com/~joelm/pi.html)

Macintosh

Cone of Silence   Prevents keystroke capturing programs from recording anything you type. Shareware. (http://www.parkbenchsoftware.com/)

Free Guard   Hides files and folders. Freeware. (http://www.msrwerks.com/applications.html)

VSE My Privacy   Encrypts private information, such as credit card numbers, passwords, confidential names and addresses, and so on, to keep it safe from prying eyes. Shareware. (http://www.vse-online.com)

ANTI-CON GAMES

Protects you from falling for Internet con games.

MegaHack   Cracks the Mega$Nets online pyramid scheme.

ANTI-SPYWARE

These programs block or disable advertiser-sponsored programs that could secretly transmit information about your computer over the Internet.

Windows

Ad-Aware   Helps detect and block advertiser-sponsored software (spyware) from retrieving information from your hard disk. (http://www.lavasoft.de)

Aureate/Radiate Remover   Removes the Radiate/Aureate spyware DLL files from your computer to prevent them from retrieving information from your hard disk. Advertiser-supported freeware. (http://www. radiate.com/privacy/remover. html)

FlowProtector   Blocks cookies, spyware, and Internet connections that could send data from your computer without your knowledge. Freeware. (http://www. flowprotector.com/usa)

OptOut   Removes the Aureate/Radiate DLL files that turn shareware into spyware. Freeware. (http://grc.com/optout.htm)

Silencer   Blocks communication between spyware and the server that the spyware is trying to send your data to. Freeware. (http://radsoft.net/bloat-busters/)

ANTI-TROJAN HORSE

These programs can help you detect, block, and remove remote access Trojan horse programs.

Windows

BODetect   A comprehensive Trojan horse detection and removal program. Shareware. (http://www.cbsoftsolutions.com/)

The Cleaner   Scans your system for Trojans. Shareware. (http://www.moosoft.com)

Jammer   Protects you against NetBus, Back Orifice 1.x, and BO2K. (http://www.agnitum.com/products/jammer/)

NetBus Remover   Finds and removes the NetBus Trojan horse that affects Windows 95/98/NT. Freeware. (No installation support.)

NetBuster   Detects and removes the NetBus Trojan horse. Will also create a fake NetBus connection to help you fool any hackers trying to access your computer using NetBus. Freeware. (http://surf.to/netbuster)

StartupMonitor   Monitors all programs that automatically start up when you boot up Windows. Use this to detect Trojan horse programs that may be secretly starting when you boot up. Freeware. (http://www.mlin.net/StartupMonitor.shtml)

Sub-Net 2.0   Trojan horse port scanner useful for analyzing and securing your Internet connection. Freeware. (http://www.sub-seven.com/freeware.shtml)

SubSeven Server Sniper   Detects and removes the SubSeven Trojan horse; can also trace an attacker over the Internet. Freeware. (http://subseven.slak.org)

Tauscan   Detects and removes remote access Trojans installed on your hard disk. Trialware. (http://www.agnitum.com/products/tauscan)

TDS: Trojan Defence Suite   Detects and removes hundreds of Trojan horses from your computer. Trialware. (http://www.diamondcs.com.au)

Trojans Database   Describes the most popular Trojan horses including their features and the ports they use to attack a computer. Freeware. (No installation support.)

Trojans First Aid Kit   Detects and removes hundreds of Trojan horses. Freeware. (http://www.snake-basket.de/)

Win Trinoo Server Sniper   Detects and removes the Trinoo Trojan, which can use your computer to launch a distributed denial-of-service attack against another computer. Freeware. (http://www.diamondcs.com.au)

ANTIVIRUS

These programs can detect, remove, and block viruses from infecting your computer.

Windows

eSafe   Multipurpose program that provides content filtering (so you can selectively block certain websites from users), an antivirus program, a desktop lockdown program (to prevent unauthorized access to your computer), and an anti-vandalism program to keep malicious worms and viruses from attacking your hard disk. Trialware. (http://www.ealaddin.com)

F-Prot   DOS-based antivirus program. Freeware. (http://www.f-secure.com/)

Mail Cleaner   Scans your Outlook or Outlook Express email for viruses hidden as file attachments. If it finds one, the program deletes the suspect email and notifies you of its action. Freeware. (http://www.mailcleaner.com)

Norton Antivirus 2000   Well-known leading antivirus program. Trialware. (http://symantec.com)

ScripTrap   Blocks the running of malicious scripts, such as viruses written with VBScript. Freeware. (http://keir.net/scriptrap.html)

Script Defender   Protects against all forms of malicious code (such as macro viruses) that run scripting languages such as VBScript or JavaScript. Freeware. (http://www.analogx.com)

SurfinGuard   Monitors programs for suspicious behavior; if malicious behavior is detected, SurfinGuard kills the suspect program. Freeware. (http://www.finjan.com)

Virus Trap   Helps detect and capture viruses by offering "bait" files for viruses to infect. Once a "bait" file has been infected, the program alerts you so you can send the trapped virus to an antivirus company for further analysis. Freeware. (http://www.diamondcs.com.au/)

Macintosh

Agax   An expandable, free antivirus program that offers both standard virus-scanning and more advanced background protection. Freeware. (http://www.defyne.org/agax/)

Disinfectant   Adds basic virus protection by scanning files when opened and monitoring your system for unusual activity. Freeware. (http://macinfo.its.queensu.ca/MacSDistribution/Disinfectant.html)

McAfee VirusScan   One of the most popular antivirus programs in the world. Shareware. (http://www.mcafee.com)

BULK EMAILERS

This program is typical of the type of programs that spammers use to flood email accounts with their advertisements.

Windows

Express Mail Server   A bulk emailing program. We don't like these any more than you do, but you might check out this example. Demoware. (http://www.homeuniverse.com)

CACHE AND COOKIE CLEANERS

Clean your browser's cache and wipe out any cookies with these programs.

Windows

AdSubtract SE   Selectively blocks unwanted ads or cookies. Free for personal use. (http://www.adsubtract.com)

Complete Cleanup   Deletes temporary files, cookies, and web cache files to guard your privacy. Trialware. (http://www.softdd.com)

Cookie Crusher   Automatically accepts or rejects cookies for you. Trialware. (http://www.thelimitsoft.com)

Cookie Pal   Manages your cookies. Shareware. (http://www.kburra.com)

CyberClean   Removes cookies, history files, bookmarks and cache files, and registry entries that refer to recently visited websites. Trialware. (http://www.thelimitsoft.com)

SurfSecret   Removes cookies and Internet surfing debris. Trialware. (http://www.surfsecret.com)

Window Washer   Cleans up any files created by your browser, such as cookies or lists of recently visited websites, to prevent others from tracking your Internet usage. Trialware. (http://www.webroot.com)

Macintosh

MacWasher   Cleans up cookies or lists of recently visited websites to prevent others from tracking your Internet usage. Trialware. (http://www.webroot.com)

DESKTOP SECURITY

Generate secure passwords and protect your computer while you're away with these programs.

Windows

Password Generator   Generates random passwords. Freeware. (http://ben-jaminsoftware.hypermart.net/)

ISS Complock II   Password-protects your computer to prevent someone from booting it up without your knowledge. Shareware. (http://www.techniclabs.com/)

Magic Folders   Hides files and folders from view to keep a thief from finding them. Shareware. (http://www.pc-magic.com/)

Quicky Password Generator   Helps you create a unique and difficult-to-guess password (which may also be difficult to remember). Freeware. (http://www.quickysoftware.com)

PGP Desktop Security   Protects your data across your network and the Internet by encrypting information in email, hard drives, and more. Trialware. (http://www.mcafee.com)

Security Officer   In addition to monitoring the programs run on your computer, this program can also protect your files from being modified or deleted. Shareware. (http://www.compelson.com)

WinGuardian   Logs all programs run along with keystrokes typed in each program. Trialware. (http://www.webroot.com)

DISASSEMBLERS

These programs can tear a program apart and reveal its assembly language source code so you can see how the program works.

Windows

IDA Pro Disassembler   Shows you the assembly language source code of an executable file. Demoware. (http://www.datarescue.com)

Letun Disassembler   Disassembles Windows executable files. Shareware.

DNS LOOKUP

Verify a domain's existence with these tools.

Cyberkit   Ping, TraceRoute, WhoIs, Finger, and more in one easy-to-use utility. Postcardware. (http://www.cyberkit.net)

DNS Workshop   Converts between IP addresses and Internet host names. Trialware. (http://www.evolve.co.uk/dns)

Domain Searcher   Searches for and investigates domain names. Trialware. (http://www.igsnet.com/igs/dsearch.html)

ENCRYPTION CRACKER

Crack files encrypted with DES.

BrydDES   Brute force cracker for the DES encryption algorithm. Freeware. (No installation support.)

FILE ENCRYPTION

These programs will scramble your data using a variety of algorithms, to keep your files safe.

Windows

Absolute Security   Protects the confidentiality of sensitive information. Shareware. (http://www.pepsoft.com)

Blowfish-C   C source code implementation of the Blowfish encryption algorithm. Freeware. (http://www.counterpane.com)

Blowfish-Java   Java source code implementation of the Blowfish encryption algorithm. Freeware. (http://www.counterpane.com)

CuteZip   Compression utility that includes 128-bit encryption using the Twofish algorithm. Trialware. (http://www.cuteftp.com/products/cutezip/)

Encrypted Magic Folders   Hides files and folders and protects them with encryption. Shareware. (http://pc-magic.com/)

GNU Privacy Guard   A complete and free replacement for PGP. Freeware. (http://www.gnupg.org)

Kryptel Lite   A free version of Kryptel, a file encryption program. Freeware. (http://inv.co.nz)

PC-Encrypt   Encrypts and compresses any type of file used in Windows 95/98 and NT. Shareware. (http://www.pc-encrypt.com)

PGP   The popular PGP encryption program for protecting your files. Freeware. (http://www.pgpi.org)

PGP Personal Privacy   Protects your email, files, folders, disk volumes, and network communication from prying eyes with one integrated product. Trialware. (http://www.mcafee.com)

ScramDisk   Encrypts your hard disk with various encryption algorithms including IDEA, Blowfish, DES, and Square. Freeware. (http://www.scramdisk.clara.net/)

Twofish-C   C source code implementation of the Twofish encryption algorithm. Freeware. (http://www.counterpane.com/twofish.html)

Twofish-Java   Java source code implementation of the Twofish encryption algorithm. Freeware. (http://www.counterpane.com)

Twofish-VB   Visual Basic source code implementation of the Twofish encryption algorithm. Freeware. (http://www.counterpane.com/twofish.html)

Macintosh

PGP   The popular PGP encryption program for protecting your files. Freeware. (http://www.pgpi.org)

Tresor   File encryption program for protecting individual files and entire folders using IDEA. Shareware. (http://warlord.li/)

VSE My Privacy   Encrypts private information, such as credit card numbers, passwords, confidential names and addresses, and so on, to keep it safe from prying eyes. Shareware. (http://www.vse-online.com)

Linux

GNU Privacy Guard   A complete and free replacement for PGP. Freeware. (http://www.gnupg.org)

PGP   The popular PGP encryption program for protecting your files. Freeware. (http://www.pgpi.org)

FILE INTEGRITY CHECKERS

These programs can help you detect changes in your files that could indicate a hacker has gotten into your computer.

Windows

Veracity   A network intrusion detection tool that uses cryptography to detect unauthorized changes to files. Trialware. (http://www.veracity.com)

Macintosh

Veracity   A network intrusion detection tool that uses cryptographics to detect unauthorized changes to files. Trialware. (http://www.veracity.com)

Linux

Tripwire   Monitors and protects your data against changes. Freeware. (http://www.tripwire.com)

Veracity   A network intrusion detection tool that uses cryptographics to detect unauthorized changes to files. Trialware. (http://www.veracity.com)

FILE SHREDDERS

These programs can securely delete files to prevent all but the best-funded authorities from recovering your data.

Windows

BCWipe   Shreds your files and disks to eliminate traces of your data. Free for non-commercial use. (http://www.jetico.com)

CyberScrub   Securely shreds and deletes confidential files beyond recovery. Shareware. (http://www.cyberscrub.com)

Eraser   File shredder with Visual C++ source code. Freeware. (http://www.tolvanen.com/eraser)

Evidence Eliminator   Securely shreds files and disks. Defeats forensic analysis software. Trialware. (http://www.evidence-eliminator.com)

Shredder 95/98/NT   Completely destroys files and even free space beyond any hope of recovery. Shareware. (http://www.gale-force.com/shredder)

Shred-It   Shreds your files and folders beyond recovery. (http://www.mireth.com)

Shred-X   Removes all traces of your files. Shareware. (http://www.bsoft.ic24.net)

Macintosh

Burn   File shredder to keep your deleted files from being recovered. Freeware. (http://www.thenextwave.com/burnHP.html)

NetShred   Shreds your web cache and other related files to prevent someone from tracking your Internet usage. Shareware. (http://www.arccom.bc.ca)

Shred-It   Shreds files and folders beyond recovery. Shareware. (http://www.mireth.com)

Linux

Wipe   Includes C source code. Freeware. (http://gsu.linux.org.tr/wipe)

FORENSICS

These programs can retrieve information from deleted files and formatted disks.

Windows

Directory Snoop   Recovers erased files and data from individual clusters. Can also wipe sensitive data from a disk to prevent recovery. Shareware. (http://www.briggsoft.com/dsnoop.htm)

File Scavenger   Scans a disk to find previously deleted files that can still be recovered. Shareware. (http://www.quetek.com/)

NTIDoc   Lists all files and creation dates and times stored in a directory. Freeware. (http://www.secure-data.com)

Omniquad Detective   Searches and examines a hard disk for information. Shareware. (http://www.omniquad.com)

HEX EDITORS

Programs that peek inside files and disk sectors so you can see what's inside them or so you can modify their contents.

Windows

FRHED   Windows-based hex editor with Microsoft Visual C++ source code. Freeware. (http://www.kibria.de)

Freeware Hex Editor   Hex editor for peeking inside files and disk clusters. Freeware. (http://www.chmaas.handshake.de/delphi/freeware/xvi32/xvi32.htm)

Hex Workshop   A powerful hex editor for examining the contents of files and disk clusters. Shareware. (http://www.bpsoft.com)

UltraEdit   Hex editor with a dictionary for spell-checking. Trialware. (http://www.idmcomp.com)

VEDIT   Hex editor that can edit files up to 2 gigabytes in size. Includes a manual stored as an Acrobat PDF file. Trialware. (http://www.vedit.com)

HONEYPOT TRAPS

Programs to help you catch and counterattack hackers.

Windows

NetBuster   Detects and removes the NetBus Trojan horse. Will also create a fake NetBus connection to help you fool any hackers trying to access your computer using NetBus. Freeware. (http://surf.to/netbuster)

Tambu UDP Scrambler   Watches ports for hacker probes and floods attackers with a flurry of messages. Freeware. (http://www.xploiter.com/tambu)

INTRUSION DETECTION

These programs can help you block or monitor the ports on your computer to determine if a malicious hacker is trying to access or probe your computer.

Windows

Anti-Hack   Monitors your open ports to detect unauthorized access attempts. Shareware. (http://www.carbosoft.com/anti-hack.htm)

AntiSniff   Detects port sniffing on a network. Freeware. (http://www.atstake.com/)

Attacker   Monitors your ports for suspicious behavior and notifies you when someone tries to connect to your computer through a Trojan. Freeware. (http://www.keir.net/)

BlackICE Defender   Intrusion detection and a personal firewall. Demoware. (http://www.networkice.com/)

Jammer   Monitors ports on your computer to detect attempted break-ins. Shareware. (http://www.agnitum.com/jammer)

McAfee Personal Firewall   Secures your computer from hackers. Trialware. (http://www.mcafee.com)

Netmon   Monitors your ports for suspicious behavior and detects the more common Trojan horses. Freeware. (http://members.tripod.com/circlet)

NukeNabber   Monitors your computer ports to alert you when someone may be trying to access your computer using a Trojan horse. Freeware. (http://www.dynamsol.com/)

Port Blocker   Blocks open ports on your computer to prevent them from being used by hackers or Trojan horses. Freeware. (No installation support.)

ProtectX   Monitors your ports to detect and remove any Trojan horses that could be used to access your computer. Shareware. (http://www.archimedean.com/)

Rainbow Diamond Intrusion Detection   Detects suspicious activity through your ports. Demoware. (http://www.brd.ie/)

SuperScan   Port scanner that probes your computer to detect any open ports that could be vulnerable to a remote attack, such as through a Trojan horse. Freeware. (http://www.keir.net/)

ZoneAlarm   Firewall that protects your computer from port scanners and remote access Trojans. Freeware. (http://www.zonelabs.com/)

Macintosh

TrashScan   Monitors the ports on your Macintosh to make sure an intruder isn't secretly accessing your computer over a network or the Internet. Freeware. (http://trashscan.hypermart.net)

IRC CLIENTS

These programs connect you to Internet Relay Chat (IRC) rooms so you can chat in real time with people all over the world.

Windows

mIRC   Very popular Windows IRC client. Shareware. (http://www.mirc.co.uk/)

Pirch98   Shareware. (http://www.pirchat.com)

Visual IRC   Easy-to-use IRC program. Donationware. (http://www.visualirc.net/)

Macintosh

Ircle   Popular Macintosh IRC client. Shareware. (http://www.ircle.com)

ShadowIRC   Open source IRC client. Shareware. (http://www.shadowirc.com)

Linux

Bitch-X   The most popular Linux IRC client. Free (GPL). (http://www.bitchx.com/)

ircit   IRCIT (IRC for the Information Terrorists) is a full-featured, text-mode, macro-extensible modern IRC client. Free (GPL). (http://www.asymmetrica.com/software/ircit/)

KEYSTROKE LOGGERS

See what others are doing with your computer in your absence.

Windows

2Spy   Logs all activity on your PC so you can see what others may be doing on your computer in your absence. Shareware. (http://www.zoranjuric.com)

AppsTraka   Records all programs run, when they were used, and all keystrokes typed to help you detect unauthorized users on your computer. Shareware. (http://appstraka.hypermart.net)

Ghost Keylogger   Secretly records keystrokes so you can see what someone may have been doing on your computer. Demoware. (http://www.keylogger.net)

iOpus STARR   Monitors the use or abuse of your PC. Shareware. (http://www.iopus.com/)

Key Interceptor   Logs all typed keys. Freeware. (http://www.ultrasoft.ro/)

KeyKey   Records keystrokes in Windows or a DOS box. Shareware. (http://mikkoaj.hypermart.net)

Omniquad Desktop Surveillance   Runs as an invisible agent, which unobtrusively captures keystrokes and records screen contents for replay. The program also compiles activity reports that include all user activities: websites, chat rooms, newsgroups, games, files, and folders. Trialware. (http://www.omniquad.com)

PC Activity Monitor   Records keystrokes to help you monitor what people are doing on a computer without your knowledge. Shareware. (http://www.key-loggers.com)

RedHand   Secretly monitors your computer to determine which programs someone may be using without your knowledge or permission. Can also limit users to performing only certain functions on a computer. Shareware. (http://www.harddrivesoftware.com)

Security Setup II   Restricts different users from accessing certain features, such as disabling the Control Panel and limiting users to running only certain programs. Shareware. (http://www.security-setup.dk)

WinWhatWhere Investigator   Quietly monitors and reports date, time started, time elapsed, program captions, and keystrokes. Shareware. (http://www.winwhatwhere.com)

Macintosh

Cone of Silence   Prevents keystroke capturing programs from recording what you type. Shareware. (http://www.parkbenchsoftware.com)

Free Guard   Hides files and folders. Freeware. (http://www.msrwerks.com/applications.html)

Keystroke Recorder   Records each keystroke into a file for later viewing. Shareware. (http://www.campsoftware.com/camp)

SuperLock Pro   Prevents unauthorized access to your Macintosh by recording any break-in attempts, sounding an alarm, automatically going into sleep mode, and stopping someone from rebooting your computer. Shareware. (http://www.trivectus.com)

MP3 TOOLS

These programs allow you to play or record MP3 files.

Windows

Audiograbber   Grabs music from CDs digitally. Freeware. (http://www.audio-grabber.com-us.net/)

AudioCatalyst   Transforms your CD files to MP3s. Shareware. (http://www.xingtech.com/mp3/audiocatalyst/)

CD'n'Go   Extracts and encodes digital MP3s. Freeware. (http://www.cdngo.com)

HyCD Play & Record   Lets you create your own MP3 audio CDs. Demoware. (http://www.hycd.com)

MP3 JumpGate   Lets you play, create, decode, and mix MP3s. Freeware. (http://www.worldusa.com/mp3/mp3studio.shtml)

MuzicMan   Organizes and plays MP3 files. Shareware. (http://www. muzicman.com)

Rosoft CD Extractor   Creates WAV and MP3 files. Advertiser-supported freeware. (http://www.theripper.com-us.net/)

Winamp   Popular MP3 player. Freeware. (http://www.winamp.com)

Macintosh

Macast Lite   Plays MP3 files on your Macintosh. Shareware. (http://www. macast.com/lite/)

SoundJam MP Free   MP3 player (encoding features are time-limited). Shareware. (http://www.soundjam.com)

Linux

cdparanoia   MP3 ripper. Freeware. (http://www.xiph.org/paranoia)

MPG123   A real-time MPEG audio player. Freeware. (http://www.mpg123.de/)

ripperX   Extract CD audio and encode it to MP3 format. Freeware. (http://rip-perx.sourceforge.net/)

PACKET SNIFFERS

Analyze information traveling across a network with these programs.

Windows

Sniffer   Intercepts and analyzes packets transmitted over a network. Network Sniffer can take plug-ins for different protocols, including IP, TCP, and UDP. Shareware. (http://www.ufasoft.com/)

TraceWolf Packet Sniffer   Opens all packets passing through your modem or Ethernet card and displays header and data fields. Demoware.

PARENTAL CONTROL

Limit and monitor Internet access and program use on your computer.

Windows

ENUFF   Limits and monitors computer use. Shareware. (http://www.akron-tech.com)

IamBigBrother   Filters what your kids can access on the Internet. Demoware. (http://www.chatnanny.com)

PASSWORD RECOVERY

These programs can recover forgotten passwords from password-protected files.

Windows

007 Password Recovery   Retrieves passwords hidden behind asterisks. Freeware. (http://www.iopus.com)

Advanced Zip Password Recovery   Retrieves a password from a password-protected ZIP file using bruteforce, dictionary, and plain text attacks. Shareware. (http://www.elcomsoft.com/azpr.html)

Fast Zip Cracker   Executes a brute force attack to retrieve a password from a password-protected ZIP file. (http://www.netgate.com.uy/~fpapa/)

John the Ripper   Password cracker to help you detect weak UNIX passwords. Freeware. (http://www.openwall.com/john)

Password Recovery Toolkit   Helps recover passwords from password-protected files created by a variety of popular programs including Quicken, Lotus 1-2-3, WordPerfect, and Outlook. Demoware. (http://www.lostpassword.com)

Passware Kit   Retrieves passwords from password-protected files created by programs such as Quattro Pro, Microsoft Money, Excel, and Windows NT. Demoware. (http://www.accessdata.com)

Peek-a-Boo   Retrieves a password hidden behind asterisks. Freeware. (http://www.corteksoft.com)

Revelation   Displays passwords hidden behind asterisks. Freeware. (http://www.snadboy.com)

The Ultimate Zip Cracker Retrieves the password for any password-protected ZIP, ARJ, Excel, or Word file. Shareware. (http://www.vdgsoftware.com/uzc.html)

Unix/Linux

John the Ripper Password cracker to help you detect weak UNIX passwords. (http://www.openwall.com/john/)

PORT SCANNERS

Analyze ports on your network and detect vulnerabilities with these programs.

Windows

AATools Scans a network for vulnerable computers and open ports. Shareware. (http://www.glocksoft.com)

AntiSniff Detects port sniffing on a network. Freeware. (http://www.l0pht.com/antisniff)

NetBrute Searches for shared resources, detects open ports on a computer or network, and tests a website for password security. Freeware. (http://www.rawlogic.com/products.html)

PortBlocker Blocks open ports on your computer to prevent them from being used by hackers or Trojan horses. Freeware. (http://www.analogx.com)

SATAN (Security Administrator Tool for Analyzing Networks) Recognizes several common networking-related security problems and reports the problems without actually exploiting them. Freeware. (http://www.fish.com/satan/)

TJ Ping Ping, traceroute, and lookup utility. Freeware. (http://www.topjimmy.net/tjs)

Linux

Nmap Linux-based port scanner regarded as the most comprehensive port scanner currently available. Freeware. (http://www.insecure.org)

Snort A lightweight network intrusion detection system, capable of performing real-time traffic analysis and packet logging on IP networks. C/C++ source code available. Freeware. (http://www.snort.org)

READERS

Disguise what you're reading by displaying the entire text of an ASCII document on your screen in large letters, one word at a time, at speeds up to 1,000 words per minute, so that it's virtually impossible for anyone to see at a glance what you're reading.

> **AceReader**   Read or skim text on your computer. Demoware. (http://www.stepware.com)

REMOTE MONITORING

These programs can help you remotely monitor a computer (such as your own) without the knowledge of anyone using it.

Windows

> **Spector Pro**   A remote access program that has moved away from its original remote access Trojan horse roots. The current version of the program allows you to control another computer from a remote location. Shareware. (http://www.netbus.org)

> **PC Spy**   Monitor your computer while you are away by capturing and saving screen images. Shareware. (http://www.softdd.com)

> **Q-Peek**   View the desktop of a computer from anywhere on the Internet or on your local network using a standard web browser. Shareware. (http://www.qpeek.com)

ROLLBACK PROGRAMS

These programs can return your computer to a previous state to help you recover from all types of malicious attacks such as virus, Trojan horse, or hacker attacks.

Windows

> **Aladdin FlashBack**   Saves all previous versions of your files so you can retrieve previously created or deleted data at any time. Trialware. (http://www.aladdinsys.com)

> **ConfigSafe**   Tracks changes in your computer so you can return to a previous state at any time. Demoware. (http://www.imagine-lan.com)

Macintosh

Aladdin FlashBack   Saves all previous versions of your files so you can retrieve previously created or deleted data at any time. Trialware. (http://www.aladdinsys.com)

SPAM FIGHTERS

These programs block or filter email to reduce or eliminate spam from clogging your email account.

Spam Buster   Advertiser-supported freeware. Filters your email to remove spam. (http://www.contactplus.com/)

SpamKiller   Filters your email to remove spam from known spamming addresses, while allowing email from a list of addresses that you define. Shareware. (http://www.spamkiller.com/)

SpammerSlammer   Tags suspected spam so you can delete or read it if you choose. Freeware. (http://www.n2plus.com/)

WebCrypt   Unique program that encrypts your HTML code so spammers can't retrieve email addresses from your website. Shareware. (http://www.moonlight-software.com)

STEGANOGRAPHY

Hide data in graphics or sound files with these programs.

Windows

dc-Steganograph   A very small DOS-based program that hides data in PCX images. Freeware. (http://members.tripod.com/~Nikola_Injac/stegano/)

Gif-It-Up   Hides data in GIF files. (No installation support.)

Hide and Seek Encrypts data using Blowfish and then hides it in GIF files. Freeware.

Hide4PGP   Works with PGP to encrypt and hide data in bitmap or sound files. Freeware. (http://www.heinz-repp.onlinehome.de/Hide4PGP.htm)

Hide in Picture   Hides and encrypts data in a bitmap file. Freeware. (http://www16.brinkster.com/davitf/hip/)

Invisible Secrets   Hides files in other files not usually suspected of encryption, including JPEG, PNG, and BMP. (http://www.invisiblesecrets.com/)

MP3Stego   Hides data in MP3 audio files. (Includes C source code.) Freeware. (http://www.cl.cam.ac.uk/~fapp2/steganography/mp3stego/)

S-Tools   Hides data in bitmap, GIF, or WAV files. Freeware. (http://members.tripod.com/steganography/stego/s-tools4.html)

Steganos Security Suite   Encrypts email using ordinary encryption or steganography to hide your email from prying eyes and can shred files beyond recovery. Trialware. (http://www.steganos.com)

wbStego   Hides data in graphic, ASCII, HTML, or Adobe Acrobat files. Trialware. (http://wbstego.wbailer.com/)

Java

Stego   Hides and recovers encrypted data in GIF files. Free (Open Source). (http://www.stego.com/)

SYSTEM LOCKS

These programs can keep unauthorized users from accessing your computer in your absence.

Windows

DesktopShield 2000   Secures your PC when you're not using it. Freeware. (http://www.dilawri.com/software/sysprotect/)

Workstation Lock   Password-protects your system at startup without using a screensaver. Shareware. (http://posum.com)

Macintosh

SuperLock Pro and **SuperLock Lite**   Prevents unauthorized access to your Macintosh by recording any break-in attempts, sounding an alarm, automatically going into sleep mode, and stopping someone from rebooting your computer. Shareware. (http://www.trivectus.com/)

SYSTEM RESTORER

This program can help your computer recover from an accident, malfunction, or malicious attack.

Windows

System Safe   Automatically detects and repairs corrupted system files so you can restore your computer after an accident or hacker, virus, or Trojan horse attack. Shareware. (http://systemsafe.now.nu/)

VOICE ENCRYPTION

Use this program to encrypt voice transmissions over the Internet or other networks.

Windows

PGPFone   Encrypts voice transmissions over the Internet or other networks. (Includes C/C++ source code.) Freeware. (http://www.pgpi.org/)

Macintosh

PGPFone   Encrypts voice transmissions over the Internet or other networks. (Includes C/C++ source code.) Freeware. (http://www.pgpi.org/)

VULNERABILITY SCANNERS

Vulnerability scanners combine the features of an ordinary scanner with a database of all known weaknesses that hackers commonly exploit. The scanners list weaknesses that they find in a network and then offer suggestions for closing these possible openings.

Windows

Kane Security Analyst   A network security assessment tool that provides a fast, thorough analysis of network security for Windows NT and Novell NetWare. Trialware. (http://www.intrusion.com)

Retina   Scan, monitor, and fix vulnerabilities within a network's Internet, Intranet, and Extranet. Windows NT. Trialware. (http://www.eeye.com)

Linux

The Security Administrator's Integrated Network Tool (SAINT) An updated and enhanced version of SATAN, designed to assess the security of computer networks. Freeware. (http://www.saintcorporation.com/products/saint_engine.html)

WEB SITE PROTECTION

These programs can help protect your website from getting attacked or abused.

WebAgain Automatically fixes vandalized web pages. Trialware. (http://www.lockstep.com)

WebCrypt Helps stop linkbacks to your web pages that eat up your bandwidth, and blocks spammers who use spiders to get email addresses from your site. Trialware. (http://www.moonlight-software.com/)

B

A HACKER'S GALLERY OF ROGUE TOOLS

WITH SO MANY HACKER TOOLS AVAILABLE ON THE INTERNET, IT'S QUITE POSSIBLE THAT HACKERS MAY ATTACK YOUR COMPUTER WITH SOME OF THE MORE POPULAR HACKER PROGRAMS ONE DAY. Since most people aren't likely to see, let alone use, these hacker tools, this appendix contains screenshots from a selection of recent and previously popular hacker tools. This will give you a historical and present-day perspective of the tools that hackers use when they attack someone (maybe even you) over the Internet.

INTERNET HACKER TOOLS

Hackers are generally lazy but intelligent, which means they don't like doing something boring that they can program the computer to do for them instead. As a result, hackers have unleashed a variety of tools designed to make their lives easier (but their victims' lives more miserable). Some of these tools include scanners (to find open ports on vulnerable computers), remote Trojan horse programs (to take over a computer through the Internet), and password crackers (designed to exhaustively try out different password combinations until they finds one that works). To see what types of tools hackers may use against you, browse through the following:

AOHell

Released around 1995, AOHell (see Figure B-1) defined the standard for online harassment programs and quickly spawned numerous copycats for harassing other online services including CompuServe, Prodigy, and the Microsoft Network. Written in Visual Basic 3.0, AOHell was a relatively simple program that helped hackers send spoofed email, create phony credit card numbers for making fake AOL accounts, con AOL users out of passwords and credit card numbers, and send insulting messages to others in chat rooms.

Although AOHell initially caused problems for America Online users, the program is now obsolete. Few hackers are currently developing AOHell copycat programs, preferring to channel their energy towards creating more sophisticated

Figure B-1

AOHell, the first and original online harassment tool.

Internet hacking tools such as port scanners or harassment tools that cause chaos on IRC or in ICQ chat rooms.

BO2K – Back Orifice

With a name deliberately chosen to mock Microsoft's Back Office program, Back Orifice caused a sensation when released in 1998 as one of the first remote access Trojan horse programs that could remotely control another computer over a phone line or through the Internet (see Figure B-2).

Developed by a hacker group calling themselves the Cult of the Dead Cow, Back Orifice (www.bo2k.com) made headlines again in 1999 when it was released at DefCon 7.0 with improvements, including the option of adding plug-in programs written by others, and the complete C/C++ source code so that anyone could study and modify the program. Ironically when introduced at DefCon, the Back Orifice 2000 CD was infected by the Chernobyl (CIH) virus.

Although Back Orifice still poses a threat to computers, the buzz surrounding BO2K has faded. Still, the program has spawned numerous remote access copycats programs that have improved upon the original Back Orifice design, and despite its age, Back Orifice still remains a favorite tool for hackers to probe computers connected to cable or DSL modems.

Crack Whore

One of the new breed of website hacking programs, Crack Whore uses a brute force/dictionary attack against a website to find the password to a legitimate account (see Figure B-3). Since so many people use weak, easy to guess passwords, programs like Crack Whore are surprisingly successful far more often than they should be.

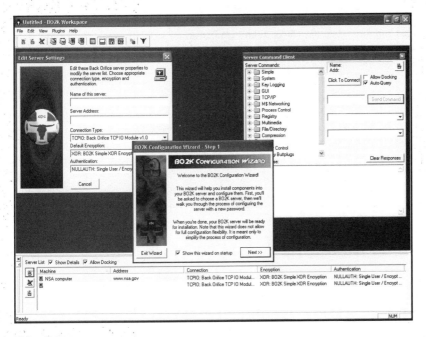

Figure B-2

Back Orifice 2000 is the latest incarnation of the popular and ground-breaking remote access Trojan horse.

Figure B-3

Crack Whore probes a website for easily-guessed passwords to give a hacker access to a system.

Once hackers have access to a legitimate account, they can either modify web pages and other data directly or attempt to burrow through the system and either gain access to additional accounts or elevate the current account to get greater access to the rest of the computer hosting a particular website.

Death 'n Destruction

One of the simplest denial-of-service (DoS) hacking tools, Death 'n Destruction sends endless streams of useless data to a victim's computer port (usually port 139), effectively overwhelming the target computer and causing it to crash or disconnect from the Internet (see Figure B-4).

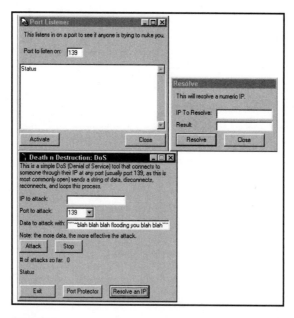

Figure B-4

Death 'n Destruction can flood a computer with useless data as a primitive, but effective, form of a denial-of-service attack.

ICQ War 2000

With the popularity of instant messaging services (and the dwindling popularity of online services), hackers quickly turned their attention from writing online harassment programs such as AOHell clones and started writing ICQ harassment tools instead (see Figure B-5).

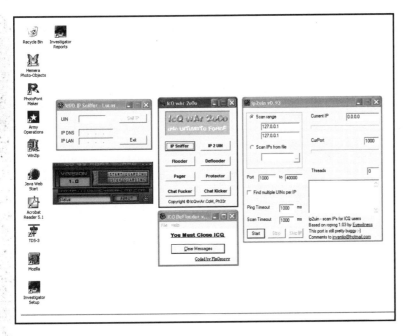

Figure B-5

ICQ War 2000 provides multiple features for harassing someone (and protecting yourself) while using ICQ.

ICQ War 2000 is one of many multi-purpose ICQ harassment programs that can flood a victim with messages, track down a person's IP address, and disrupt chat rooms with insults and obscenity.

John the Ripper

One of the more popular password cracking programs available, John the Ripper runs under UNIX and MS-DOS to crack weak UNIX passwords and systems such as Linux, FreeBSD, OpenBSD, Solaris, Digital UNIX, AIX, HP-UX, and IRIX.

John the Ripper can automatically detect DES, MD5, and Blowfish encrypted UNIX passwords and use a brute force attack to uncover easy-to-guess passwords (see Figure B-6). Once hackers have a password, they can log in to a valid account and establish a foothold on a computer.

NetBus

Originally developed as a remote access Trojan similar to Back Orifice, newer versions of NetBus are now being marketed as a legitimate remote access administrative tool. Despite this change of focus by the NetBus programmers, hackers continue to

```
John the Ripper  Version 1.6  Copyright (c) 1996-98 by Solar Designer

Usage: //E/TEMP/JOHN-16/RUN/john [OPTIONS] [PASSWORD-FILES]
-single                    "single crack" mode
-wordfile:FILE -stdin      wordlist mode, read words from FILE or stdin
-rules                     enable rules for wordlist mode
-incremental[:MODE]        incremental mode [using section MODE]
-external:MODE             external mode or word filter
-stdout[:LENGTH]           no cracking, just write words to stdout
-restore[:FILE]            restore an interrupted session [from FILE]
-session:FILE              set session file name to FILE
-status[:FILE]             print status of a session [from FILE]
-makechars:FILE            make a charset, FILE will be overwritten
-show                      show cracked passwords
-test                      perform a benchmark
-users:[-]LOGIN|UID[,..]   load this (these) user(s) only
-groups:[-]GID[,..]        load users of this (these) group(s) only
-shells:[-]SHELL[,..]      load users with this (these) shell(s) only
-salts:[-]COUNT            load salts with at least COUNT passwords only
-format:NAME               force ciphertext format NAME (DES/BSDI/MD5/BF/AFS/LM)
-savemem:LEVEL             enable memory saving, at LEVEL 1..3
```

Figure B-6

John the Ripper is a command-line program that can find weak passwords on UNIX-based systems.

use earlier versions of NetBus (see Figure B-7) to secretly access other computers. In addition, many hacker websites provide the original Delphi source code so anyone can make modifications to create a new version of NetBus or write an entirely different remote access Trojan horse.

Nmap

Considered one of the best scanning tools for probing a system, Nmap incorporates almost every scanning technique known into one single program (see Figure B-8). Depending on the scanning option you use, Nmap can offer you speed or stealth (to prevent a target computer from knowing it's being probed) using a variety of different protocols (ICMP, UDP, TCP, etc.). You can safely assume that given enough time, Nmap can find an opening in practically any computer.

Nmap runs on UNIX-based operating systems such as Linux and FreeBSD, and comes with full C/C++ source code that you can study and modify. With an active programming community behind it, Nmap is likely to continue for some time as the most powerful scanning tool available to both system administrators and hackers.

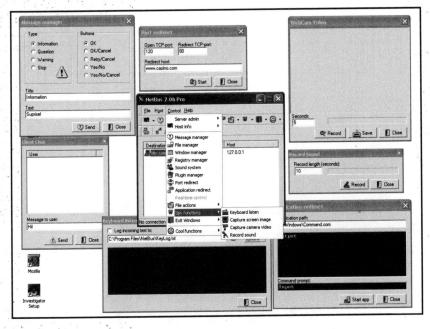

Figure B-7

NetBus is one of the more popular remote access Trojan horse programs.

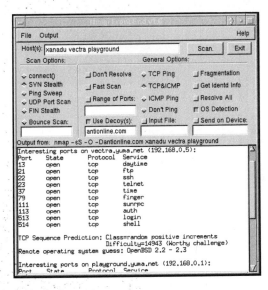

Figure B-8

Nmap provides a variety of scanning techniques to help you probe the vulnerabilities of a computer.

SubSeven

While development of Back Orifice has slowed to a crawl, a new Trojan horse named SubSeven has taken its place as the most popular Trojan horse to use (see Figure B-9). SubSeven's programmers continue to add new features to the program, such as a text-to-speech module, a spy program for retrieving passwords and other data used by instant messaging programs, and the ability to retrieve a variety of information from an infected computer such as the user's name, address, and even Windows CD key number.

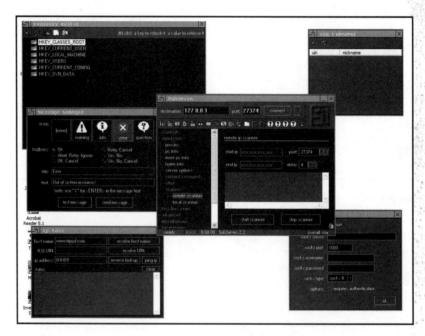

Figure B-9

SubSeven has surpassed Back Orifice as the most popular remote access Trojan horse currently in use.

To help stay in touch with other users, SubSeven's programmers even offer a mailing list and IRC chat room. With the popularity of SubSeven, more computers could eventually be infected by SubSeven than other remote access Trojan horse.

UpYours

For a brief period, email bombs surged in popularity. The idea was to flood a single email account with multiple messages or to subscribe a victim to multiple mailing lists, usually to topics that included child pornography, sexual bondage, or necrophilia.

In 1996, a hacker named "johnny xchaotic" made the headline news when, on two separate occasions, he email bombed various organizations and prominent people including Bill Gates, the Ku Klux Klan, Pat Buchanan, Bill Clinton, the Church of Scientology, and Newt Gingrich.

Email bombing quickly faded as ISPs shut down their mail forwarding services and removed websites that offered email bombing programs. While still an effective tool, email bombing programs like UpYours can reveal an attacker's IP address, further reducing the appeal of attempting a large-scale email bombing attack (see Figure B-10).

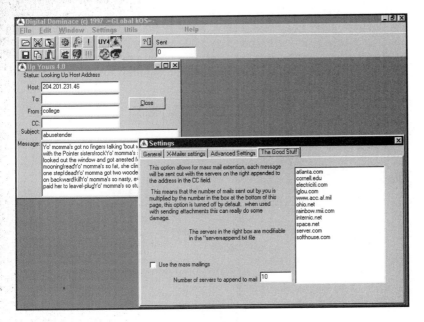

Figure B-10

UpYours was one of the original email bombing programs that provides a variety of options for email bombing a victim.

PHONE PHREAKING TOOLS

In the early days of computers before the Internet, hackers had to communicate through the telephone lines. Since making multiple long-distance phone calls for extended periods of time cost money, hackers soon learned to manipulate the telephone company's computers to make free phone calls or wipe out previously recorded charges on their phone bills.

These early hackers, dubbed phone phreakers, also developed tools to help them control and cause havoc over the telephone lines. While most hackers spend their time creating Internet tools, a few phone phreakers still exist and many hackers still find that phone phreaking tools can help them sneak into a computer through the telephone lines when the usual Internet connections are too heavily protected by firewalls and intrusion detection systems.

Master Credit Card Generator

Master Credit Card Generator created seemingly valid credit card numbers using the same formula that the credit card companies use. By using a program such as Master Credit Card Generator, hackers could create fictitious credit card numbers to help them set up Internet accounts through online services such as America Online. Once the online service verified that the credit card number wasn't valid, they would shut down the hacker's account, but with the aid of a few dozen more credit card numbers, hackers could simply create new accounts over and over again.

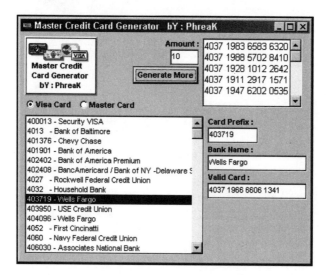

Figure B-11
Master Credit Card Generator helped hackers create fake Internet accounts at no cost.

CyberPhreak

In the early days of the telephone network, the telephone company's switches communicated by emitting specific tones to one another. If you knew which tones to use, you could play those tones into an ordinary telephone and literally reprogram the telephone company's computers. Although these tones no longer work on the newer telephone networks, a program like CyberPhreak shows a typical tone box generator program that phone phreakers have created.

CyberPhreak (see Figure B-12) mimicked the two common telephone color boxes that phone phreakers once used to manipulate the telephone networks: blue boxes and red boxes. A blue box emitted the 2600 Hz tone (which is where the hacker magazine 2600 got its name) while a red box emitted tones into a payphone to trick a pay phone into thinking you inserted a nickel, dime, or quarter.

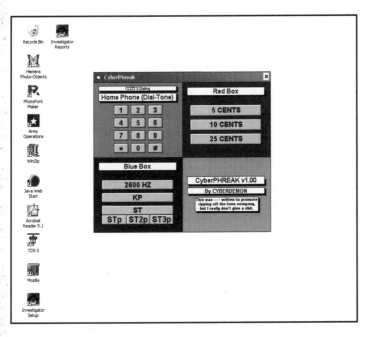

Figure B-12

CyberPhreak can make your computer generate tones to trick the telephone company's computers into giving you free phone service.

Shit Talker

More of a harassment tool than a hacker tool, Shit Talker (see Figure B-13) lets you use the sound capabilities of your computer to create a computer-generated voice that reads insults to someone on the telephone, which can be perfect for dealing with annoying telemarketers.

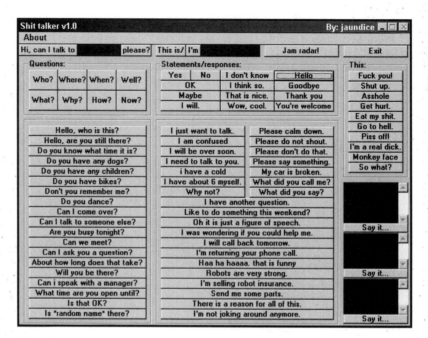

Figure B-13

Shit Talker can turn your computer into an annoying voice harassment tool.

ToneLoc

An old MS-DOS based war dialer that's still used by hackers today, ToneLoc provides a variety of options for hunting out a modem (see Figure B-14). Despite the growing use of the Internet, many corporations and organizations still provide phone modems for connecting to their network, particularly for sales people who need to use remote access programs like PCAnywhere or Carbon Copy to access a computer through the phone lines.

Once a hacker has found a connected modem to attack, the last line of defense is usually a password, which can often be guessed. As a result, many hackers use wardialers to connect to a network and bypass any firewalls that may be in the way.

VIRUSES

By their nature, most viruses attack your computer without your knowledge. However, some viruses display whimsical pictures or messages on the screen just for fun (or to warn you that it just wiped out all your data). Since few people will ever see a virus, here are some of the more interesting ones that have infected computers in the past.

```
         ToneLoc 1.10 by Minor Threat & Mucho Maas (Sep 29 1994)

ToneLoc is a dual purpose wardialer.  It dials phone numbers using a mask that
you give it.  It can look for either dialtones or modem carriers.  It is useful
for finding PBX's, Loops, LD carriers, and other modems.  It works well with
the USRobotics series of modems, and most hayes-compatible modems.

USAGE:
ToneLoc  [DataFile]  /M:[Mask] /R:[Range] /X:[ExMask] /D:[ExRange] /C:[Config]
                     /#:[Number] /S:[StartTime] /E:[EndTime] /H:[Hours] /T /K

    [DataFile]   - File to store data in, may also be a mask      Required
    [Mask]       - To use for phone numbers   Format: 555-XXXX    Optional
    [Range]      - Range of numbers to dial   Format: 5000-6999   Optional
    [ExMask]     - Mask to exclude from scan  Format: 1XXX        Optional
    [ExRange]    - Range to exclude from scan Format: 2500-2699   Optional
    [Config]     - Configuration file to use                     Optional
    [Number]     - Number of dials to make    Format: 250        Optional
    [StartTime]  - Time to begin scanning     Format: 9:30p      Optional
    [EndTime]    - Time to end scanning       Format: 6:45a      Optional
    [Hours]      - Max # of hours to scan     Format: 5:30       Optional
                   Overrides [EndTime]
    /T = Tones, /K = Carriers (Override config file, '-' inverts) Optional
```

Figure B-14

ToneLoc is a DOS-based wardialer that can search a range of phone numbers to determine which ones are connected to a modem.

AIDS virus

Although most viruses try to hide their presence on a computer, the AIDS virus (see Figure B-15) blatantly announces its presence with a message designed to taunt the user. Despite its threatening message, the AIDS virus is rare, so unless you're still running any version of MS-DOS, chances are good your computer will never risk infection by this particular virus.

Ambulance virus

Not all viruses deliberately damage files. Some of them, like the Ambulance virus (see Figure B-16), simply infect computers so they will display an animation of an ambulance rushing across the screen, complete with the wail of a siren. While not dangerous, the Ambulance virus can still demonstrate that even harmless viruses can still be a nuisance.

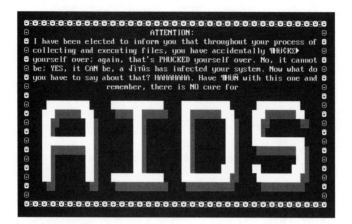

Figure B-15

The AIDS virus attempts to frighten a user after it has infected a computer.

```
CLINT     WAV    32300  07.05.93    20.25
WHIP      WAV     6006  23.04.92     2.01
POP       WAV     4486  05.11.91     4.50
SYSINI    WRI    58496  01.10.92     7.11
PRINTERS  WRI    37760  01.10.92     7.11
WININI    WRI    23168  01.10.92     7.11
NETWORKS  WRI    22528  01.10.92     7.11
EXCEL     XLB      267  26.08.93    16.15
F-EXCEL   ~EX    32352  03.12.93    17.31
F-COREL   ~EX    32736  01.10.92     7.11
F-WORD    ~EX    32736  01.10.92     7.11
F-AMIPRO  ~EX    32352  03.12.93    17.31
F-WP      ~EX    32352  03.12.93    17.31
GDW       SCR   489888  00.06.93    13.20
GDWREAD   TXT     4667  17.08.93    14.19
F-PROT    BAK      454  11.01.94    13.28
MOSAIC    <DIR>         20.01.94    19.22
MOSAIC    BAK    10691  11.11.93    15.32
MOSAIC    INI    10683  20.01.94    19.50
APPLICA0  GRP     4693  23.01.94    15.33

                              free
```

Figure B-16

The Ambulance virus does nothing but make noise and draw an ambulance rushing across your screen.

Boza virus

Sometimes a virus deliberately announces its presence simply to boast that it has succeeded in infecting another computer. The Boza virus (see Figure B-17) infects computers and then displays a simple dialog box that announces its claim to fame as the world's first Windows 95 computer virus.

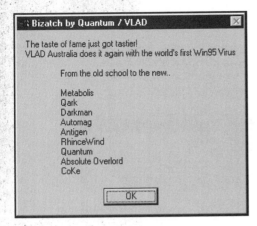

Figure B-17

The Boza virus does nothing but remind people that it was the first Windows 95 virus in the history of the world.

Casino virus

Once a virus has infected a computer, it can trash any files at any time. Since random hard disk trashing can get boring, the Casino virus (see Figure B-18) makes a game out of its infection. After an infection, the Casino virus displays a video slot machine on the screen for the user to play. If the user plays and wins, the Casino virus leaves the hard disk alone. If the user tries to exit out of the video slot machine game or plays the game and loses, the Casino virus trashes the hard disk.

```
       DISK DESTROYER · A SOUVENIR OF MALTA

          I have just DESTROYED the FAT on your Disk !!
    However, I have a copy in RAM, and I'm giving you a last chance
                 to restore your precious data.
   WARNING: IF YOU RESET NOW, ALL YOUR DATA WILL BE LOST - FOREVER !!
             Your Data depends on a game of JACKPOT

          CASINO DE MALTE JACKPOT


             [£]    [?]    [¢]

              CREDITS : 5


          £££ = Your Disk
          ??? = My Phone No.

          ANY KEY TO PLAY
```

Figure B-18

The Casino virus threatens to trash a hard disk if the user fails to win at the video slot machine.

Senna Spy Internet Worm Generator 2000

In much the same way as hackers tried to create special programs for mass-producing viruses and Trojan horses, hackers have now created the Senna Spy Internet Worm Generator 2000 for mass-producing worms that use the VBScript language (see Figure B-19).

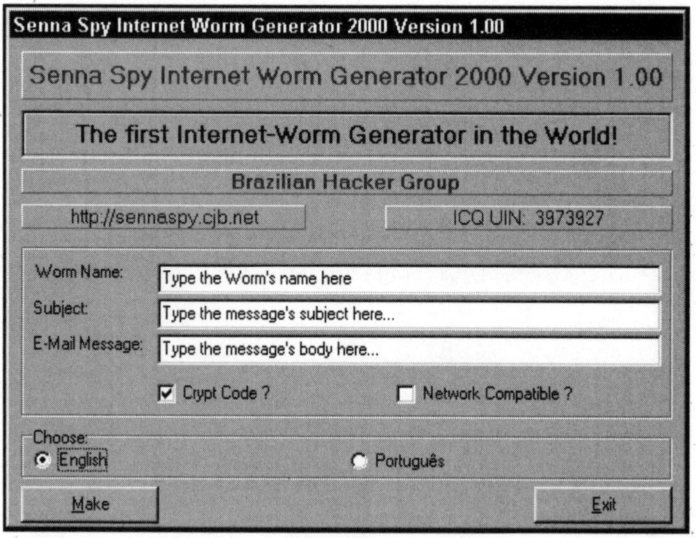

```
┌─────────────────────────────────────────────────────────────┐
│ Senna Spy Internet Worm Generator 2000 Version 1.00          │
├─────────────────────────────────────────────────────────────┤
│  ┌─────────────────────────────────────────────────────────┐ │
│  │ Senna Spy Internet Worm Generator 2000 Version 1.00      │ │
│  └─────────────────────────────────────────────────────────┘ │
│  ┌─────────────────────────────────────────────────────────┐ │
│  │   The first Internet-Worm Generator in the World!       │ │
│  └─────────────────────────────────────────────────────────┘ │
│               Brazilian Hacker Group                         │
│  ┌──────────────────────────┐  ┌───────────────────────────┐ │
│  │ http://sennaspy.cjb.net   │  │  ICQ UIN: 3973927         │ │
│  └──────────────────────────┘  └───────────────────────────┘ │
│  Worm Name:     ┌──────────────────────────────────────────┐ │
│                 │ Type the Worm's name here                │ │
│  Subject:       │ Type the message's subject here...       │ │
│  E-Mail Message:│ Type the message's body here...          │ │
│                 └──────────────────────────────────────────┘ │
│          ☑ Crypt Code ?          ☐ Network Compatible ?      │
│  ┌─Choose:───────────────────────────────────────────────┐   │
│  │ ◉ English                    ○ Português              │   │
│  └───────────────────────────────────────────────────────┘   │
│  ┌──────────────┐                      ┌──────────────┐      │
│  │    Make      │                      │    Exit      │      │
│  └──────────────┘                      └──────────────┘      │
└─────────────────────────────────────────────────────────────┘
```

Figure B-19
Senna Spy Internet Worm Generator 2000 simplifies the creation of VBScript worms.

While the program can create worms quickly and easily, the worms it creates are not necessarily malicious; they simply provide a skeleton program that can retrieve addresses stored in Microsoft Outlook to email themselves to other people. If you want to customize the worm to add a malicious payload of some sort, you'll still need to understand the VBScript language. Still this program is likely to help an aspiring worm programmer understand the basics to retrieving Outlook addresses and getting the worm to email itself to others.

VBS Monopoly Worm

While not one of the more dangerous digital threats out there, the VBS Monopoly worm may be one of the more amusing ones. Written in Visual Basic Script, this worm consists of three files: a picture named MONOPOLY.JPG and two additional Visual Basic scripting files MONOPOLY.WSH and MONOPOLY.VBE.

The MONOPOLY.WSH files executes the MONOPOLY.VBE file, which sends out an email message to everyone in the user's Outlook Address Book. The message has the following subject and message:

Subject: `Bill Gates joke`

Message: `Bill Gates is guilty of monopoly. Here is the proof. :-)`

After executing the MONOPOLY.VBE file, the worm displays the MONOPOLY.JPG file (as shown in Figure B-20) and displays the message:

`Bill Gates is guilty of monopoly. Here is the proof.`

Figure B-20
The VBS Monopoly worm displays a picture of Bill Gates after it infects your computer.

VBS Worm Generator

This is a sophisticated worm generator that offers pull-down menus for mass-producing custom worms that can start infecting the Internet as soon as you release them into the wild (see Figure B-21). Some of its replication methods include sending itself to email addresses stored in Microsoft Outlook and through IRC by infecting the mIRC or Pirch IRC programs.

To avoid detection, the VBS Worm Generator tries to encrypt its VBScript code. For payloads, the program allows a hacker to display a message and picture, crash

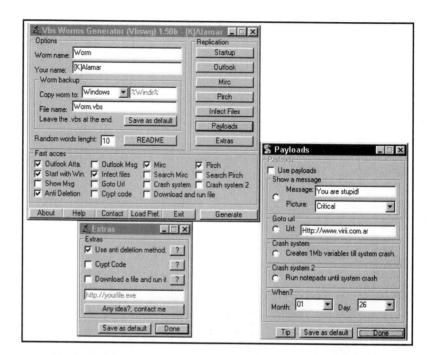

Figure B-21

The VBS Worm Generator can mass-produce custom worms to spread to your enemies.

the computer, or gain access to a website. Since the VBS Worm Generator provides the complete VBScript source code to a worm, hackers can just modify the code and create custom worms nearly as fast as the VBS Worm Generator can produce them.

Virus Creation Laboratory (VCL)

Released in 1992, the Virus Creation Laboratory (VCL) was written by a hacker dubbed the Nowhere Man (see Figure B-22). VCL provided pull-down menus so users could customize a virus with little or no knowledge of programming. In theory, VCL sounds formidable but in reality, bugs and its limited features kept VCL from creating any new viruses that could seriously threaten anyone.

Most of the viruses VCL creates either don't work or don't spread. On top of that, VCL viruses are easily identified by nearly all antivirus programs. Although the threat that hackers could mass-produce viruses using VCL initially panicked the antivirus community, the limited capabilities of VCL have guaranteed the program a place as an interesting but unsuccessful footnote in computer virus history.

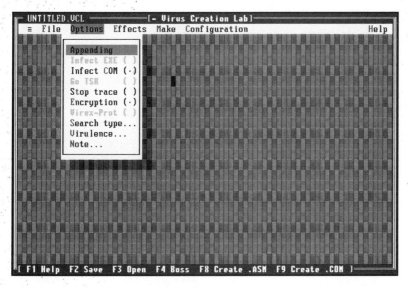

Figure B-22

The Virus Creation Laboratory offered a graphical user interface for mass-producing computer viruses.

Other hackers have tried to create similar virus-making toolkits, such as the ScareMaker Project (see Figure B-23), but like the Virus Creation Laboratory, the viruses and worms these toolkits create are rarely successful.

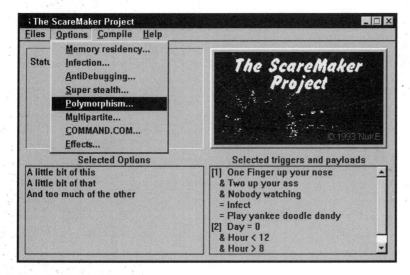

Figure B-23

The ScareMaker Project was an attempt to create a Windows version of the Virus Creation Laboratory.

C

A BIT OF HISTORY: PHONE PHREAKING AND OTHER PHUN

IN THE DAYS BEFORE THE INTERNET, MOST HACKERS COMMUNICATED THROUGH THE TELEPHONE SYSTEM. Instead of using the Internet, people crowded into online services with odd names like The Source and GEnie, and not so odd names like CompuServe and America Online. Instead of setting up web sites, people set up electronic bulletin board systems (BBS). Most importantly, instead of linking computers together through high speed cable, DSL, or satellite Internet connections, people had to connect to one another through the much slower telephone lines.

The problem wasn't necessarily the slowness of the telephone system. The problem was that the cost of multiple long distance phone calls quickly added up. To avoid paying the least amount of money to the telephone company as possible, many people simply figured out various ways to manipulate the telephone company's computers to remove charges from their bills or grant themselves free telephone service so they could make as many long distance phone calls as they wanted.

These early hackers were called *phone phreaks*, and their methods were known as *phone phreaking*. On the noblest level, phone phreaking was about exploring, experimenting, and learning as much as you could about the telephone system out of sheer curiosity. On a more malicious level, phone phreaking meant making free phone calls at somebody else's expense, denying phone service to valid customers, or even wrecking telephone company equipment.

Unlike computer hacking, which can often be practiced in isolation on a single personal computer, phone phreaking requires more extensive preparation that includes software, hardware, and social engineering expertise. One moment you may be reprogramming the phone company's computers, another you may be soldering wires together to alter a pay phone, and still another you may be chatting with a telephone employee to get the passwords for a different part of the phone system. Like computer hacking, phone phreaking is an intellectual game where players try to learn as much as they can about the system (usually) without breaking any laws to do so.

NOTE: *Although much of the phone phreaking methods described in this part of the book are obsolete, much of the techniques that phone phreakers invented, such as social engineering, are still valid today. So read this section with the eye of a historian to see how people hacked their way through the telephone company's computers armed with nothing more than their wits and a rotary telephone.*

A SHORT HISTORY OF PHONE PHREAKING

In the early days of the phone system, you picked up a telephone and talked to an operator who put your call through. As more people got phone lines, the phone company began to replace its operators with special switching equipment. When you dialed a number, your telephone sent a signal to the switching equipment, which routed your call to its destination. Such switching systems could handle more calls more efficiently than human operators, but they also opened the door to phone phreaking. Trying to trick a human operator into letting you make a free phone call to Brazil was nearly impossible, but tricking a mindless machine into letting you make free phone calls only required sending signals identical to the phone company's. If you knew the right signals, the switching systems would blindly obey your orders.

Perhaps the most famous phone phreak was a man nicknamed Captain Crunch because of his accidental discovery of a unique use for a toy whistle found in a box of Cap'n Crunch cereal. He found that blowing this toy whistle into his phone's mouthpiece emitted a 2600 Hz tone, which was the exact frequency used to instruct the telephone company's switching systems.

Other people soon discovered this secret, and some even developed the ability to whistle a perfect 2600 Hz tone. For those unable to obtain the original Cap'n Crunch toy whistle, entrepreneurs started selling devices, known as blue boxes, that simply emitted the 2600 Hz tone. With the introduction of personal computers such as the Apple II, phone phreaks started writing computer programs that could emit the proper 2600 Hz tone from their computer's speaker.

Blue boxes worked as long as the telephone company relied on their old electromechanical switching systems. But eventually these were replaced with newer electronic switching systems (known as ESS), which rendered blue boxes (and the infamous 2600 Hz tone) useless for manipulating the telephone system (although blue boxes may still work on older phone systems outside the United States).

Of course, the introduction of ESS brought a whole new set of problems. With the older electromechanical switching systems, a technician had to physically manipulate switches and wires to modify the switching system. With ESS, technicians could alter the switching system remotely over the phone lines.

Naturally, if a technician could perform this feat of magic over the telephone, phone phreakers could do the same—if they only knew the proper codes and procedures to use. Obviously the telephone company wanted to keep this information secret, and the phone phreakers wanted to let everyone know how the telephone system works (which is partly what the ongoing struggle between the telephone company and phone phreakers is all about).

To learn more about phone phreaking, visit one of the following phone phreaking websites: Hack Canada (http://www.hackcanada.com), Phone Losers of America (http://www.phonelosers.org), Phone Rangers (http://www.phonerangers.org), or

United Phone Losers (http://www.phonelosers.net). Or try the alt.phreaking and alt.2600.phreakz newsgroups for messages about phreaking.

POSSIBLY TRUE STORIES ABOUT PHONE PHREAKING

If you have a telephone, anyone in the world, including the legions of phone phreakers just goofing around with the telephone system, can call you. Steve Wozniak reportedly once called the Vatican and pretended to be Henry Kissinger. Other phone phreakers have attempted to call the Kremlin through the White House hot line and have rerouted a prominent TV evangelist's business number to a 900-number sex hot line. Because a large part of phone phreaking lore involves performing progressively more outrageous acts and then boasting about them, the following phone phreaking stories may or may not be true. Nevertheless, they will give you an idea of what phone phreakers can achieve given the right information. The three stories are "urban myths" circulating around the Internet and are reprinted here verbatim.

The toilet paper crisis in Los Angeles

One thing that was really easy to do was pop into the AutoVerify trunks by accessing the trunks with that "class mark." You couldn't just dial an 800 number that terminates into Washington DC; you also had to pop over to a trunk class marked for "auto-verification."

This is used when a phone user has to reach someone and the line is busy. The normal procedure goes like this: The operator selects a special trunk, class marked for this service, and dials either the last five digits of the phone number, or a special TTC code like 052, followed by the whole seven-digit number. After that, the operator hears scrambled conversation on the line. The parties talking hear nothing, not even a click.

Next, the operator "flashes forward" by causing the equipment to send a burst of 2600 Hz, which makes a three-way connection and places a beep tone on the line so that both parties originally on the line can hear the initial click (flash, in this case) followed by a high-pitched beep. At this point, the parties can hear you, and you can hear them. Usually, the operator announces that it's an emergency, and the line should be released. This is called an "emergency interrupt" and is a service normally reserved for emergencies. It's available today for a $2 fee ($1 in certain areas).

Earlier, I had mapped every 800 number that terminated in Washington DC by scanning the entire 800-424 prefix, which then indicated Washington DC.

That scan found an impressive quantity of juicy numbers that allowed free access to Congressional phone lines, special White House access numbers, and so on.

While scanning the 800-424, I got this dude whose bad attitude caught my attention. I determined to find out who it was. I called back and said, "This is White Plains tandem office for AT&T, which subscriber have we reached?"

This person said, "This is the White House CIA crisis hot line!"

"Oh!" I said, "We're having problem with crossed lines. Now that I know who this is, I can fix it. Thank you for your time—good-bye!"

I had a very special 800 number.

Eventually my friends and I had one of our info-exchanging binges, and I mentioned this incident to them. One friend wanted to dial it immediately, but I persuaded him to wait. I wanted to pop up on the line, using AutoVerify to hear the conversation.

Our first problem was to extract what exchange this number terminated in, because AutoVerify didn't know about 800 numbers.

At that time, all 800 numbers had a one-to-one relation between prefix and area code. For instance, 800-424 = 202-xxx, where xxx was the three-digit exchange determined by the last four digits. In this case, 800-424-9337 mapped to 202-227-9337. The 227 (which could be wrong) was a special White House prefix used for faxes, telexes, and, in this case, the CIA crisis line.

Next we got into the class marked trunk (which had a different sounding chirp when seized) and MF'ed KP-054-227-9337-ST into this special class marked trunk. Immediately we heard the connection tone and put it up on the speaker so we would know when a call came in.

Several hours later, a call did come in. It did appear to have CIA-related talk, and the code name "Olympus" was used to summon the president. I had been in another part of the building and rushed into the room just in time to hear the tail end of the conversation.

We had the code word that would summon Nixon to the phone. Almost immediately, another friend started to dial the number. I stopped him and recommended that he stack at least four tandems before looping the call to the White House.

Sure enough, the man at the other end said "9337."

My other friend said, "Olympus, please!"

The man at the other end said, "One moment sir!" About a minute later, a man that sounded remarkably like Nixon said, "What's going on?"

My friend said, "We have a crisis here in Los Angeles!"

Nixon said, "What's the nature of the crisis?"

My friend said in a serious tone of voice, "We're out of toilet paper, sir!"

Nixon said, "WHO IS THIS?"

My friend then hung up. We never did learn what happened to that tape, but I think this was one of the funniest pranks — and I don't think that Woz would even come close to this one. I think he was jealous for a long time.

To the best of my recollection, this was about four months before Nixon resigned because of the Watergate crisis.

The Santa Barbara nuclear hoax

General Telephone, once the sole phone service for Santa Barbara, used older equipment. Some calls into certain exchanges got routed through inter-region exchanges. A lot of these used the older 2600 Hz–pulse method of signaling.

One of my phone-phreak friends got the bright idea of dialing out on two lines at once to see what happens. Normally, one line would be busy, and the other one would get through. But sometimes, this would jam the lines on both sides of the trunk but still indicate the trunk was free. In telephone talk, this creates a "glare" condition, where one side glares at the other. Calls coming in would just terminate into emptiness, and the trunk would appear to be free to the trunk selector.

Eventually calls came in that terminated to our phone(s). One of my pranky friends said the following to a caller: "What number are you calling? This is a special operator!" The other person said they were calling Santa Barbara and gave us the number. My friend asked, "What area is that in?" then said, "We've had a nuclear accident in that area, please hang up so we can keep the lines open for emergencies only."

Pretty soon, others called—some reporters and other official types. When calls really started to pour in, we broke the connection.

That next day, the Los Angeles Times carried a short news article headlined "Nuclear hoax in Santa Barbara." The text explained how authorities were freaked out and how puzzled they were. The phone company commented, "We don't really know how this happened, but it cleared right up!" Five years later, Santa Barbara replaced that old faulty equipment with newer electronic systems.

The President's secret

Recently, a telephone fanatic in the Northwest made an interesting discovery. He was exploring the 804 area code (Virginia) and found that the 840 exchange did something strange. In all of the cases except one, he would get a recording as if the exchange didn't exist. However, if he dialed 804-840 followed by four rather predictable numbers, he got a ring!

After one or two rings, somebody picked up. Being experienced at this kind of thing, he could tell that the call didn't "supe," that is, no charges were being incurred for calling this number. (Calls that get you to an error message or a special operator generally don't supervise.) A female voice with a hint of a southern accent said, "Operator, can I help you?"

"Yes," he said, "What number have I reached?"

"What number did you dial, sir?"

He made up a number that was similar.

"I'm sorry. That is not the number you reached." Click.

He was fascinated. What in the world was this? He knew he was going to call back, but before he did, he tried some more experiments. He tried the 840 exchange in several other area codes. In some, it came up as a valid exchange. In others, exactly the same thing happened—the same last four digits, the same southern belle.

He later noticed that the areas where the number worked were located in a beeline from Washington, DC, to Pittsburgh, Pennsylvania. He called back from a pay phone.

"Operator, can I help you?"

"Yes, this is the phone company. I'm testing this line and we don't seem to have an identification on your circuit. What office is this, please?"

"What number are you trying to reach?"

"I'm not trying to reach any number. I'm trying to identify this circuit."

"I'm sorry, I can't help you."

"Ma'am, if I don't get an ID on this line, I'll have to disconnect it. We show no record of it here."

"Hold on a moment, sir."

After about a minute, she came back. "Sir, I can have someone speak to you. Would you give me your number, please?"

He had anticipated this and had the pay phone number ready. After he gave it, she said, "Mr. XXX will get right back to you."

"Thanks." He hung up the phone. It rang. INSTANTLY! "Oh my God," he thought, "They weren't asking for my number — they were confirming it!"

"Hello," he said, trying to sound authoritative.

"This is Mr. XXX. Did you just make an inquiry to my office concerning a phone number?"

"Yes. I need an identi- . . ."

"What you need is advice. Don't ever call that number again. Forget you ever knew it."

At this point my friend got so nervous he just hung up. He expected to hear the phone ring again, but it didn't.

Over the next few days, he racked his brains trying to figure out what the number was. He knew it was something big — so big that the number was programmed into every central office in the country. He knew this because if he tried to dial any other number in that exchange, he'd get a local error message, as if the exchange didn't exist.

It finally came to him. He had an uncle who worked in a federal agency. If, as he suspected, this was government related, his uncle could probably find out what it was. He asked the next day and his uncle promised to look into it.

When they met again, his uncle was livid. He was trembling. "Where did you get that number?" he shouted. "Do you know I almost got fired for asking about it? They kept wanting to know where I got it!"

Our friend couldn't contain his excitement. "What is it?" he pleaded. "What's the number?"

"IT'S THE PRESIDENT'S BOMB SHELTER!"

He never called the number after that. He knew that he could probably cause quite a bit of excitement by calling the number and saying something like, "The weather's not good in Washington. We're coming over for a visit." But my friend was smart. He knew that there were some things that were better unsaid and undone.

GETTING STARTED

To start phone phreaking, you need access to a telephone other than your personal phone. Phreaking from your own phone will not only cost you in phone charges, but will also provide the telephone company with a convenient way to track you by tracing your phone line. To be a true phone phreak, you need access to the telephone system and a way not to get billed.

"SHOULDER SURFING" CALLING CARD NUMBERS

The crudest level of phreaking is known as *shoulder surfing*, which is simply looking over another person's shoulder who is typing in a calling card number at a public pay phone.

The prime locations for shoulder surfing are airports because travelers are more likely to use calling cards rather than spare change to make a call. Given the hectic nature of a typical large airport, few people will notice someone peering over their shoulder while they punch in their calling card number, or listening in as they give it to an operator.

Once you have another person's calling card number, you can charge as many calls as you can to it until the victim receives the next billing statement and notices your mysterious phone calls. As soon as the victim notifies the phone company, they will usually cancel that calling card number, and you'll have to steal a new calling card number. Since it is theft, true phone phreakers look down on calling card number stealing as an activity unworthy of anyone but common thieves and juvenile delinquents.

TELEPHONE COLOR BOXES

The simplest method to access the telephone system anonymously is through a pay phone. One of the earliest ways phone phreaks learned to manipulate the telephone system was through telephone "color boxes." These boxes emit special tones or physically alter the wiring on the phone line, allowing anyone to make free phone calls, reroute phone lines, or otherwise raise havoc with the phone system.

Although the Internet abounds with different instructions and plans for building various telephone color boxes, just remember that many of them no longer work with today's phone system—although they might work in other countries or in rural areas. To satisfy your curiosity, though, here are some descriptions of various color boxes that others have made and used in the past. But first, a warning from a phone phreaker regarding the legality of building and using such boxes:

> You have received this information courtesy of neXus. We do not claim to be hackers, phreaks, pirates, traitors, etc. We only believe that an alternative to making certain info/ideas illegal as a means to keep people from doing bad things - is make information free, and educate people how to handle free information responsibly. Please think and act responsibly. Don't get cockey, don't get pushy. There is always gonna be someone out there that can kick your ass. Remember that.

Aqua box

The surest way to catch a phone phreak is to trace his phone calls. One technique the FBI uses is called a Lock-in-Trace, which allows the FBI to tap into a phone line much like a three-way call connection. Because every phone connection is held open by electricity, the Lock-in-Trace device simply cuts into a phone line and generates the same voltage as when the phone line is being used. The moment you hang up, the Lock-in-Trace device maintains the voltage of the phone line as if the phone were still in use, thus allowing the FBI (or anyone else) to continue tracing the origin of a particular phone call.

The aqua box simply lowers the voltage level on a phone line, preventing the Lock-in-Trace device from maintaining the necessary voltage to keep the line open (and possibly even shorting out the Lock-in-Trace device itself). It should block any attempt by the FBI (or anyone else) to trace your phone call.

Beige box

A beige box mimics a lineman's handset, which means that you can do anything a telephone company lineman can. Just open up any of the telephone company's protective metal boxes (usually found on a street corner), attach your beige box to an existing phone line (preferably not your own, which would defeat the whole purpose of the beige box), and you can make free long-distance calls at your neighbor's expense or eavesdrop on their calls.

Black box

Before you receive a phone call, the voltage in your phone line is zero. The moment someone calls you and the phone starts ringing, the voltage jumps to 48V. As soon as you pick up the phone, it drops to 10V, and the phone company starts billing the calling party.

A black box keeps the voltage on your phone line at a steady 36 volts so that it never drops low enough to signal the phone company to start billing—incoming callers never get billed for talking to you.

Cheese box

A cheese box tricks the phone company into thinking that your ordinary phone is actually a pay phone that can make outgoing calls but can't accept incoming calls. Cheese boxes were supposedly invented by bookies as a way of making calls to people while making it impossible for others (such as the police) to call them.

Crimson box

A crimson box is a device that lets you put someone on hold so that they can't hear you but you can still hear them. Great for listening to what telemarketers say to their co-workers when they think you're not listening.

Lunch box

The lunch box connects to an ordinary phone and turns that phone into a transmitter. That way you can use a receiver and eavesdrop on other people's phone calls while listening from a safe distance away.

Red box

Each time you drop a coin into a pay phone, the pay phone sends a tone over the line. When you toss in enough coins, the telephone company opens up the line so you can place a call. The red box simply generates the same tones that the pay phone generates when it receives a coin. By playing the tones from a red box into the mouthpiece of a pay phone, you can fool the phone company into thinking that you dropped coins into the pay phone, thus allowing you to make a free phone call.

Many of the above color boxes were developed to work with the older phone systems, which means they may not work with your phone systems. Of course, if you happen to live somewhere remote that hasn't updated its phone system, or if you're living in a country that still uses obsolete telephone equipment, you might experience better results. Since phone phreaking is about experimenting, you could try these telephone color boxes at your own risk and see what happens.

COLOR BOX PROGRAMS

To make a telephone color box, you often needed to solder or connect different wires together. But with the popularity of personal computers, people soon wrote programs to mimic the different telephone color boxes. By running a telephone color box program on a laptop computer, you can experiment with the phone system from any pay phone in the world.

Of course, personal computers aren't the only tools available to phone phreaks. If you visit the Hack Canada (http://www.hackcanada.com) Web site, not only can you learn about hacking the Canadian phone system, but you can also download the source code to telephone color box programs (dubbed RedPalm) that run on a PalmPilot handheld computer.

By using the RedPalm program, you can make your PalmPilot emit tones that mimic the sounds made when you put real money into a Canadian payphone. The tones make the pay phone respond as if you had dropped in a nickel, dime, or quarter, letting you make phone calls for free.

In addition to using a personal computer or PalmPilot to run telephone boxing programs, a group of hackers calling themselves TeamKNOx has released a program called PhreakBoy, which mimics red and blue telephone boxes and includes C source code. The PhreakBoy program even runs on Nintendo GameBoy systems.

WAR DIALERS AND PRANK PROGRAMS

Besides writing programs to mimic telephone calling boxes, phone phreakers also created special programs called war dialers or demon dialers. War dialers are an old, but still effective, method for breaking into another computer.

War dialers work by hunting for telephone lines connected to a modem and a computer, which means that every person, corporation, and organization are potential targets. Because most people don't advertise their modem numbers, war dialers dial a range of phone numbers and keep track of any of the dialed numbers that respond with the familiar whine of a computer modem. A hacker can then use this list and dial each number individually to determine what type of computer he has reached and how he might be able to break in to it.

For example, many businesses have special phone lines that allow traveling employees to control their desktop computers with their laptop computers and special remote-control software, such as pcAnywhere, RapidRemote, or CarbonCopy. If a hacker finds this special phone number and uses a copy of the same remote-control software, guess what? With the right password, the hacker can take over the desktop computer too and then erase or copy all of its files.

Since war dialers can dial a number over and over again, they can also be used to harass people. Some of the more unusual harassment programs include a pager program that repeatedly dials a victim's pager number and randomly types in a phone number. Other phone harassment programs dial a single number over and over again at random intervals or play a computer-generated voice to insult a caller the moment he or she picks up the phone. (Just remember that with caller ID, available in most parts of the country, a victim can track your phone number, so it's not a good idea to call from any phone number that can be traced back to you.)

VOICE MAILBOX HACKING

Voice mail is the corporate alternative to answering machines. Rather than give each employee a separate answering machine, voice mail provides multiple mailboxes on a single machine. Because a voice mail system is nothing more than a programmable computer, phone phreaks quickly found a way to set up their own private voice mailboxes buried within a legitimate voice mailbox system.

The first step in hacking a voice mail system is finding the system's phone number — something a war dialer can do for you. (Many voice mailboxes even have toll-free numbers, so don't forget to scan those numbers too.) If you have legitimate access to a voice mail system, you could practice hacking into it so you have a better idea of what to expect when you work on somebody else's.

When you call a voice mail system, you might have to press a special key, such as * or #. Then a recording will usually ask for a valid mailbox number, typically three or four digits. After choosing a mailbox number, you'll need a password to access the mailbox, play back messages, or record your own messages.

People will usually choose a password that's easy to remember (and easy to guess). Some people base their password on their mailbox number, so try typing the mailbox number itself or backward (if the mailbox number is 2108, try 8012 as the password). Other people might use a password that consists of a repeated number (such as 3333) or a simple series (6789).

Once you manage to guess a password, you'll have free access to the voice mailbox, which means you can play back or erase any stored messages. Of course, if you start erasing somebody's messages, they'll notice fairly quickly and get the system administrator to change the password to lock you out again.

Most voice mail systems always have several empty mailboxes, either leftovers from previous employees or extra capacity for anticipated newcomers. Voice mailbox hackers simply hunt around a voice mailbox system until they find an unused mailbox that they can claim for themselves.

After they've claimed a voice mailbox, hackers can send and retrieve messages from their buddies all over the world. Many companies are providing mailboxes for hackers without even knowing it while other companies ignore or tolerate this minor transgression. As long as the hackers don't mess up the voice mail system for legitimate users, it's often cheaper just to pretend they don't exist on the system at all.

CELLULAR PHONE FRAUD AND TV SATELLITE DESCRAMBLING

With the introduction of cellular phones, a whole new realm has opened up for phreaks. Unlike a beige box, which requires a physical connection to make a free call on an existing phone line, cellular phone theft requires only a radio scanner.

Even when your cellular phone isn't in use, it must constantly transmit its electronic serial number (ESN) and mobile identification number (MIN) so the cellular network knows where to send an incoming call. With a radio scanner and additional data-capture equipment, a thief can capture and store the ESN and MIN of a legitimate cellular phone. Later, the thief can program the stolen ESN and MIN into another cellular phone. All calls made from this "cloned" cellular phone now get billed to the victim's cellular phone.

(The cellular phone equivalent of shoulder surfing calling card numbers is to sign up for cellular phone service using a fraudulent name. Then just use the service until the cellular phone company cuts you off for nonpayment.)

To prevent cellular phone "cloning," phone companies now use encryption. When a user makes a call with these newer cellular phones, the cellular network asks for a special code. Legitimate cellular phones will be able to supply the proper authentication code; cloned cellular phones will not.

Cable and satellite TV companies face a similar problem: Cable and satellite TV broadcasts often get intercepted by people using special receivers and descramblers. By browsing the Internet, you can even find companies that sell plans, instructions, and actual kits for building your own cable or satellite TV descrambler (for educational or legitimate purposes only, of course!).

The corporations continue to develop more sophisticated methods for protecting their broadcasts, and the video pirates always come up with new methods for cracking the protection schemes. Video pirates often claim that if the broadcasting companies lowered their prices, fewer people would steal their services. Broadcasting corporations make the counter-claim that the cost of fighting the pirates keeps prices artificially high.

The question is, if video pirates and cellular phone cloners disappeared overnight, would corporations lower their prices? If you think so, then perhaps video pirates and cellular phone thieves deserve to be caught. But if you think that corporations would keep their prices the same whether they had to absorb the cost of fighting thieves or not, then video pirates and cellular phone thieves might be considered modern-day Robin Hoods after all.

Be careful if you steal service from the telephone or cable TV companies. Stealing service for yourself is enough to earn you a free trip to the police station, but if you get greedy and try to resell the service to other people, you're really asking for trouble.

Of course, if your government restricts the flow of information, stealing from the telephone and cable TV companies may be the only way to communicate with others and receive news from the rest of the world. Ultimately, you have to decide if you're breaking the law out of greed or rebellion against unfair government laws. And take the consequences.

D

GLOSSARY

Adware   Programs that display advertisements, often retrieved off the Internet. *See* Freeware, Open source, and Shareware.

AES (Advanced Encryption Standard)   An encryption standard defined by the United States government. *See* DES.

Anonymous remailer   A program or website that strips away an email address from a message and then forwards it, allowing you to send email without revealing your identity or location.

Antivirus program   A program that detects and removes computer viruses.

AOL (America Online)   The most popular (and hated) online service in the world.

Assembly language   A low-level machine programming language. Each specific family of microprocessors (such as Intel or Motorola microprocessors) has its own assembly language that allows maximum flexibility in controlling the computer. Most viruses are written in assembly language, although a few are written in BASIC, C, or Pascal.

Back door   A hidden entry point into a computer or program. Hackers often create back doors in a computer so they can return later and quickly bypass any security or log-in procedures normally required.

Back Orifice   One of the most popular remote access Trojan horse programs. *See* RAT and Trojan horse.

Black hat hacker   Term describing a hacker who uses his or her skills for malicious purposes, such as deleting files and crashing computers. *See* White hat hacker.

Blowfish   Popular encryption algorithm freely available for anyone to use.

Boot sector   The part of the disk that identifies the disk type (floppy or hard), the size of the file allocation table, the number of hidden files, and the number of files in the root directory. Every disk has a boot sector, which makes every disk vulnerable to boot viruses. *See* Boot virus.

Boot virus   A virus that infects the boot sector of a disk.

Brute-force attack   A method of discovering a password by exhaustively trying all possible combinations of words and numbers until you find the right one.

C/C++   Popular programming languages used to write most operating systems and programs such as Linux, Windows, and Microsoft Word. C was the original language used to develop Unix, while C++ is an object-oriented version of C.

Censorware   Generic term for programs, such as parental control programs, that block or limit access to certain websites and Usenet newsgroups. *See* Parental control software.

Checksum   The numeric result of some calculation (for example, a one-way hash function) based on the physical contents of a file, that uniquely identifies that particular file. If the file changes in any way, its checksum also changes. Checksums are often stored in a separate file that may be encrypted, hidden, or saved on a separate floppy disk. Antivirus and anti–Trojan horse programs use checksums to identify when a file may have been altered (and thus possibly infected). Similarly, computer forensics experts often use checksums to verify that a file hasn't been changed since the computer was first seized by the police.

Clusters   One or more sectors on a disk, containing all or part of a file. *See* Slack space.

CMOS (complementary metal-oxide semiconductor)   A battery-powered chip that stores information about a computer's configuration. Many viruses target this chip because it can keep your computer from working properly.

Cold boot   To turn a computer off and then back on again. *See* Warm boot.

Companion virus   A now obsolete type of MS-DOS virus that stores itself as a separate file, usually as a .com file. Companion viruses name themselves after an infected program file, such as wp.exe, but with the .com file extension.

Compiler   A program that converts source code into an executable program. *See* Decompiler.

Cracker   1. A malicious hacker. 2. A type of program that can defeat encryption or copy protection.

Cracking   Defeating a program's copy-protection method or bypassing any password or encryption scheme.

Credit card generator   A program that creates credit card numbers using the same mathematical formula used by the credit card companies.

Cross-platform   Capable of running on multiple operating systems.

Decompiler   A type of program that reconstructs a program's original source code from an executable file. Decompilers exist for Visual Basic, Java, and other programming languages. *See* Disassembler.

Delphi   Rapid-application development tool based on the Pascal programming language. Often used to write remote access Trojan horse programs. *See* RAT and Visual Basic.

Denial-of-service attack   The tying up of a computer's resources to prevent its use by others. Often abbreviated as *DoS*.

DES (Data Encryption Standard)   An encryption method. DES can be cracked and is thus considered useless for encrypting valuable or sensitive information. *See* AES.

Desktop-monitoring program   Program designed to spy and record the activities of a person on a computer without his or her knowledge. *See* Spyware.

Dictionary attack   A way of finding a password by trying a list of common passwords such as Star Trek lingo, names of cars, or titles of popular movies.

Direct action virus   A virus that does something immediately each time you run it, such as attack your hard disk or display a message on the screen.

Disassembler   A program that generates assembly language source code from an executable program file. *See* Assembly language and Decompiler.

Email bombing   Clogging up an email account by sending a large number of email messages or several huge files. *See* Fax bombing and Phone call flooding.

Encryption   A method of scrambling data to make it unreadable by others. *See* AES and DES.

EXE file   A common name for a file that contains a program such as a word processor or a game. An EXE file is a relocatable program that can be used to store larger programs.

False negative   When a program, such as an antivirus or anti–Trojan horse program, fails to detect a result. When an anti-virus program fails to detect a legitimate virus, that result is called a false negative.

False positive   When a program, such as an antivirus or anti–Trojan horse program, incorrectly claims an error. When an anti-virus program incorrectly identifies a virus where none exists, the result is called a false positive.

Fast infector   A type of virus that infects program files whenever the computer loads or examines the virus file.

FAT (file allocation table)   Part of the disk that contains information about the size and location of all the other files on the disk. Each time you format a disk, it creates two identical FATs, which store information on the clusters used by each file stored on the disk. If your disk's FAT gets messed up, the files are still on the disk, but your computer will no longer be able to find or use them.

Fax bombing   Sending multiple messages to a fax machine to prevent others from using it. *See* Email bombing and Phone call flooding.

File infector   Another name for *program infectors*.

Firewall   Utility designed to keep intruders out of a network or individual computer.

Flooder   A malicious program designed to overwhelm a target computer with more data than it can handle. *See* Denial-of-service attack and Email bombing.

Forensics   The science of recovering deleted files for evidence.

Fortress phone   Slang name for a pay phone, referring to its extensive defenses designed to keep people from breaking into it.

Freeware   Software that can be copied, distributed, and given away without payment of any kind. *See* Adware and Shareware.

Gnutella   Program designed to allow people to "share" audio and video files with each other over a distributed network. *See* Napster.

Hacker   Slang name given to someone extremely knowledgeable about computers. Pejorative in some circles—but not here. *See* Cracker.

Hacking   The process of examining and experimenting with something, such as the telephone system or a computer, in order to find out how it works. Hacking often occurs without the owner's knowledge or permission.

Hacktivism   Form of protest that uses computer skills, mostly focusing on website defacing, to spread a message. *See* Web site defacing.

Hate group   An organization or collection of people who advocate violence and discrimination against another group of people. Usually motivated by religious or racial differences.

Heuristic analysis   Sometimes called rule-based or artificial intelligence analysis, it uses intelligent guesswork, which more often than not finds the solution faster than a standard algorithm. Antivirus programs use heuristic analysis to examine a file, and based on typical virus characteristics, make an educated guess as to whether a file is infected or not.

Hex editor   A program that can directly examine and modify the contents of a file or disk.

Honeypot   A phony target used to tempt hackers. Often used to keep hackers logged on to a system long enough to trace their location, or to lure a hacker into a harmless part of a network so that he or she can't get out and cause real damage. Also called a *goat file*.

ICQ   Popular instant messaging program.

Identity theft   Passing yourself off as another person electronically.

Information warfare   Popular term to describe hacking on an individual, commercial, and international level.

Integrity checker   A program that examines each file and calculates a numeric result based on that file's size, time, and date stamp. If the integrity checker notices that the file's size, time, or date has changed, it assumes the file may have been infected by a virus or modified by a hacker. *See* Checksum.

Intrusion-detection system   Program designed to detect the presence of a hacker who has already penetrated a system. Often abbreviated as *IDS*.

IRC (Internet Relay Chat)   A loosely structured network where people can type and send messages to each other in real time.

Java   Cross-platform programming language used to create web page applets and full-blown applications.

Keystroke recorder   A program that records keystrokes and/or mouse clicks on a computer, usually without the user's knowledge.

Linux   A free version of Unix designed for personal computers. Although Linux can be copied and distributed without restriction, many companies sell their own versions of Linux that include technical support, software, or other value-added services.

Logic bomb   A type of program, often buried within another program, that is set to go off on a certain date or by a specific event, erasing data or crashing the computer. Logic bombs are often inserted by disgruntled programmers willing to sabotage their own programs to get back at their employers.

Macro virus   A virus written using the macro programming language of a particular program. The most common macro viruses are written in WordBasic or Visual Basic for Applications, although a few macro viruses have been written in the macro programming language for WordPerfect and Lotus 1-2-3. *See* Visual Basic for Applications.

Master Boot Record (MBR)   The information stored on a hard disk that tells the computer how the hard disk is partitioned. Most hard disks have only one partition but can usually be divided into as many as four partitions.

Michelangelo virus   A virus that made headlines in all the major newspapers worldwide in 1992. The Michelangelo virus isn't as common as many other viruses.

MP3   Acronym that stands for Moving Picture Experts Group (MPEG) Audio Layer-3, a file compression format for storing digital audio. *See* Napster and Gnutella.

Multipartite virus   A type of virus that can infect both files and boot sectors.

Mutation engine   A programming tool kit designed to help virus writers create polymorphic viruses, which can modify themselves to avoid detection by antivirus scanners. *See* Polymorphic virus.

Napster   Program designed for "sharing" MP3-compressed audio files over the Internet. *See* Gnutella and MP3.

Newbie   Slang term to describe a novice or beginner.

Nuker   A malicious program designed to crash another computer.

Online harassment program   A program designed to harass users on specific online service, such as America Online, or in chat rooms. Such programs are often used to trick people into giving up their credit card numbers or passwords.

Open source   A type of program where the source code can be studied and modified with no or few restrictions. Any changes made to an open source program are meant to be shared with others. Linux is an example of an open source program. *See* Adware, Freeware, and Shareware.

Overwriting infector   A type of file-infecting virus that erases part of a file while infecting it.

Packet sniffer   A program that surreptitiously captures information flowing through the Internet. Often used to intercept credit card numbers and passwords.

Parasitic infector   A type of file-infecting virus that attaches itself to the beginning or end of a file.

Parental control software   Programs that block access to certain Internet resources (such as websites or FTP sites) that may contain adult-oriented material. Can also filter email or chat rooms, and control access to certain programs stored on the computer. *See* Censorware.

Partition table   The part of a hard disk's boot sector that defines the size and partition of the hard disk, the operating system each partition uses, and the partition the computer uses to boot from.

Patch   A program designed to correct a flaw or bug in a program. *See* Service pack.

PGP (Pretty Good Privacy)   One of the most popular and effective encryption programs used on the Internet. *See* Encryption.

Phishing   To trick or fool chat room attendees into revealing their passwords, credit card numbers, or other valuable information. Often a special feature provided in an online harassment program. *See* Online harassment program.

Phone call flooding   Dialing a single phone number over and over again. Often used to harass a specific company or individual, such as a company or individual that sent unwanted email. *See* Fax bombing.

Phreaking   Manipulating the phone system.

Pirated software   Illegally copied software. Check any computer in any organization, and you'll probably find at least one pirated program somewhere.

Polymorphic virus   A virus that modifies itself each time it spreads in order to avoid detection by antivirus scanners. *See* Mutation engine.

Ponzi scheme   A con game where early investors receive their money when others invest money into the scheme. Similar to Social Security. *See* Pyramid scheme.

Pop-up/under ads   Advertisements that appear on your screen when you're browsing the Internet. Pop-up ads cover the web page that you're viewing while pop-under ads hide and only appear when you close your browser window.

Port   An "opening" in your computer used to send and receive data. When a computer connects to the Internet, it opens several ports, where each port performs a specific function, such as sending and receiving web pages or email. *See* Scanner.

Private-key encryption   Method of encrypting and decrypting data that uses a single key. *See* Public-key encryption.

Program infector   A virus that infects program files, such as word processors or spreadsheets.

Public-key encryption   Method of encrypting and decrypting data that uses two separate keys: a private key (known only to one person) and a public key that anyone can use. Data encrypted with one key can only be decrypted using the other. *See* Private-key encryption.

Pyramid scheme   A con game where one person receives money from two or more other people in exchange for the promise that they can make money if they recruit others to give them money too.

RAT (remote access Trojan)   A program that allows hackers to access your computer from a remote location. *See* Trojan horse.

Rollback program   Utility that restores a hard disk's contents back to a previous state. Often used to repair damage caused by erratic software installations but can also be used to repair damage caused by hackers, viruses, or Trojan horses.

Rootkit   A collection of one or more programs designed to hide a hacker's tracks on a computer and install additional back doors to ensure that the hacker can get back into that computer at a later time.

SATAN   An acronym that stands for Security Administrator Tool for Analyzing Networks. SATAN is a program designed to probe a website for security weaknesses.

Scanner   1. A type of antivirus program that contains a database of known virus characteristics. By comparing files to this database, a scanner can accurately determine the exact type of virus that may be infecting your computer. 2. A type of program that searches the Internet or a network for computers.

Script kiddie   Derogatory term used to describe hackers who use programs written by other people without understanding the technical details.

Service pack   A collection of several programs designed to correct multiple flaws or bugs in a program. *See* Patch.

Shareware   A method of software distribution that lets you freely copy and try the program without payment. If you use the program regularly, you are legally obligated to pay for it. *See* Adware, Freeware, and Open source.

Signature   The unique structural characteristic of a virus or Trojan horse, much like a fingerprint on a person. Every virus and Trojan horse has a unique signature, which antivirus and anti–Trojan horse scanners use to detect and identify it.

Slack space   The unused space in a cluster, which often contains keystrokes or other fragments of a file that can be recovered and used as evidence. *See* Clusters.

Slow infector   A virus that only infects files when they are created or modified. By doing this, slow infectors avoid detection by antivirus programs, such as integrity checkers. *See* Fast infector.

Sniffer   A program that copies data as it the data passes through a network.

Source code   The actual commands that make up a program. If you have the source code of a virus, you can modify its behavior. Virus source code is usually written in assembly language or Visual Basic for Applications, online harassment programs are usually written in Visual Basic, and Trojan horses are usually written in C/C++ or Delphi. *See* Assembly language, C/C++, and Visual Basic for Applications.

Spam   Slang name for unwanted email.

Sparse infector   A virus that infects files only occasionally to avoid detection by antivirus programs.

'sploit   Slang term for "exploits." Often used by hackers to identify the latest vulnerabilities found in a particular program, such as an operating system or firewall.

Spyware   Programs that retrieve information from a hard disk and send that information to another computer. Often used by advertiser-sponsored shareware programs or desktop-monitoring programs designed to spy on people using a computer. *See* Adware.

Stealth   A virus that tries to avoid detection by antivirus programs.

Steganography   The science of hiding information like text in another medium, such as a graphic file, sound file, or another text file. *See* Encryption.

Trigger   The event that causes a virus to act. The trigger can set off the virus on a certain date (Friday the 13th, or April 15) or when certain conditions have been met (such as when the hard disk is 80 percent full).

Trojan horse   A type of program that pretends to be a useful (usually well-known) program while it really does something else, such as erase files from your computer. Unlike computer viruses, Trojan horses can't duplicate themselves.

Unix   Operating system originally developed at Bell Laboratories in the early 1970s. Unix is one of the most popular operating systems in the world, developed primarily for larger computers, such as mainframes and minicomputers, although a free version of Unix, called Linux, has been gaining popularity on personal computers. *See* Linux.

Vaccine   A type of antivirus program that claims to protect files from virus infection.

Virus monitor   A program that hides in your computer's memory and watches for signs of a virus infection.

Visual Basic   A program sold by Microsoft that lets you visually design a program and then write BASIC commands to make the program work.

Visual Basic for Applications   A special version of Visual Basic, often abbreviated as VBA, designed for creating programs within Microsoft applications such as Word, Excel, PowerPoint, and Access.

War dialer   A program that can dial a range of phone numbers, searching for a modem on the other line. Can also be used to repetitively dial a single phone number, thereby harassing the recipient. Also called a *demon dialer*.

Warez   Slang term for pirated software, usually games. Also called *appz*.

Warm boot   To restart a computer without turning it off and on again. Most computers have a restart or reset button, or you can press CTRL-ALT-DEL.

Web bug   A tiny, invisible graphic file used to track a person's activities on the Internet.

Website defacing   Modifying or replacing web pages with new ones that often display profanity, pornography, or political messages. *See* Hacktivism.

Web spoofing   To intercept a user's request to view one website and display a different Web site with the intent to deceive.

White hat hacker   Term used to describe a hacker who uses his or her skill for constructive purposes, such as hunting down pedophiles or guarding against malicious (black hat) hackers. *See* Black hat hacker.

Worm   A type of program that copies itself from computer to computer. Unlike a virus, a worm doesn't infect a file or disk but simply reproduces itself.

Wrapper   A program that can combine two separate programs into a single file, most often used to combine a Trojan horse installation program with an installation program for a legitimate program. Also called a *binder* or *joiner*.

INDEX

INDEX

THE BOOK OF WI-FI
Install, Configure, and Use 802.11b Wireless Networking

BY JOHN ROSS

A practical and plain English guide to a fun but tricky technology. Shows how to build and use wireless networks at home, at work, or in your neighborhood. Includes detailed information on setting up and configuring access points, network interface cards, cables and antennas, and wireless software. Also discusses how to secure your wireless access point with encryption, password protection, and virtual private networks (VPNs). Covers Windows, Macintosh, Linux, Unix, and PDAs. For beginners on up.

2003, 288 PP., $29.95 ($44.95 CDN)
ISBN 1-886411-45-X

THE ART OF INTERACTIVE DESIGN
A Euphonious and Illuminating Guide to Building Successful Software

BY CHRIS CRAWFORD

Renowned author Chris Crawford demonstrates what interactivity is, why it's important, and how to design interactive software, games, and websites that work. Crawford's mellifluous style makes for fascinating and idea-inspiring reading that encourages you to think about design in new ways.

2002, 408 PP., $29.95 ($44.95 CDN)
ISBN 1-886411-84-0

Phone:

1 (800) 420-7240 OR
(415) 863-9900
MONDAY THROUGH FRIDAY,
9 A.M. TO 5 P.M. (PST)

Fax:

(415) 863-9950
24 HOURS A DAY,
7 DAYS A WEEK

Email:

SALES@NOSTARCH.COM

Web:

HTTP://WWW.NOSTARCH.COM

Mail:

NO STARCH PRESS
555 DE HARO STREET, SUITE 250
SAN FRANCISCO, CA 94107
USA

Distributed in the U.S. by Publishers' Group West

UPDATES

Visit **http://www.nostarch.com/stcb3.htm** for updates, errata, and other information.

Ken Yeh
6/11/03